CONFESSIONS

MY SECRET LIFE OF SCANDAL, CORRUPTION, HYPOCRISY AND DIRTY

OF A POLITICAL

ATTACKS THAT DECIDE WHO GETS ELECTED (AND WHO DOESN'T)

HITMAN

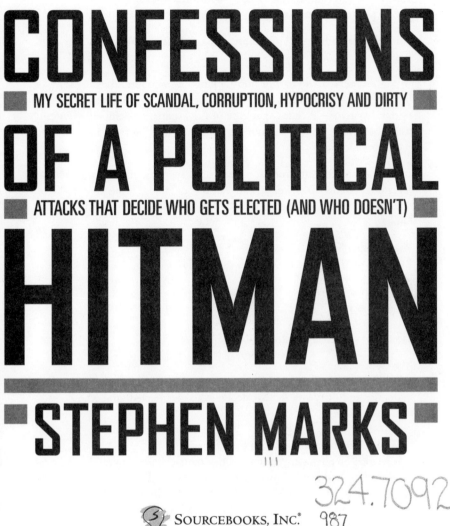

CONFESSIONS

MY SECRET LIFE OF SCANDAL, CORRUPTION, HYPOCRISY AND DIRTY

OF A POLITICAL

ATTACKS THAT DECIDE WHO GETS ELECTED (AND WHO DOESN'T)

HITMAN

STEPHEN MARKS

SOURCEBOOKS, INC.®
NAPERVILLE, ILLINOIS

Published by Sourcebooks, Inc.
P.O. Box 4410, Naperville, Illinois 60567-4410
(630) 961-3900
Fax: (630) 961-2168
www.sourcebooks.com

Library of Congress Cataloging-in-Publication Data

Marks, Stephen.
   Confessions of a political hitman : my secret life of scandal, corruption, hypocrisy and dirty attacks that decide who gets elected (and who doesn't) / Stephen Marks.
      p. cm.
   ISBN-13: 978-1-4022-0854-6 (hardcover)
   1. Marks, Stephen. 2. Political consultants--United States. 3. Political candidates--Research--United States. 4. Political campaigns--Corrupt practices--United States--History. 5. Elections--United States--History. 6. Scandals--United States--History. 7. United States--Politics and government--1993-2001. 8. United States--Politics and government--2001- I. Title.

Jk2281.M366 2007
324.7092--dc22
                                            2007043368

Printed and bound in the United States of America.
BG 10 9 8 7 6 5 4 3 2 1

DEDICATION

Dedicated to the memory of Dave Hanna, one of the
smartest politicos I ever met.

CONTENTS

ACKNOWLEDGMENTS

First I'd like to thank the folks at Sourcebooks for giving me the opportunity to write this book, with special thanks to a great editor, Peter Lynch, for making it readable. I'd also like to thank my agent Craig Wiley for his unwavering confidence in the project.

Thank you to my friend Dave Carew for his help with writing and research; and to Mendy and Hannah Caldwell for their help with every aspect of the book.

Special thanks to Richard Billmire, Jon Taurisano, and Phoebe Stephens for keeping me sane with their friendships during my years in Washington. Also special thanks to all the clients and good folks who've hired me; who've given me all the great opportunities and great experiences I've had in politics.

Finally I'd like to thank my parents for too many reasons to mention here.

INTRODUCTION

Washington, DC, is a realm of strange euphemisms. For instance, raising taxes is called "revenue enhancement." Sparing convicted criminals from serving jail time is called "alternative sentencing." George Orwell would be proud.

Likewise, the euphemism used for the digging up of dirt on politicians is "opposition research"—which is where I come in. I'm sorry to say (to the disappointment of my more blood-thirsty readers) that, in spite of the title, I'm not really a political hitman—I don't literally murder people. No, the weapons I use to defeat targeted politicians each Election Day are provided by the politicians themselves: their own records as public officials, their records as professionals in their chosen field, their financial records, their personal lives, and so on. Anything in their background that would cause citizens to vote against them, I use. In other words, I assassinate them with their own words and deeds, digging dirt wherever I can find it.

Ironically, whenever campaigns effectively use a negative item against a political opponent, it's referred to as a good "hit." So I am a "hitman" of sorts.

All political campaigns and campaign committees have different departments with straightforward names such as "Finance" (the folks who raise money), "Communications" (the folks who deal with the media), and so on. But what do they call the department (or person) hired to dig up dirt on the opposition? This murky part of politics never came into public view until the Nixon years, when Republican political hacks took "dirty tricks" to a more sophisticated level as they broke into the Watergate Office Building for the purpose of digging up dirt on the Democrats at their Democratic National Committee (DNC) headquarters in that now infamous building. Back in those days, there was never any formal name for political operatives who did that sort of work, and everything was done rather loosely. G. Gordon Liddy and his fellow Watergate henchmen proudly referred to themselves as "Rat Fuckers."

Well, fortunately, things are a bit more civilized today. Respectable political hacks can't use that sort of so-called "politically incorrect" language. Hence the term "opposition research." And this makes sense to me—after all, you can't have the folks who dig up dirt for political campaigns and campaign committees answering their phones saying "Rat-fucking department, can I help you?" or ""Dirt-digging division, how can I be of assistance to you today?"

So, as a matter of practicality and civility, we dirt diggers are stuck with "opposition research" to describe what we do. It does have kind of an innocent ring to it, don't you think?

There's nothing offensive about the word research. In fact, that's how campaign workers in this department generally answer the phone—dropping the unnecessary word opposition and simply calling the department "Research."

But among political hacks, opposition research is simply referred to as "oppo" for short. Such as "We need some oppo on this guy. Quickly!"; or, "What kind of oppo is out there on this jerk?"

This is where Oppo Man originated.

In the real world, I was Stephen Marks, mild-mannered author of this book. But in the fantasyland of my work I transformed into Oppo Man, offspring of the superheroes of my youth, Superman, Batman, and Spiderman. I was a legend in my own mind, fighter for truth, justice, and the American way, battling all crooked politicians. Sometimes I dreamt of myself as Oppo Man wearing a ski mask with only one hole for only one eye, waving my finger at the wicked politicians, warning them, "I've got my eye on you." Then, in the dream, Oppo Man faded into a strange-looking character, half librarian and half James Bond. In a way, that's what the life of a political hit man really is: half librarian for all the grunt work looking through old press clippings, court documents, financial records, and the like, and half secret agent for all the other stuff we dig up.

But the more I did this work, the more difficult it became to distinguish between Stephen and Oppo Man. Where did Stephen end and Oppo Man begin? Where did the real world end and my fantasy world begin? Most of the time it was impossible to tell. And this truly hit home for me one perfect summer afternoon in August 2002.

I was in the Texas state comptroller's office digging up dirt on some of the statewide candidates. Each state's comptroller is responsible for keeping the financial records of all state agencies, and it's always a good place to find government waste, taxes, audits, and other potentially incriminating paper trails left by politicians.

As I sat working, it brought back some of my fondest memories as Oppo Man. Four years earlier, in 1998, I had sat in the same state comptroller's office, and the dirt I dug up helped the Texas Republican Party win control of all statewide candidates for the first time in Texas history. It helped elect the Republican Lieutenant Governor Rick Perry, who would later become governor (a job he holds to this day) when Bush ascended to the presidency, as well as helping Republicans win the offices of Attorney General, State Comptroller, and Land Commissioner.

Except in 2002 there was one thing a bit different about this particular trip to the comptroller's office. A beautiful young staffer took me to a vacant meeting room on the second floor so I could have some privacy as I went through the documents I had come to "research." Once in the meeting room, though, instead of poring through the government documents I was ostensibly there to examine, I was instead poring over this beautiful young woman. We were having sex right there in the meeting room!

Four years earlier, I had flirted with this woman when I met her at the comptroller's office. I had asked her out a few times, with no success. There was always lots of sexual tension between us, but never any action. But on that particular day she was happy to see me, and the next thing I knew there was all kinds of action.

Now keep in mind that this was Oppo Man, who is hired for his discretion, his subtlety, his ability to do things under the radar, where no one can see him. Being caught doing something this flagrantly reckless would have destroyed my entire career in politics on the spot. And, in retrospect, since this sexual escapade in the Comptroller's office was shortly after 9/11, there was a chance there would be hidden security cameras in these rooms. (Fortunately for Oppo Man, there were not.)

My job required—in fact demanded—intense secrecy, since hiring a dirt digger from DC to come into the hinterlands to dig up dirt for any political campaign could badly hurt whomever had employed me. The public doesn't take kindly to DC political hacks like Oppo Man coming onto their turf to dig up dirt on their politicians. And you know what the worst part of that incident was? Despite knowing it was the most reckless and stupid thing I'd ever done in my career, and despite having so many regrets regarding so many stupid things I've done in my both my personal and professional life, I had zero regrets regarding this particular act of stupidity. Why? Because I got away with it!

So let's get this straight from the get-go. Oppo Man lived his life and did his job exactly like the politicians on whom he dug up dirt—with little conscience, if any. I came into the business bright-eyed and idealistic, just like politicians do, smugly believing that I was really different than the rest of those seedy political hacks. Well, it sure didn't take long for Oppo Man's ethics and hypocrisy to deteriorate to the level of the nasty, awful politicians I loved digging up dirt on for so many years.

In retrospect, this incident was not only indicative of what I had become, but was also certainly one of the signs at that time that I had no business doing this type of work anymore. They were signs I didn't see then, since I was still badly hooked on, and needed, the action. But it wouldn't be long before I'd see the signs; they slowly but surely took their toll on me, both physically and emotionally, to the point where I lost all my personal and political innocence.

Chapter One

THE BEGINNING OF THE END: JACK ABRAMOFF, JOHN KERRY, AND AL GORE

"You're up all night and down every day"

—ELLIOTT SMITH, FROM THE SONG "BALLAD OF BIG NOTHING"

I t was the day after Election Day 2004. Despite only twelve years in a successful career as a political hitman—and doing for those twelve years what I believed at the time to be the first truly constructive endeavor in my life—I had become disillusioned with the entire political process, and to make matters worse, my physical health was deteriorating more rapidly than my political idealism.

"Stephen, this has got to stop. You cannot continue doing this for a living," Dr. Butler told me in frustration. "It's killing you physically and mentally, and not only that, you're way too high-strung for this type of work."

Shooting back in knee-jerk fashion, I responded sarcastically, "And what type of work is that, doctor?"

"Working on the dark side. You living in the shadows, digging up dirt on politicians. Living out of a suitcase, skulking around the country from state to state, keeping crazy hours at night, and feeling like a wild man every day.

Having to be so secretive, since you can't let anyone know what you're doing . . ."

The good doctor was now foaming at the mouth. "Who in their right mind does this kind of crap for a living? The stress will kill you, not to mention your asthma."

He had a point.

✷ ✷ ✷

It was November 2, 2004, early in the morning after Election Day, when John Kerry finally called George W. Bush and gracefully told him "Congratulations, Mr. President." Bush had unbelievably once again pulled the rabbit out of the hat— *déjà vu* all over again as America stayed up all night while a single state decided Bush's fate and his place in history.

These were heady times for Republicans in the nation's capitol, who for the first time in fifty years (with the exception of a brief five-month period in early 2001) would take complete control of the White House and both houses of Congress. But times were not so flush for me. Despite my success as a political hitman, my life was unraveling.

Up to that date, I had built a successful career in a mostly unknown field. I was "re-born" as a political hitman in 1994 for the sole purpose of helping to elect a Republican Congress, the first in my lifetime, which we did on Election Day 1994. I did my part by digging up dirt on Democratic political opponents for the National Republican Congressional Committee (NRCC).

I continued in this line of work for ten more years, working for the Republican National Senatorial Committee and dozens of other political clients as a private consultant, helping more politicians (mostly Republicans) get elected and re-elected with the help of the dirt I dug up on their political opponents. I also wrote a political expose on the Pat Buchanan Presidential campaign that would reveal political corruption to the American people. I also dug up dirt for corporate clients to use against their competitors, no different and no less dirty than political dirt-digging.

Why did I do this work? Dr. Butler was quite correct about the negative impact that being Oppo Man was having on my mental and physical health. But the doctor was dead *wrong* in his belief that I was the man "in the shadows," living "on the dark side." While this may have been true in the literal sense, in a much more important and deeper sense, it's the politicians and most of the press who cover them that really live in the shadows. It is the politicians who deceive at best and lie at worst, about where they really stand on the issues and about their private and professional lives.

So, who is left to expose them? The press sometimes does, but usually can't because of their lack of resources. There are many excellent journalists and investigative reporters in America, but the average political press man or woman doesn't have an entire month to research a politician's veracity about his voting record in Congress, as Oppo Man does

Other times, the press is just plain lazy. For instance, when Congressman X sends out a press release boldly bragging that it was he, the great congressman, who was responsible for sponsoring the great legislation that was going to put away thousands of pedophiles, how many members of the media will actually look at the first three lines of the legislation, where they could clearly see that Congressman X did indeed sponsor the legislation—along with two hundred other members of Congress? How many members of the press will follow that up with a full research package on every one of that same congressman's votes over x number of years to see how he really votes on all the issues? How many members of the press will find that, ten years prior, that very same congressman who now brags about sponsoring tough-on-crime legislation had in fact voted against key anti-crime legislation, which resulted in thousands of dangerous criminals walking the streets, including the pedophiles he now brags about putting away?

If the only "news" the public gets about politicians is from the politician's bogus press releases, and the press is working under the handicap of not having the resources to research the truth, who is left to tell the public what's really going on?

You guessed it. The political hitman.

A political hitman is forced to live in the shadows in order to uncover the truth that will eventually lead the American public out of the shadows; to force politicians into the light of truth.

I know what you're thinking:

• Is all this negative political stuff really good for America?
• Is it really good for America to know all the personal foibles of every politician?

These are excellent questions. Each reader must come to his or her own conclusions after finishing this book. But you must keep one important fact in mind. Saying the public should *not* be privy to certain sensitive matters regarding those that represent our democracy is an insult to America's collective intelligence. Armed with all the facts, the public can generally figure out which are relevant and which are not. We saw this in 1998, when President Clinton's popularity rose during the Monica Lewinski fiasco. Not only that, the backlash against the hypocrisy of the Republicans attacking Clinton at that time resulted in the Democrats gaining congressional seats in 1998, less than two months before Clinton was impeached in the House of Representatives.

In retrospect, the voters had it just about right regarding Clinton, and in the end, his historical accountability and punishment were also just about right. The Republicans were correct in their assertion that Bill Clinton lied under oath in a federal courthouse and obstructed justice, and therefore deserved impeachment. But the Democrats were right, too— it was all about sex, so he didn't deserve to be removed from office. This historical result came from congress' actions (impeachment in the House, acquittal in the Senate), made possible largely as a result of the public's wishes.

Thus, while most Americans didn't believe the president's transgressions were serious enough to warrant his removal from office, the public still had the right to know about those transgressions. So unfortunately, the investigative reporters and political hitmen who bring all this negativity into American politics are a necessary evil if the public has "*the right to know*" the truth before they can make educated votes regarding who their leaders will be.

The logical questions here would be: "What are the actual nuts and bolts of this process used by the political hitman?" and "How does this process work that forces negativity into American politics?" Well, it's a fairly simple, straightforward three-step process, used the same way in all political campaigns:

- Step I: The political hitmen dig up the dirt.
- Step II: The dirt is then given to the pollsters, who through sophisticated polling can determine which pieces of dirt are the most damaging in the minds of the voters.
- Step III: The pollsters give their results to the media advertising folks, who put the most damaging two or three negative issues into the TV, radio, and direct-mail pieces that do their best to rip their political opponent into shreds.

The third step is truly impressive. I marvel at the unbelievable talents of campaign media spinsters. They have the rare skill to take pages and pages of opposition research and transform it into simple thirty-second and sixty-second TV and radio spots the public can clearly understand. When it's all over, the truth has been exposed—and quite often the opponent has suffered a serious blow to his or her campaign, one from which they sometimes never recover.

The bottom line of the process is this: Despite the American voters' claims that they are "turned off" by negative campaigning, those same voters nonetheless still respond to negative campaigning by often voting against the candidate being attacked, and it is that same negative campaigning that wins elections.

Negative campaigning is far more important to the results of American elections than anything positive the candidates say about themselves. (I will offer proof of this assertion in the chapters "Proof That Negative Campaigning leads to Electoral Victory" and "The Unpredictable Nature of Opposition Research and Negative Campaigning."

The last question concerning the "process" would be "Who hires political hitmen?"

We get hired by all kinds of clients:

- Directly from a political campaign, looking for dirt on their opponent
- Political committees, such as the Republican and Democratic National Committees (RNC and DNC), the National Republican and Democratic Senatorial Committees (NRSC and DNSC), the National Republican and Democratic Congressional Committees (NRCC and DCCC), etc.
- PACs and special interest groups such as the NRA or Chamber of Commerce on the right, and labor unions and trial lawyers on the left
- Other political hitmen who either don't want the job or are unable to travel for family reasons
- Newer clients include the more recent so-called "shadowy" 527 groups (living proof that the McCain-Feingold Act was a joke and resulted in the exact opposite of its original intention, not to mention its questionable constitutionality)

Campaigns often hire us to dig up dirt not only on their opponents, but on their own candidates, so they know what attacks to expect from the opposition! As silly as the euphemism "opposition research" is for digging up dirt on political opponents, the mirror euphemism for digging up dirt on "our guy" in the race is just as bad—we call this research on our own candidates "vulnerability studies."

By "researching" both opposing candidates in many races, I was able to learn the hard way many times that the person I originally thought was the "good guy" in the race was in fact the "bad guy." This was a hard pill to swallow in the beginning when I actually believed that the Republicans were always the good guys and the Democrats were always the bad guys. However, I learned fast that the politicians of both parties are about equal—roughly one-third good folks, one-third assholes, and one-third somewhere in between (which is probably the same, or close to the same, breakdown in other walks of life). However, the most bitter pill for me to swallow was something I knew subconsciously but refused to admit for many years: that Democrats are not even close to Republicans when it comes to personal hypocrisy. While Democrats are indeed hypocrites in so many areas, they can't hold a candle to the GOP when it comes to the hypocrisy of their so-called "family values." (More on that later, in the chapter "Sex, Lies and Republican Hypocrisy.")

✷ ✷ ✷

Despite my growing disillusionment with the Republican Party, my two greatest moments as Oppo Man came during the 2000 and 2004 presidential elections, when my TV ads arguably helped elect and re-elect George W. Bush as president. This was achieved in part through some creative dirt-digging on Al Gore and John Kerry, and subsequent use of the material to write and produce TV attack ads against the two Democratic nominees. The ads arguably swung enough votes in Florida to help W. win in 2000, and possibly swung enough votes in Ohio in 2004 to defeat Kerry.

The creation of my anti-Gore ad and the election of George W. Bush in 2000 was probably my finest moment as Oppo Man. I had researched and produced my best opposition research in the form of a powerful anti-Gore ad that received massive airplay and publicity in the closing week of the 2000 election. The national media picked up on it, and it was subsequently seen on TV in all fifty states. It received much attention in the print media as well. The ad showed footage of Al Gore defending "Reverend" Al Sharpton as Gore pandered to an African-American audience during the 2000 campaign. This footage was followed with grainy footage (featuring some pretty scary music) showing Al Sharpton urging college students to kill cops (or "off the pigs" as the "Reverend" so eloquently put it). This was followed by footage of Sharpton referring to America's Founding Fathers as the "Scum of Europe," then some gruesome photos of killers and rapists Sharpton had defended (remember, this was the pre-2004 Sharpton, before he transformed his image from radical, race-baiting rabble-rouser to mainstream black leader four years later when he ran for president in 2004).

In those days, there did not exist the nasty 527 groups like MoveOn.org or Swiftboat Veterans that were created during the 2004 Bush-Kerry race. In 2000 they were simply called Independent Expenditures (IE), made by so-called "independent" folks. This was of course laughable, since we were anything but independent. And since one was not allowed by law to say anything positive about our favored candidate in the television ad (as is the case with 527 ads), we had no choice but to bash the opposing candidate unmercifully. A perfect job for Oppo Man.

How did I know my ad was working? Everyone was attacking it. On *Hannity and Colmes*, the normally unflappable Alan Colmes screamed, "This ad is shameful." In the pre-election issue of *Time Magazine* less than a week before the 2000 election, Viveca Novak described my ad in her piece entitled "And Now for the Nasty Stuff," while the the *New York Daily News* referred to me as "shadowy." Even those leaning to the right, such as Bill O'Reilly, said to me on *The O'Reilly Factor*, "I don't like your ad."

I like to think that my ad moved at least 169 votes in Florida, which would have helped win the state for Bush (he won the state by 336 votes).

Of course I'm hardly claiming to be personally responsible for Bush winning Florida, since there were countless other more important factors in play. In fact, its even possible that my ad may have cost W. votes; we'll never know. That's because at the same time as my ad was appearing, it may have provided some political cover for an ad the NAACP was airing at the same time, which was truly the most disingenuous and venomous ad in political history. The NAACP ad implied that then-Governor Bush was responsible for the tragic death of James Byrd, the black man that was dragged to his death in Jasper, Texas, by some white racist yahoos. According to the NAACP, it was Bush's fault, because as Governor of Texas he had not passed "Hate Crimes" legislation. And that supposedly caused Mr. Byrd's death? The killers only received the death penalty, which the NAACP opposes, but none of that mattered to the race-baiters at the NAACP.

So the reason it was believed by some that my ad was harmful to Bush was because to some degree it gave the despicable NAACP ad political cover, as some of the liberal press lumped the two ads together, as did *Time Magazine* in their story "And Now For the Nasty Stuff."

Maybe they're right; maybe my ad did hurt Bush by reinforcing the NAACP ad and causing a higher-than-normal black turnout—indeed, the highest in history, with Al Gore receiving 94 percent of the black vote, even a higher percentage than the first "black president," Bill Clinton. Or maybe the naysayers were wrong. Maybe my ad did indeed move at least the 169 Democratic, independent, and/or undecided voters needed to put Bush over the top in 2000.

I'll never know. But it's certainly interesting food for thought.

After the 2000 election, independent expenditure ads such as mine attacking Al Gore were outlawed by McCain-Feingold. As a result, the so-called 527 Groups were created as a legal loophole around McCain-Feingold and a way to continue sinking tens of millions of dollars into ads attacking both Bush and Kerry. 527s were the brainchild of ultra-liberal George Soros and MoveOn.Org, who lowered the boom against President Bush. Other 527 ads followed, the most notable being the anti-Kerry "Swiftboat" ads that attacked Kerry's record in Vietnam and in my opinion cost Kerry the election; hitting him at this strength (his serving in Vietnam, whereas Bush had not) and blunting his momentum or "bump" after the Democratic Convention.

But the mother of all negative 527 ads in 2004 (in my never-humble opinion) was created and aired by me. My ad brought back the ghost of Willie Horton, which drove the liberals crazy. Having researched John Kerry in 1996 while working for his U.S. Senate opponent at the time, then-Republican Governor William Weld, I had lots of dirt on Kerry that wasn't known to the American public in 2004. For instance, in 1982, John Kerry, as a private attorney, secured the early parole of a career criminal, George Reissfelder of Boston, who had pled guilty to the attempted murder of a police officer in Florida. He had committed this crime after escaping a Massachusetts prison during a furlough, just as had Willie Horton.

Kerry argued that Reissfelder had been wrongly convicted of murder in Massachusetts and had unfairly served jail time for a crime he probably did not commit (all of which was true). Kerry subsequently convinced the Florida Parole Board that, since Reissfelder had served time for a crime he didn't commit, the parole board should make it up to him by granting him early parole for his attempted murder of a police officer in Florida.

Back in those days, politicians in general and parole boards in particular were much more sympathetic to criminals than they are today. Consequently, the Florida Parole Board agreed with Kerry, granting Reissfelder parole after serving only five years of his fifteen-year sentence.

After being paroled, Reissfelder immediately proved to everyone that Kerry exercised poor judgment in helping secure his freedom. It wasn't long after his release that Kerry's "poster boy" continued his criminal ways, quickly involving himself with a Mafia-controlled drug ring in Boston. He was wanted for questioning by the police in regards to the Gardner Museum heist, the largest museum robbery in U.S. history, a case still open and featured on the TV show "Unsolved

Mysteries." When law enforcement couldn't locate Reissfelder, a local mobster told the cops to try his residence again. This time he was found dead from "cocaine poisoning"—a suspected mob hit that was never proven.

My 527 ad pointed out that despite the fact that Reissfelder did indeed serve time he probably shouldn't have, Kerry nonetheless secured early parole from prison for a man who had pled guilty to trying to kill a Florida police officer. The ad continued with the point that Reissfelder subsequently continued to live a life of life of crime until his death, also being involved with organized crime, all true facts.

The ad ended with a picture of George Reissfelder morphing into a picture of Willie Horton, the obvious message being that both men had committed heinous crimes while out on furlough while serving jail time in Massachusetts. The ad ended the Reissfelder story with a voice-over saying "John Kerry's support of Michael Dukakis' furlough program should come as no surprise. After all, guess who was Michael Dukakis' lieutenant governor? That's right, John Kerry." At that last moment in the ad, as Reissfelder morphed into Willie Horton, John Kerry simultaneously morphed into Mike Dukakis.

I thought, and still do, that the ad was brilliant.

Beltway liberals did not agree, and all hell broke loose. Willie Horton had been a dead political issue since 1988 but still festered beneath the surface of many liberal psyches. Many liberals to this day are angered by nothing more severely than the memory of Willie Horton, and how the Horton issue single-handedly destroyed Michael Dukakis' presidential candidacy in 1988. Their anger derived from their belief that the ad was inherently racist because Horton was black. And that's precisely why I believed my ad was brilliant: in this case, George Reissfelder was *white*, which I believed negated the argument for this ad.

However, none of this logic impressed the liberals. I was invited onto Alan Colmes' radio program to "debate" former Dukakis campaign manager Susan Estrich on the issue. Both Colmes and Estrich are normally thoughtful liberals, but not this time. The normally calm and unflappable Colmes and the normally calm Estrich went completely crazy, tag-teaming me, screaming at me while not allowing me to get a word in edgewise. Colmes eventually cut me off for good, ending the "debate."

After the Reissfelder ad, I released two more 527 ads against Kerry. The first showed Kerry to be soft on crime, using a clip from his own 2004 convention acceptance speech bemoaning how America was putting too many people in jail. The second was a repeat of the anti-Gore ad from 2000, this time showing Kerry sucking up to Sharpton in 2004. Sharpton, who had called the 2000 ad "slanderous," intelligently ignored my ad this time.

The 2004 anti-Kerry ads aired throughout several key states, including Ohio, during the campaign's closing months—a time when most polls showed Kerry slightly ahead in that state. Yet the state, and subsequently the election, was won by George W. Bush, giving him his second consecutive razor-thin victory determined by a single state. Of course I have absolutely no idea whether or not my ad helped Bush win the state. The margin of victory in Ohio in 2004 was roughly 130,000, versus the 336 votes that Bush carried Florida by in 2000.

But once again it's interesting food for thought.

There was another effect of these ads, though, one that affected me personally and the course of my thinking as Oppo Man. The Reissfelder episode made me realize something important I never had before thought of: that my actions as Oppo Man sometimes had unexpected consequences. And these consequences sometimes hurt innocent people.

After the ad aired, I immediately received death threats from Reissfelder's surviving relatives. They claimed that the charges in my ad were lies, which was of course bullshit. However, they also legitimately pointed out that the ad opened up old wounds for them, since Mr. Reissfelder had died twenty-two years earlier. They were right that the ads opened up old wounds, and that was something I had never before considered.

A few weeks after the ad aired, I received a surprisingly friendly telephone call from Mr. Reissfelder's niece, a young woman serving in the military at that time. She explained to me that she had never known that her uncle had been involved in any of this, and politely asked me to send her some proof. I sent her copies of some news articles that I had used to fact-check my ad, and she thanked me. I felt a sort of kinship with her, since one of my own uncles had been a mobster, and I never found about his past until after his death, when I was in my early twenties.

Unfortunately, good people are sometimes related to people who do bad things, and these good people sometimes get hurt in the process. But does that mean in order to protect the good people, we should make believe the bad people and/or their acts don't exist or never existed? These questions started to weigh on me, especially after that 2004 election and despite Bush's victory.

☆ ☆ ☆

I know what you're wondering: Why didn't I just quit and make a clean break after that 2004 election? Like I said earlier, I was still hooked; I still needed the action. Actually, the truth is that despite all the negatives of a highly negative-oriented job, there was still quite a lot to like about it. Which is why Dr. Butler's opinion about how terrible this job was for me didn't matter. He didn't have the full story.

I actually loved the so-called "dark side" of being a political hitman, even if it did indeed mean sometimes living in the shadows. I loved living out of a suitcase, particularly the feeling I had checking into all those nice hotels in each strange new city, eating in any restaurant I wanted to as many times as I wanted to, all being paid for by the client.

I loved the travel. I loved seeing America; the different scenery; the different cultures, the different food, the different music, and all the diversity that makes this country so great. Since I had never traveled much before becoming Oppo Man, I had no idea how truly diverse and beautiful this country is.

And of course, there was the ultimate perk of the job: all those women I met in all those cities. You see, on the one hand there was Stephen Marks; on the other was his alter-ego, the political hitman Oppo Man. But Oppo Man had his own separate alter-ego, for whom chasing women was just as much a full-time job for him as being Oppo Man

Dr. Butler could not possibly understand (nor would I ever have the balls to tell him) how much I loved what he considered the difficult parts of my job. He couldn't possibly understand that I loved getting on airplanes at 6:15 a.m. after not having slept all night, and waiting for all the other passengers to take their seats before I casually sauntered onto the plane. Quickly scanning the passengers, like clockwork I would head to the most attractive woman on the plane who happened to be sitting next to a vacant seat. And do you know why they would always be sitting next to a vacant seat? Because unless the flight is completely full, every single passenger will be sitting in either an aisle or window seat, including all the attractive women. No one sits in the middle seats if they can avoid it, except for one person: Oppo Man.

I wasn't supposed to tell anyone I met on the road what I was really up to, so I would make up any cover story my imagination could conjure. But sometimes I would slip up. And when I did, it was always over a woman. Luckily, I survived those slip-ups. I *loved* the travelling. I was Roger Williams "King of the Road," Ricky Nelson's "Travellin' Man," and Johnny Cash's "I've Been Everywhere Man" all wrapped into one, if you know what I mean.

Unfortunately, I didn't survive the lifestyle, which would eventually catch up with me. My personal metamorphosis was from a swaggering ladies' man to a remorseful, borderline sex addict who eventually could no longer remember most of the women he had been with, nor how many women he had hurt. Despite knowing intellectually that using woman sexually was morally wrong, I couldn't control myself.

So when the time came that I finally met a woman with whom I truly did fall in love, I didn't even realize it until it was too late. While I was seeing her, I was still in the fantasyland of my Oppo Man mode, continuing to see other women while I was seeing her. It took me two full years to realize that I really was in love with her and only wanted to be with her and no one else. But by the time I figured it out it was much too late. By that point she wanted nothing to do with me. It finally all caught up with me. My private life was a disaster.

This mirrored my political metamorphosis. I had gone from born-and-bred liberal New Yorker, to Beltway Republican right-wing political hack, finally landing where I am now, and where I believe most of America is: squarely and passionately in the center, deeply afraid of America's political extremes, both of which I now believe border on fascism.

My right-wing political beliefs began to crack in 1995, not long after I became Oppo Man and within that first year of the Republican takeover of Congress. I couldn't believe how many "family values" Republican congressmen's marriages began to fall apart due to adultery. The charade began to crack open even wider in 1996, when both Republican presidential and vice presidential candidates Bob Dole and Jack Kemp were unable to attack Bill Clinton as they ran against him; since both had prior philandering problems of their own. The charade escalated into high comedy right after the 1998 elections, in what should have been the Republican Party's finest hour, as Bill Clinton was about to be impeached. Instead, the most recognizable face of the 1995 "Republican Revolution," Newt Gingrich was himself exposed as a "family values fraud" and forced to resign in the wake of his own infidelities becoming public. It was the same old song and dance with Gingrich's successor as Speaker, Bob Livingston, who also had philandering problems. Finally came the "coup de grace"—the Republicans in the Senate chose not to remove Clinton from office for fear of their own sexual and other ethical hypocrisies becoming public. This collapse of the Republican Party's moral high ground coincided with my own self-doubt as to the "rightness" of the Republican Party, later reinforced with yet more self-doubt regarding the hypocrisy in my own personal behavior as Oppo Man. Both the Republican Party's and my own personal hypocrisy are discussed in morbid detail later in this book.

But all the self-doubt about what I was doing, and the question of whether or not I was really working for the "good guys" or the "bad guys," came to its climax in 2006 with the breaking of the Robert Abramoff scandal.

$$* \quad * \quad *$$

It was midday on January 3, 2006, and the tune "Miss Misery" by Elliott Smith was floating through my headphones. Out of the corner of my eye I saw my TV screen flash: news alert! Ninety percent of the time, these "alerts" turn out to be bullshit, so I continued to listen to the music. But then the words "News Alert" on the screen were replaced by "Republican Lobbyist Pleads Guilty to Conspiracy Charges." Video footage appeared showing a big man in handcuffs, flanked by the federal agents while being led to a big black car. "I hope it's not someone I know," I thought as I stared at the screen.

The man under arrest looked ridiculous, wearing a dark, double-breasted trench coat, his head covered by a Fedora hat flopping all around in the wind. He looked like a goon from an old Edward G. Robinson movie. Then I went numb as the man's name flashed across the screen: Jack Abramoff.

My mind immediately went back to 2000 and 2001, when I did some work for a client on behalf of Abramoff's partner, Michael Scanlon. Scanlon had already pled guilty to conspiracy charges back in November 2005. Although I felt bad for Mike at the time, I thought little of it—until now.

On the TV, Chris Matthews began screaming that more indictments were to follow regarding multimillion dollar payoffs made to Abramoff and Scanlon by casino-owning Indian tribes. I became nervous. Very nervous. I had worked closely with Scanlon on that casino project. Before I could stop to think clearly, Matthews was again screaming, this time even louder. He said even more indictments were to follow regarding Abramoff's and Scanlon's work for New York businessman Adam Kidan and his SunCruz casino boats. Suddenly my nervousness turned into a freezing sweat; I had worked closely with Scanlon on that project, too. I also knew about the involvement of Kidan and Abramoff.

I stood frozen as Chris Matthews blurted the litany of federal charges brought against Abramoff. And when he shouted the words "mail fraud," I was sweating so profusely that I had to turn the television off. That's when "The Incident" came back to me.

In the spring of 2001, I was working for that client on behalf of a PR outfit called Capitol Campaign Strategies for Michael Scanlon. One day I was told to take a trip to rural Kenner, Louisiana, to conduct research on a casino and the Coushattas Indian tribe that owned it. But before going to the casino, I was to go to New Orleans. For what, I had no idea. I was simply to go.

Upon arriving in New Orleans, I was instructed to go to the FedEx office at the New Orleans airport and pick up a box Scanlon had sent me. This didn't seem strange; clients often send background information on the people I'm researching via FedEx. When I'm traveling, I usually read it once I get to my hotel before I conduct my research. This time, however, was different. There was a note on the box instructed me to take the box to the airport's regular post office. Once there, I was to open the box, which included several hundred stamped envelopes, and simply hand over the envelopes to the post office to be mailed.

And that was it. That was my job for the whole time in New Orleans! Weird.

Now, I always follow orders meticulously. But that didn't stop me from opening one of the envelopes at the New Orleans post office and reading the letter. After all, no one ever specifically told me *not* to open them.

I knew better than to read the letter. It's usually best not to know what's going on when dealing with such a bizarre situation. But my curiosity got the better of me, and the temptation was made even greater by the fact that the envelopes were not sealed shut, apparently to save some postage on the bulk rate. (Unbelievably, Scanlon and his friends thought nothing of paying handsomely for my single trip to the New Orleans post office, but at the same time they were apparently too cheap to pay the extra postage to make certain someone nosy like me didn't read the letters.)

The letters were all the same: fund-raising appeals from some guy named "Poncho," who was campaigning to become president of Coushatta Indian tribe in Louisiana. The letters were sent to several hundred people with Native American-sounding names.

I didn't think much of it. I figured it was just a political ploy by Scanlon and "Poncho." See, in most parts of America, particularly in rural America, people hate Washington DC. If they knew that "Poncho" was working with a big-time DC firm on his campaign, they would immediately distrust him. So the whole ruse with my re-mailing the letters from New Orleans seemed designed so that the recipients would see the local postmark and believe "Poncho" wrote the letter, not some high-paid Washington DC PR guys. So the whole thing seemed like no big deal to me at the time. They certainly were doing nothing illegal. Or so I thought.

A few seconds after hearing the words "mail fraud" with terror, I reflected upon my involvement in "The Incident" and began to feel tremendous relief. Even though the whole thing had been fishy, I personally hadn't broken any laws. My behavior and actions were indeed bizarre, but legal.

But I also now realized that my mail "switcheroo" at the airport may have been much more than it initially seemed. What if it was part of a conspiracy, where Abramoff and Scanlon's actions were part of a quid-pro-quo for the Indian tribe election? Perhaps the reason they were working with "Poncho" was more than PR. If they helped "Poncho" win the election and get access to all those casino profits, perhaps Abramoff and Scanlon would see tens of millions of dollars in lobbying fees in return. Which is exactly what happened after "Poncho," who turned out to be Coushatta Chairman Lovelin Poncho, did indeed win the election. Poncho was never charged with anything concerning the election.

Although I had knowingly played a part in the deception that the letters came from Poncho instead of a DC-based PR firm, and I had no idea about any conspiracy nor any quid-pro-quo. I had not broken any laws.

And I have Mike Scanlon to thank for that, since he had apparently deliberately kept me in the dark about anything illegal he may have been doing. Still, had I not been kept in the dark and had known the truth, I can't honestly say that I would never have knowingly and willingly participated in all that skullduggery.

Maybe I would have. Maybe not.

As of this writing, my mail switcheroo and the fact that it was part of the Abramoff/Scanlon role in an internal Indian election, which resulted in their subsequent trouble for illegally making tens of millions of dollars from Indian tribes, has not been made public. I have no problem revealing the information at this time, since I'm certain that by now the prosecutors have the information. Scanlon and Abramoff, after all, have already pled guilty and are both serving time in the federal pen.

But this incident nonetheless created a lot of self-doubt for me, since I was an unwitting pawn in the breaking of some pretty serious federal laws by my supposed "good guy" clients. And despite his apparently illegal actions, Mike Scanlon nonetheless is truly a good guy. Young, preppy, and, unlike Mr. Abramoff, very unpretentious, Scanlon is one of the nicest people I ever dealt with on Capitol Hill. After leaving some boilerplate Capitol Hill staff positions, he formed the PR and lobbying firm Capitol Campaign Strategies, and his career took off. Over time he moved away from campaign work and more toward politically connected corporate clients. When he needed dirt on one of his corporate client's competitors, that's when I came into the picture.

Since I dealt exclusively with Scanlon, I knew little about Abramoff; only that he worked with Scanlon and had a lot of money. At that time, I had no idea that Abramoff and Scanlon were even lobbyists. As far as I knew, Capitol Campaign Strategies was a PR firm, and they were simply political hacks like me. I couldn't have been more wrong.

Another job I did for a client on behalf of Scanlon was extremely bizarre, and also involves never-before-revealed information relevant to the Abramoff scandal. My job was to "research" Gus Boulis, a fascinating guy who had ignored the niceties of immigration law and arrived in Florida from Greece as a teenage stowaway in the 1960s. Within a few years, he made millions with his restaurant chain "Miami Subs," and subsequently made even more millions with SunCruz, the Florida casino boat chain.

Boulis sold SunCruz to Jack Abramoff and Adam Kidan, but the deal quickly went sour when Boulis tried to back out of it. This is where I was brought in. Capitol Campaign Strategies was hoping to find dirt on Boulis that could be used against him. Criss-crossing the state of Florida in January 2001, I had to analyze Boulis' courthouse records in Tallahassee, Tampa, Miami, Fort Lauderdale, Palm Beach, and the Florida Keys. Not exactly the worst places to be in January.

The research into Boulis exposed a plethora of shady business dealings and complex legal problems, not to mention his two families, one with a wife and two kids, the other with a common-law wife (mistress) of eighteen years and two kids. Definitely a man of action, Gus Boulis, and definitely a man with more balls than brains. I like that; sounds like someone else I know.

Yet all my research pointed to Boulis being the "bad guy" in this SunCruz dispute, and that Kidan and Abramoff were the good guys. Most strongly reinforcing this belief were lawsuits against Boulis throughout Florida, some of them very serious. There were federal lawsuits against Boulis that were settled, including two for racketeering, and an even stranger case that featured the feds suing Boulis for fraudulently owning a casino boat company using dummy corporations to hide his ownership, which was illegal since he was not a U.S. citizen. This case was originally settled with Boulis agreeing to sell his stake in the company, but then he fought the settlement as the court sealed and closed the case.

Since I had already heard rumors that Boulis was letting mobsters use SunCruz to launder drug money, the lawsuit was no big surprise to me. But his plea arrangement resulting in zero jail time and the case being sealed certainly was. What was the court hiding? I had no idea.

That changed quickly, though. On February 6, 2001, I was sleeping in my Fort Lauderdale hotel room after another day of researching Boulis. Suddenly, I was awakened by a call in the wee hours of the morning. "Get the hell out of Dodge," I was told. To this day I can't even remember specifically who it was that called me that morning, although it was certainly one of the cohorts for whom I was working while researching Boulis.

Not having any idea what was going on, I immediately got dressed, packed, and was on the first plane out of town.

As I settled into my plane seat, I was still confused as I opened the morning *Miami Herald* and read the headline:

"Florida Development Mogul Gunned Down in Fort Lauderdale." Gus Boulis had been assassinated in a mob-style hit.

Once the shock wore off, it all finally made sense to me, although there were still some questions. Did Boulis' original settlement with the feds include Boulis ratting out mobsters? Was he in cahoots with mobsters and letting them use SunCruz to launder money? Did the mobsters find out he was a rat, and was that why he was killed?

Only years later would we find out that there was a connection between the killings and Abramoff's partner, Adam Kidan. It also became clear that the reason Boulis was trying to get out of the settlement was because he somehow found out that the men to whom he had agreed to sell SunCruz, Abramoff and Kidan, were politically connected frauds with bogus financial statements. That they were in reality unable to afford to pay Boulis for SunCruz. And that Abramoff and Kidan had the help of a corrupt Republican congressman, Bob Ney of Ohio, in these dealings.

Once I was safely "out of Dodge," I realized why it was a good idea to leave town so quickly. Even an opposition researcher is required to give the court clerk his or her correct name and ID while checking out or making copies of court documents. I had just finished looking at every court document in Florida involving Boulis. My name was now attached to each of those documents and to the public record, and that would look suspicious. Anyone looking to cover their tracks on the Boulis murder might come looking for me.

My phone rang a few days later, and a man identifying himself as a detective with the Fort Lauderdale police politely asked me what I was doing checking out all of Mr. Boulis' court documents, including a copy I had requested of Boulis' mug shot in Fort Lauderdale that had been taken after a domestic violence arrest. Figuring the call was most likely being recorded, I told him the truth. I was researching public records for a private client, which is perfectly legal. When asked, I declined to divulge the name of my client. That, too, is my legal right. He was a total gentleman, but to this day I have no idea of whether or not he actually worked for the Fort Lauderdale police.

Bizarre statements by the Fort Lauderdale police media spokespeople seemed to indicate that they had little desire to solve the case. For the first six weeks after Boulis' death, all the press reports indicated that he had many enemies that wouldn't mind seeing him dead.

Then, out of the blue, on March 20, 2001, the press reported that despite the Boulis case arguably being the most important and mysterious murder in the history of Fort Lauderdale, the Fort Lauderdale police had a grand total of two detectives working the case. Not only that, they appeared to be classic "Keystone Cops." One of the two, Detective Jack King, contradicted press reports by claiming that Boulis was a nice guy, and that despite media reports of federal investigations and numerous legal fights, Boulis appeared to be a man without much to hide.

"We expected to find someone who was somewhat shady, and would prove to have a lot of enemies and we didn't find that with Gus," King said. Unbelievable.

I would return to Fort Lauderdale and the Broward County Courthouse for one last visit, for the same clients (still believing them to be the good guys in this case), when I briefly monitored the legal battle taking place between Boulis' wife and mistress over his estate. Finally, enough time passed and the entire episode faded from my memory.

That is, until the incredible twist almost four years later, on September 28, 2005, when the Fort Lauderdale police made arrests for the Boulis murder. Three mobsters were charged, including at least one connected to SunCruz and Kidan (Kidan denied that he played any role in the murder and cooperated with the police). The logical questions now are: How did the feds crack the Boulis murder case so quickly while the Fort Lauderdale cops for four long years found nothing? And why was the case cracked at practically the exact time of the Kidan and Abramoff federal indictments? The timing seems more than coincidental.

We now know that Abramoff and Kidan have admitted to altering financial documents in order to purchase SunCruz. Their documents were bogus, and they never even made the first down payment. And that's the reason Boulis was trying to back out of the deal; he would have been stiffed. But after Boulis' death, it became moot. And Boulis' fears were proven correct, as Abramoff and Kidan shortly plundered SunCruz into bankruptcy, using millions in SunCruz funds to live lavish lifestyles.

In the end, Boulis, despite all his shady business dealings and his mob-style murder, was in reality the "good guy," at least in this case. And at the same time, I was working for the "bad guys."

To this day, these cases give me pause. It still bothers me that I arrogantly believed I was in total control during these two jobs, when the facts of course reveal the exact opposite. I had absolutely no idea what was really going on. I was merely a pawn helping bad guys break the law. Even worse is the scary fact that to this day I still have no idea what events may or may not have been caused by my actions during these projects and others over the years. This is so troubling that it goes to the root of my existence as Oppo Man: Even a smart guy like Oppo Man doesn't know what he doesn't know. So he's not all that smart after all, is he?

* * *

The self-doubt that began in early 2005 with the Abramoff scandal grew with a vengeance throughout the rest of 2006. For the first time I began to see what the rest of America had already been seeing for some time: that Bush's Iraqi adventure, which had been not only such a noble cause but also so very winnable, had been a failure thus far. It was also debatable as to whether or not we were winning the equally winnable "war on terror," this despite five years passing since 9/11. The self-doubt was given its final exclamation point on Election Day 2006, as the Republican Party I had worked so hard for over twelve years lost control of both houses of Congress due to Bush's failures in Iraq.

As mentioned earlier, these political events, and the political metamorphosis I was personally going through, would ironically coincide with the metamorphosis in my personal life, which had become just as much of a disaster as the Republican Party's political fortunes (or, should I say, misfortunes).

So that's where Oppo Man is now. Finally realizing the hard way that his personal life has been a disaster; worse than that of most of the degenerate politicians he "researched" with such glee. So it's finally time to stop.

The fall of the Republican Party during this historic period was due to the moral decay and personal hypocrisy of the party's members themselves. The same exact thing for Oppo Man, as the skeletons in his closet rivaled those of any of the politicians he tired to bring down. Just like the so-called dirty politicians I worked so hard to defeat, it's time to put Oppo Man into forced retirement.

I had been trying stop this insanity since the 2000 election, but never had the discipline to stop. I had promised myself I would stop after the 2004 election. And now, at the end of the 2006 election, the timing was perfect for me to retire Oppo Man, who had come into existence in 1994 due to a major event in American history: the Republican takeover of both houses of Congress for the first time in generations due to the massive unpopularity of the sitting Democratic president, Bill Clinton. And now, come the time to put Oppo Man to rest, the historical symmetry was exactly the same, yet the polar opposite; the *Democratic* recapture of both houses of Congress, again due to the massive unpopularity of the sitting *Republican* president: George W. Bush.

Yes, the timing was perfect, but I still didn't know if I had the discipline to stop. So I figured out a creative way to put Oppo Man to rest once and for all. Write a book. Expose the hypocrisy of politicians on both sides of the aisle, politicians of all political stripes and ideologies.

Writing a book also seemed the right thing to do for practical reasons. After all, the subject has never been written about in mainstream publishing. Also, outside the beltway, the actions and role of opposition research is completely unknown. Inside the beltway, its known but still considered mysterious and shady. I figured I needed to write this book for several reasons:

To let America know the truth about opposition research and the use of negative campaigning.

To expose our corrupt political system for what it has unfortunately become (despite the paradox that it is still by far the best political system in the history of the world). As long as men and women are imperfect, our best political system will be imperfect as well.

To expose the corrupt politics and shady politicians of both political parties, as well as the corruption and hypocrisy of political hacks like myself.

To share my political and personal metamorphosis. The good and the bad.

After reading this book, you will not only be better educated about what's really going on in American politics on all levels, from the local to the national, but you can also decide for yourself whether or not all the negativity that permeates American politics as we know it today is a necessary evil to create an educated voter, or instead is something we can all do without.

Chapter Two

A POLITICAL JUNKIE IS BORN

"Its almost eleven. Ya gotta go to sleep!"

Helen Marks, also known from time to time as "Mom," yelled at me in her unique dialect of Brooklynese. Although I was eleven years of age, and she had every right to tell me to go to bed, I was still annoyed. She didn't seem to care that I would miss all the action of the 1968 California Democratic Primary.

It was now almost five years since the death of my beloved President John F. Kennedy, and I couldn't believe what I was seeing. I couldn't believe that little brother Bobby would have the gall, the balls, to run for president simply on his dead bother's coattails. It made me sick, and I hated Bobby for it, because I adored his brother John so much. Unlike most JFK fans who enthusiastically supported Bobby's candidacy to carry the torch, my eleven-year-old mind didn't quite function that way.

Unlike his brother the former president, who appeared to be a great guy (most people of all political stripes who knew him personally would later attest that this was in fact true),

Bobby was nothing of the sort. He was the surliest politician I'd ever seen, with that perpetual scowl on his face. To make matters worse, he had been my U.S. senator from New York after leaving his job as attorney general in 1964. And now he wanted to be president? Not only that, he wanted the job but was too lazy to even run for it the hard way—instead, he let Eugene McCarthy do all the heavy lifting and all the dirty work to knock LBJ out of the race, then casually sauntered into the race on a red carpet.

Oh how I hated this bum! He wanted to be president? How dare he?

The true sign of any political junkie is his or her desire, or more likely his or her *need,* to stay up all night to watch election results. So this was the first night in my eleven-year-old life where I felt that itch. But because of my bedtime and the three-hour time difference between New York and California, it would unfortunately be impossible for me to see live from the West Coast whether or not Bobby would win California and most certainly cruise into the presidency, or lose California, in which case he would be honor-bound to exit the race. So, roughly at midnight, I stopped fighting with my mother, finally going to bed in a foul mood. Foul not only for having to go to bed early and miss all the action, but foul for a more fundamental reason: Deep down inside, I knew the same thing that all political junkies across America knew that night—that Bobby was destined to win California, and win big, leading to his final destiny and destination: the White House. As I pulled the covers over my head to go to sleep, I blurted out an unusual prayer; "I hope the scumbag gets assassinated."

The next day, Wednesday, June 6, 1968 was a total fog. Conflicting press reports. "He's gonna be okay, he's up and talking to the doctors," from one news outlet. "He's a vegetable, he'll be like that the rest of his life," from another. Of course in reality he had never regained consciousness, and in my young mind, I was totally responsible. I made it happen. And now God was paying me back and showing me how evil I was.

For the first time in my life I prayed for real—a level of prayer I never knew existed. "Pease dear God, I didn't really mean it. Please let him live. I'm so sorry. Please?"

Watching the news on TV that night made it worse. No hard news on Bobby's condition, but instead nonstop news coverage of the Bobby I never knew. Here again was Bobby fighting organized crime, staring down crime boss Jimmy Hoffa. Here again was Bobby fighting racism and segregation, standing up to George Wallace as Wallace backed down and allowed black students to enter the University of Alabama for the first time in its then-sordid history. Here was Bobby helping to heal America just hours after the murder of Martin Luther King Jr. just a few months prior, on a flatbed truck in Indianapolis compassionately calming the angry and upset black crowd.

I couldn't believe how wrong I had been. This was not a spoiled brat presidential wannabe taking advantage of his older brother's tragic death. No, this was the impending death of a giant. Oh my God, what had I done?

Despite my pleas that next night, I could do nothing but hide my head under the covers, hoping my parents wouldn't catch me crying. And then it came: the haggard doctor coming out to meet the press. He didn't have to say a word, and for several moments, he couldn't. But it didn't matter; his face said it all. He finally began speaking and was very brief. I don't remember any of what he said, except for some reason, his closing four words as he took off his glasses:

"Mr. Kennedy was forty-two."

* * *

I continued, during my teens and early twenties in the 1970s, to be a political junkie, mostly following local New York politics. The first political "dirty trick" I ever witnessed, in 1973, would always come in as a handy memory in my career when I needed creative ways to leak damaging material, even if it meant deliberately misleading voters.

One late night in 1973 as we were about to go to sleep, a loud political sound truck came blaring down the road, passing through our white ethnic Brooklyn street. With loud Puerto Rican salsa music blaring in the background, a man with an obvious Puerto Rican accent was screaming into the microphone, *"Vote for Herman Badillio for mayor! More welfare! More food stamps!"* Badillio was the well-respected and well-liked Puerto Rican congressman from the Bronx who was running for mayor at the time; he had become America's first Puerto Rican congressman back in the 1960s.

My father immediately got angry and shouted "Why are they coming through the street at this late hour waking everyone up?!" But even at sixteen years of age, it was obvious to me what was going on. It was *not* the Badillio campaign responsible for the sound truck, but a primary opponent, knowing it would anger the residents of this white ethnic neighborhood. I couldn't believe people didn't see through this dirty trick, and felt quite proud that I did. The problem with me, though, was not only did I figure it out, I thought it was brilliant and it didn't offend me one bit.

Like most Brooklynites back in the day, I was a liberal Democrat and was glad to see Nixon go. I was for the most part ambivalent about the 1976 Carter-Ford race, although it made me very uncomfortable hearing Jimmy Carter talking nonstop about what a great born-again Christian he was. (In retrospect, it's amazing how liberals since the 1980 election of Ronald Reagan have complained so bitterly about the role evangelicals play in electing Republicans, constantly screaming about the "separation of church and state." Yet they had no problem when Democrat Jimmy Carter's campaign was the first to focus primarily on the fact that their candidate was a born-again Christian.)

It was after Carter's election that my first political metamorphosis began. It was because of Carter's sheer ineptitude that I became a Republican in 1980 and voted for Ronald Reagan. After Iran, Afghanistan, inflation, unemployment, gas lines, interest rates, malaise, and so on, I had had enough.

Besides Carter, the man most responsible for my transformation was "The Great Communicator" himself, who articulated conservatism in a way that for the first time in my lifetime not only did not come off as mean-spirited, but made a lot of sense. Ronald Reagan turned me into a Republican through simple logical persuasion. As a lifelong Democrat who was now voting Republican, I was no different than the millions of other Americans in northern ethnic states, who were now being coined "Reagan Democrats." We all changed along with the millions of normally Democratic-voting Southerners, many of whom would never have been caught dead voting for a Republican before Ronald Reagan in 1980.

Like many, if not most, Reagan voters in 1980, it started more as a vote for change against Carter than a vote for Reagan. After all, Reagan only received 51 percent of the vote in 1980. But after one year of Reagan as president, I was hooked; a true believer. I was a Republican and proud of it.

✱ ✱ ✱

I was so pumped up about the "Reagan Revolution" that I decided to run for Congress in 1982 to show my true love for the GOP. Except there was a problem: I was in a fantasy world.

I ran for Congress from my home town of Brooklyn, and never did the basic research, which would have told me that my congressional district was roughly 90 percent registered Democrat. Not just Democrat, but *Republican-hating Democrat.* It was also at the time (unbeknownst to me) the most Democratic white district in the entire nation. I learned the hard way, and as the Republican Party nominee, I got trounced by then-Congressman (and now U.S. Senator) Charles (Chuck) Schumer.

That losing campaign, however, did provide me with one of the greatest thrills of my life. All the Republican congressional candidates were invited to Washington for a one-day crash course in campaigning, and Reagan himself came in to give us a pep talk. What a thrill to see my hero in person. The man responsible for my becoming a Republican. The man who would ultimately be responsible for my later career in politics. I would never see him again until his body and casket were there for public viewing in the Capitol rotunda in 2004.

Even whilst listening to Reagan give us a dull, boilerplate speech, there was action. In these situations, there's always one wacko in the group. The nut job kept interrupting Reagan, accusing him of "selling out" to the Soviets. After Reagan's initial response, the nut job began foaming at the mouth, and still standing, he began screaming, *"The Soviets get the grain, we get the shaft!"* This time, Reagan lost his temper (or did a good job pretending to), wagged his finger at the wacko, and said "I don't know who you are," and then continued to explain his trade policy in more detail. After he was done, almost as if on cue, the rest of us erupted in applause as nut job was finally physically thrown out the door. In retrospect, it was vintage Reagan.

But my congressional run was a disaster, and I've since tried to block most of the experience of that congressional run out of my head, because of the sheer stupidity of it. However, besides getting to see Reagan in person, there is one memory that remains so very vivid. I was addressing a group of senior citizens early in the general election campaign and the audience was reacting with applause to everything I was saying—until I mentioned that I was a Republican and began to praise then-President Reagan. Before I knew what hit me, the entire audience was up on their feet, shaking their fists at me and screaming. Half of them walked out, as one old woman in the front row without any teeth kept screaming "He [Reagan] is Hitler! He is Hitler!"

It was a shock to me. I was absolutely clueless to one of the most basic facts of politics, something I would learn over and over again as Oppo Man; that a large segment of the electorate (on both political extremes) puts zero thought into their political beliefs. Just pure brainless emotion.

After my failed run for Congress in 1982, I continued to live and work in New York City. While still remaining a political junkie, I never did anything personally involving politics until 1989, when I decided to spend my spare time volunteering for the first local politician in my lifetime that really excited me.

The experience offered many "firsts" for me:

It was the first time I learned about opposition research and got a chance to do it myself, to see how good research worked and how effective it was in badly hurting different candidates in the same race.

I learned for the first time how *not* utilizing good research to its fullest advantage can be a deadly mistake.

It was the first time I got to see a professional political campaign in action.

And it was the first time I gave serious thought to making politics my career. Little did I know at the time how valuable this experience would be in my future work as a political hitman.

The candidate I volunteered for was running to become mayor of New York City. He was a former federal prosecutor extraordinaire, a latter-day Elliot Ness who'd convicted drug kingpins, crippled the mafia, cracked a complex Wall Street insider-trading conspiracy, and put away corrupt politicians. And he was a Republican to boot. Not only a Republican, but the only Republican who could possibly have a chance of becoming mayor of such a Democratic-controlled city as New

York. Little did I know, while volunteering for a campaign that would ultimately lose, that this candidate who excited me so much would go on to greatness; and in my never-humble-opinion, go on to do more good for more people than any other political figure in my lifetime with the exception for Ronald Reagan. And, as of the writing of this book, the man who I hope and believe will be America's next president, and a great one.

Of course I'm talking about fellow Brooklynite Rudy Giuliani.

Except in those days he was known as "Rudolph" Giuliani, switching to "Rudy" in 1989 when he ran for mayor. "Rudy" sounded softer than "Rudolph," and Giuliani already had an image problem of sometimes looking too "mean." He was trying to show the public a softer side.

I immediately befriended Ken Caruso, who had been one of Giuliani's top assistants at the U.S. Attorney's office, and now was his deputy campaign manager. He took a liking to me, as did Cathy Smith, the campaign's volunteer coordinator. Since I didn't yet even know what opposition research was, I asked if I could work in the press office, since that's where I believed my major strength lay.

The first problem I had, though, was spelling Giuliani's name. I kept spelling it beginning with a "Gu" instead of correctly with a "Giu." The second problem was that I kept writing his name as "Rudolph" at the time when he was first being introduced to the public as "Rudy."

I was writing press releases and thought I was doing well when I had my very first experience with office politics in a political campaign. One of the press assistants was a temperamental young lady who didn't like the fact that I was invading her "turf." How stupid and how petty, I thought at the time, not yet realizing how normal this was not only in political campaigns, but in just about any bureaucratic workplace. Even though she was a paid staffer and I was just a volunteer, she kept criticizing my work to a point where I realized she was for some stupid reason threatened by me. So I spoke to Cathy Smith, who was a pretty fair politician herself, and told her I wanted to move to the "Advance" department.

"Advance" goes to all the places the candidate will be publicly and sets up everything for the candidate in advance. For instance, if the candidate is giving a speech or campaigning somewhere, the advance team gets there beforehand and sets up all the equipment, microphones, seating arrangements, and so on. "Advance" was fun since it was not in the campaign headquarters, but out in the streets where the action was, with the *real* people. Not only that, I would get to see and meet Rudy the campaigner up-close in action for the first time.

It was fascinating watching Giuliani campaigning for public office for the first time in his life. He was a little awkward as a campaigner at first, but by the end of the campaign he was a pro. A natural. He appeared to be a little shy with people he didn't know, but he overcame it fairly easily and was, by the end of the campaign, generally likeable to the public at large. He was comfortable looking people square in the eye, and he had a great smile when he shook hands (he still does). He was equally comfortable speaking to groups, having mastered the art from his many years of press conferences as a high-profile federal prosecutor. I personally saw his progress from a slightly awkward to a very good campaigner.

Although Giuliani quickly adapted to the public campaign trail, his handling of political attacks against him was another story. I thought his Republican opponent, Ron Lauder, was a joke. But Lauder did a good job bloodying up Giuliani, spending $5 million of his own money to finance vicious campaign attack ads. The Lauder attack ads against Giuliani were the first time I saw up close how effectively negative campaigning could work, no matter how unfair and/or ridiculous the attacks.

Lauder was the heir to the Estee Lauder fortune. He was convinced to run against Giuliani by then-Republican U.S. Senator Alphonse D'Amato, who certainly must have known Lauder couldn't win, but would spend enough cash in negative ads to soften up Giuliani and make him easier to beat in the general election by D'Amato's political ally, then-Mayor Ed Koch. Even though D'Amato was a Republican and Koch a Democrat, they had always been political allies and cross-endorsed each other, going back to 1980, when Koch crossed party lines to endorse D'Amato, who barely got elected on Ronald Reagan's coattails. It also may have been personal; D'Amato was, in 1989, the most high-profile Republican politician in New York State (and like Giuliani, also Italian to boot), and perhaps Giuliani was a threat to him.

Lauder's attack ads claimed that Giuliani's men acted like Nazis regarding the alleged harassment by the U.S. Attorney's office of a death camp survivor. Giuliani's handled Lauder's attack ads in a very thin-skinned manner, responding in a defensive, angry, and nasty tone, not only toward Lauder but toward the press as well. The attacks, ridiculous as they were, appeared to catch Giuliani flat-footed, and at times it seemed he didn't know how to respond.

Lauder's negative ads did indeed work, transforming Giuliani's public image from the "knight in shining armor" he had been as a prosecutor to a mean guy. But a monkey wrench was thrown into the D'Amato-Koch plan, as Koch was knocked off by his Democratic primary opponent, then-Manhattan Borough President David Dinkins, on Primary Day, 51 percent to 42 percent. New Yorkers had become sick of the once-popular and largely successful Mayor Koch, who had spent his last term in office on the defensive as many of his political allies were hauled off to federal prison—ironically being prosecuted by then-U.S. Attorney Rudolph Giuliani. So instead of softening up Giuliani for Koch in the General Election, he was instead softened up for David Dinkins. Despite the fact that Giuliani would go on to trounce Lauder in the GOP primary, 67 percent to 33 percent, Lauder had successfully damaged Giuliani's public image so badly that the day after the primary, Giuliani trailed Dinkins by up to 21 percent in some polls.

I saw clearly how effective Lauder's negative campaigning had been against Giuliani, and learned the first two rules of opposition research:

- Lesson #1: It works! Even when the attacks are ridiculous and untrue, they can still work, especially if the candidate being attacked responds as poorly as Giuliani did in 1989.
- Lesson #2: Even when it works, it doesn't always translate into votes for the attacker, which in this case was the hapless Ron Lauder.

After Dinkins defeated Koch in the Democratic primary, an event occurred by sheer happenstance that would change my life: I was assigned to work in the campaign's "research" department. I don't recall if it was ever referred to as "*opposition* research" by the campaign, but it was the first time I learned of the shadowy euphemism and what it really meant.

Dinkins' victory over Koch seemed to catch the Giuliani campaign slightly flat-footed. It appeared they were expecting (as had I) that Koch would be their opponent. Despite Dinkins leading Koch in the polls throughout the primary season, we all nonetheless believed Koch would win. Especially surprising was the margin of Dinkins' victory over Koch. It wasn't even close—51 percent to 42 percent. During every campaign speech I personally witnessed before the primary, Giuliani primarily attacked only Koch, rarely even mentioning Dinkins. (In retrospect, it's possible Giuliani was attacking Koch and not mentioning Dinkins during the primary campaign by design. Maybe the Giuliani campaign *wanted* Koch to lose to Dinkins, which would make sense, since Koch may have been a tougher opponent in a General Election campaign because of the Jewish vote.)

I heard rumors that the Giuliani campaign had proof of Koch's homosexuality. This all occurred well before Giuliani's sexual activities became an issue and well before his high-profile divorce to local news anchorwoman Donna Hanover. Back in 1989, Giuliani appeared to be clean on that front.

Now that I was working for "Research," my first assignment after Dinkins' primary victory was to try to find the exact quotes that Dinkins had made during a campaign stop at New York City's most notorious prison, Riker's Island, to campaign among the inmates. This campaign stop sounded ludicrous to me. Not only do prisoners not vote, but it would be political suicide (or so I thought) to have a candidate for mayor of New York City stumping among some of the city's worst criminals. If Dinkins was indeed crazy enough to do such a thing, we needed to know exactly what he said when he was there. Could he possibly have said anything sympathetic to all those criminals? Anything that made Dinkins seem to be on the criminals' side, back then when the city was ravaged by crime, would have been a coup.

So off I went to Manhattan's main public library on Fifth Avenue. The exact quotes to the inmates were not reported in any of the mainstream press, but I found them in a back issue of a union publication at that library. I couldn't believe it. Dinkins had promised that, if elected, he would fight for the inmates' interests and for prisoners' rights! He intimated to all those convicts that he was "their guy." *Mind-boggling!* A respected politician, leading in the polls to become New York's next mayor, actually told some of the city's worst criminals that, if elected, he was going to go to bat for them. Years later during my twelve years as "Oppo Man," I would never see any candidate for any public office do anything this insane. Campaigning for criminals? It was not only a slap in the face to the victims of these criminals, but also a slap in the face to *all* of New York's law-abiding citizens.

I believed this was a smoking gun that would destroy Dinkins.

But I was wrong. Not because it wasn't a smoking gun, but because I believe the Giuliani campaign didn't hammer Dinkins strongly enough on the issue. While Giuliani did indeed mention it in some campaign speeches, it never became a huge campaign issue that most voters were aware of. This is how I learned Lesson #3 of opposition research and negative campaigning: If you *do* have a smoking gun against your opponent and don't use it to the fullest, you will likely pay the consequences.

I believed at that time that the campaign was not being run well. And so did Giuliani. To run his campaign, he had originally brought in DC-types who had no idea about New York City politics, which is a unique animal. He later shook up his campaign, naming his top aide Peter Powers campaign manager and bringing in Roger Ailes, now of FOX News, to do the TV ads. Both were good moves by Giuliani, but by then it was probably too late.

Despite all of Giuliani's problems during that campaign, he caught a lucky break as effective opposition research was finally used to bloody up Dinkins and make his huge lead in the polls disappear, practically overnight. Oddly enough, this great opposition research came from, of all places, the fine investigative reporting of *The Village Voice*.

The *Voice* is New York's alternative weekly newspaper, headed by investigative reporter extraordinaire Wayne Barrett. Several weeks before the election, the *Voice* broke the blockbuster negative story of the campaign: David Dinkins had not filed income-tax returns, or paid any taxes, from 1969 through 1972. He had also improperly transferred stock worth $1 million to his son for $58,000.

This double-whammy against Dinkins became a triple-whammy when it was exposed that black activist Sonny Carson, who was being paid by the Dinkins campaign, had made anti-Semitic remarks. He was then booted off the Dinkins campaign, at which point the issue was compounded when Carson told the press that he "wasn't anti-Semitic, but hated *all white people.*"

All this negativity hit Dinkins at the same time, and his once-formidable lead shaved to two points. Suddenly the race was a dead heat. This illustrates Lesson #4: Poll numbers change most drastically not due to positive issues regarding the candidates, but due to *negative* issues.

Election Day 1989 finally came, and the final results were Dinkins 51 percent, Giuliani 49 percent.

When Giuliani addressed his supporters at the Roosevelt Hotel to concede defeat, several of his supporters began yelling "No...no...no...," repeatedly interrupting his concession speech and booing every time he mentioned Dinkins. For a moment, he snapped, and again I witnessed the Giuliani temper. He angrily yelled at his own supporters who were interrupting his concession speech to be quiet, and angrily explained to them that Mr. Dinkins was now *our* mayor, the mayor for all of us, and the man who would try to bring the city together. Giuliani sincerely wished Dinkins the best, and made it at least appear that he wanted Dinkins to succeed, since he loved New York City so very much. If you believe that the true measure of a man is *not* when he's a winner, but when he faces his darkest adversity, then Giuliani measured up well in defeat.

I wish I could have handled adversity in my own life as gracefully as Giuliani did that night. After the concession speech, I was invited by Cathy Smith up to Giuliani's campaign suite to meet him, as a way of thanking me for helping out the campaign. Although I had met Giuliani several times on the campaign trail, this was the first time I got to speak to him one-on-one. It was awkward for me, since I was in such awe of the man (and still am). We only chatted for a few minutes. I gave him a copy of a cassette tape that was going to play over the PA system in the event that Giuliani won that night as he came out to address his supporters. Since he didn't win, the tape was never used, but I wanted him to have it.

It was a short, catchy song (similar to a television commercial jingle) I had written and recorded that would be played as Giuliani walked to the podium in triumph. I don't remember most of it, but I do remember the first few lines. It was pure corn:

> We're here in New York City,
> And things are lookin' fine,
> We've finally found a winner,
> In Nineteen-Eighty-Nine,
> [Blah, blah, blah]

Giuliani took the cassette tape and promised he would listen to it in private. To this day I have no idea whether or not he did.

Fast forward to exactly four years later, to Election Night 1993 at the New York Hilton Hotel, where Giuliani's campaign was holding its election-night festivities. Jazz great Lionel Hampton and his band were boogying down at the Hilton as over one thousand Giuliani supporters waited in anticipation. The eighty-one-year-old jazz legend and his band suddenly began playing louder and louder as the room erupted. Giuliani had been declared the winner. After four years of David Dinkins making New York City even more unlivable than before (which is hard to imagine, but Dinkins did it), New Yorkers finally saw the light, electing Rudy Giuliani.

* * *

Giuliani's losing 1989 campaign taught me so much about campaigning and a great deal about opposition research at the same time. The campaign also made me realize for the first time that I had excellent political instincts, or as they say, a "political antenna." In 1989, even though I was a political novice, I usually knew when the campaign was making tactical errors, particularly when it came to using, or in this case not using, opposition research as effectively as it could have. Little did I know at that time that just five years later I'd end up using this political antenna to make a living as Oppo Man for the next thirteen years.

One final note about Rudy Giuliani and New York City:

I left New York in 1990, three years before Giuliani was elected mayor. During the entire time I lived there the city was a dump; totally unlivable. Just watch ten minutes of the '70s classics "The French Connection" or "Death Wish," and you'll see what I'm talking about; a graffiti-strewn, crime-ridden dump of a city. During Giuliani's tenure as mayor and since, I have only been to New York as a visitor, since I never moved back.

When I see the beautiful city New York has become once again, it actually makes me angry. While I feel great that Giuliani single-handedly turned the city around, I nonetheless feel cheated; because all the time I was living and working there, it was *never* the city it is now. I never personally experienced the quality of life that New Yorkers do today.

When I go back to visit now, it seems like a strange city to me, definitely not the same place I lived until age thirty-three.

It definitely doesn't feel like home. Exactly as Neil Diamond wrote in the song "*I Am, I Said*": "New York's fine, but it ain't home no more."

Chapter Three

CLINTON SHOCK

B ecause of the Republicans winning the presidency easily in 1980, 1984, and 1988, I was convinced that the rest of my lifetime was going to be just like the second half of the nineteenth century, when Americans elected only Republican presidents (with the one exception of Grover Cleveland) from Abraham Lincoln in 1860 until Woodrow Wilson in 1912. I couldn't imagine a Democrat would ever get elected again as president in my lifetime.

In my mind, the American public (minus my old district in Brooklyn) was too smart to let that happen, and the proof was what happened during the 1988 Bush/Dukakis race, when Bush was able to overcome an eighteen-point deficit and pull ahead by eight points. During and after the Republican convention I believed that, no matter who was running in whatever year, once the public heard the "truth" from the GOP nominee, the race would be over, as it was in 1988.

My false sense of security was obviously shared by the 1992 Bush campaign, which never took Bill Clinton seriously.

As the Democratic Convention opened, the polls were strange indeed. Reform Party nominee H. Ross Perot was at 27 percent, President Bush at 25 percent, and Bill Clinton trailing at 22 percent. But then an even stranger thing happened. The day Clinton was to give his acceptance speech, Perot dropped out of the race. So now all those Perot supporters, who so badly wanted change, had nowhere else to go except to Bill Clinton. Clinton's nomination speech that night, while lackluster by Clinton standards, was nonetheless good enough to convince the Perot supporters that Clinton was the only real agent of change. Overnight, the formerly third-place Bill Clinton was suddenly thirty points ahead of Bush, 59 percent to 29 percent!

How could this have happened, I thought? Was Clinton's lead for real? It must have been, since he never relinquished the lead for the rest of the campaign. But despite the reality of what was going on, I was in the same fantasyland as the Bush campaign. *So what! Down 30 percentage points? It doesn't matter! Look how we overcame the eighteen-point deficit against Dukakis by tearing Dukakis apart with "Willie Horton," the "Pledge of Allegiance," and "Boston Harbor." We'll do the same thing to Bill Clinton on his draft dodging, womanizing, and overall dishonesty.*

But Bill Clinton then proceeded to break all the rules of conventional political wisdom:

- Rule # 1: It had become conventional political wisdom in all political quarters that *any* sexual indiscretion by a presidential candidate meant instant disqualification, after 1988 frontrunner Gary Hart went into the tank after the Donna Rice affair was exposed.

• Rule #2: After the Dan Quayle debacle in 1988, it became conventional political wisdom that *any* attempt to avoid the draft also meant instant disqualification.

• Rule #3: After the Joe Biden debacle of 1988, when the super-honest senator was forced out of the race for what was, in retrospect, a minor miscue (his speechwriter stole part of a speech), it became conventional political wisdom that even the most minor ethical indiscretion also meant instant political disqualification.

So much for conventional wisdom. Bill Clinton broke every single rule, and with relish. His Gennifer Flowers episode was far worse than the Gary Hart/Donna Rice affair because Ms. Flowers had tape-recorded conversations with Clinton talking about their affair. His draft-dodging episode was likewise far worse than Dan Quayle's because Clinton played the system, as opposed to Quayle, who at least served in the National Guard.

Clinton kept getting knocked down, and after each hit, he kept getting up, just like the "Joe Palooka" punching bag of my childhood. As Dan Quayle later wrote with admiration towards Clinton in his book, *Standing Firm*, "The question in life is not whether you get knocked down. You will. The question is, are you willing to get back up, and fight for what you believe in?" Quayle was right.

Ultimately, the most significant of political conventional wisdom Clinton broke was the most daunting one—challenging a sitting president who had a 91 percent approval rating after the first Gulf War, an approval rating so intimidating that the nationally known Democrats considered to be presidential timber (Mario Cuomo, Jay Rockefeller, Ted Kennedy, etc.) all decided Bush was unbeatable and took a pass.

Being the hard-core Republican I was at the time, I *hated* Bill Clinton, and I couldn't see past his lying. I now believe that he was a true visionary who was the first major politician of his time to truly understand that America was a country of passionate centrists deeply distrusting of both political extremes. While I wasn't listening to anything he was saying, Clinton was articulating this vision of what we now know as "triangulation," which was not only good *politics*, but good *policy* as well. Ironically, after twelve years as the political hack Oppo Man, I would find myself in the same political center where Clinton was back in 1992, and where I am to this day.

But at the time I hated him. I was not yet a full-fledged political hitman, yet there was an incident I recall that would foreshadow my future as Oppo Man, and hint that opposition research was my destiny. During the 1992 presidential campaign between Bush I and Clinton (which was two years prior to my becoming Oppo Man), there was an odd picture in *USA Today* with no accompanying article. It showed then-candidate Bill Clinton at a campaign rally in LA flanked by two gentlemen: one was a Mr. Charles "Q Bone" Rachal, and the other was Leon Gullette.

"Q Bone" was a convicted killer and former member of the notorious Los Angeles street gang the Crips, and Gullette was a former member of the Crips' rival street gang, the Bloods. Clinton and these two gentlemen were photographed waving their arms in the air triumphantly. The praise was in regards to their role in brokering a "truce" between the two street gangs and forming a community center with federal dollars to help former gang members.

When I saw the photo, I couldn't believe it: Clinton sharing the podium with two notorious former gang leaders from the Crips and the Bloods, one of them a convicted killer. What kind of rally was this? The photo had no accompanying news article, although a follow-up article indicated Clinton told Q Bone, "I need your help."

Help with what?

Either way, I believed the photo was a smoking gun. Whatever good deeds these two guys may have done would have been irrelevant politically. Truce or no truce, it didn't matter: A photo of Clinton standing triumphantly on a podium at a rally in Los Angeles with these two gang members shortly after the deadly riots could have been lethal for Clinton—almost as bad as Willie Horton. That is, if only the 1992 Bush campaign had the brains to use the issue against Clinton. But they never did.

I did all I could do at the time. During the three debates between Bush, Clinton, and Perot, I found out which hotel the Bush campaign honchos were staying at, and before each debate I faxed copies of the offending photo and its caption to each of Bush's top six or seven campaign advisors, pleading with them to use it against Clinton. The only one of Bush's brain trust to even respond to me was Torie Clark, then Bush's press secretary. She wrote me a simple but nice letter thanking me for the information.

Whether or not they were gun-shy and/or intimidated by the liberals' response to Willie Horton during the campaign four years prior, I don't know. Were they afraid of being labeled "racists" again? It wouldn't have mattered, since those who would have been offended by Bush using this issue would be those on the far left who would never have voted for him anyway. However, this was not the case with the "swing vote" or "soccer-mom" vote that went to Reagan and Bush the first time, but switched to Clinton in 1992. That "swing vote," I believed, would have responded to this issue, and many of those voters, I believe, would not have voted for Clinton as they did had the issue been raised. The suburban or "soccer mom" vote was deathly afraid of crime and drugs in their neighborhoods, and even more afraid of the negative influence street gangs had on their children. The fact that Clinton appeared to have embraced two notorious gang members from the equally notorious Crips and Bloods would have hurt Clinton badly with this segment of the vote. I believe many of those swing voters would have switched from Clinton to Bush just as they had four years earlier switched from Dukakis to Bush because of the Willie Horton issue. If the issue had been raised, would enough voters have defected from Clinton to change the election result? I don't know.

But maybe it would have, and here's why: during that campaign there were many big hits against Clinton, but he kept bouncing back, particularly from Gennifer Flowers and the draft dodging issue. But both those incidents involved Clinton's personal life from years earlier, which is why the public gave him so much leeway. They had nothing to do with his job as a political leader, nor any hot-button political issue.

But this was different. The political issue of crime can be deadly, as Michael Dukakis learned the hard way.

During the remainder of that campaign, as Bush was going down the toilet, I remember how I kept thinking "I wish I were running that campaign. I'd be using this photo like the 1988 campaign used Willie Horton. I'd be ramming it down their throats."

The ineptitude of that 1992 Bush campaign is regarded by many historians as the worst-run incumbent campaign in this century. Bush's 37 percent was the lowest vote total for an incumbent re-election campaign since William Howard Taft in 1912. This is particularly stunning considering Bush's 90 percent approval rating right after the first Gulf War. True Bush's final numbers were deflated from Perot siphoning off votes, but the fact still remains that 63 percent of the public didn't vote for him.

Whether or not using this issue against Clinton would have changed the results of the election, we'll of course never know. But it certainly would have moved many votes.

So, despite the fact that I was not yet a political hack and Oppo Man would not be born for another two years, this incident nonetheless showed once again that I had a good political antenna concerning negative issues, and which ones would work in a political campaign. Even if the Bush campaign didn't have the stomach to use it.

Chapter Four

THE BIRTH OF OPPO MAN
AND THE REPUBLICAN
REVOLUTION

When Clinton became president, I was still in too much shock to think straight. All I could think of was one thing: I would now commit my life to doing anything in my power to stop Bill Clinton and those "evil" Democrats, who now controlled the White House and both houses of Congress. I immediately hit the road to the nation's capital, where I went on over twenty interviews for a Republican job on Capitol Hill. Figuring my experience in writing about politics would land me a job as a press secretary, I was ready for action.

Most of the interviews, mostly with Capitol Hill senior-level staffers, went very badly, and in the beginning I couldn't understand why. I was convinced I was making a great case: They should hire me as their press secretary since, through my writing and speaking, I would help them better articulate Republican positions. It was that word "*better*" that was automatically disqualifying me from being hired. They took my use of the word "better" to mean I was calling them inept. I eventually learned the hard way that the *last* thing the person interviewing me wanted was someone who could actually improve their office. In fact, any person with an IQ over 12 would be considered a "threat" to these people (this is why Capitol Hill offices are known for deliberately "dumbing down" their staffs).

While I was suffering through this spate of bad interviews in early 1994, I was fortunate enough to meet two high-level Republican staffers who made a big difference in my life. Both were nice guys who invited me into their offices during my trips there, to give me some much-needed advice on the ways of Washington. And they were happy to let me pick their brains.

Ironically, and probably not coincidentally, both men would be largely responsible for the birth of Oppo Man.

The first man was Richard Billmire, the "Research Director" at the National Republican Congressional Committee, who was the first to explain to me why my interviews were going poorly with these six simple words: "Washington is not a meritocracy, Stephen." I had never before even heard the word "meritocracy," but I immediately figured out what it meant. He gave me some more good advice on the ways of Washington and how to improve my performance during interviews. Billmire would later become my mentor, an Oppo Man's Oppo Man.

The second man who took me under his wing during those days was Chris Hennick, then-Chairman of the Republican Governor's Association (RGA), which was an arm of the RNC. Chris had been brought to DC by fellow Mississippian and RNC Chairman Haley Barbour. Unlike Billmire, a blue-collar type and former union man from

Baltimore, Chris Hennick was the consummate "Southern gentleman." But unlike many of their high-level political hack peers, both Billmire and Hennick were smart, and unpretentious enough to give this stranger from Brooklyn their best advice on how the nation's capitol worked.

One other thing kept me in a positive frame of mind during the interview debacle: the natural beauty of the city. Whatever foul mood I was in after each interview would disappear the moment I walked outside from whatever Capitol Hill building I was in. The sight of the U.S. Capitol and the adjacent mall with its reflecting pool, and all it represented, were the most physically and emotionally beautiful sights I had ever seen. No matter how many failed interviews, the moment I saw the Dome again, with the sun almost always reflecting off one of its sides, my anger immediately disappeared and I would believe more strongly that this was the city for which I was destined. My unconditional love for the city and what it represented made me even more determined every day to make myself a success in politics, no matter how many obstacles or how I had to do it. Some would say it's because I'm a Taurus; stubborn.

*   *   *

As 1994 unfolded, both U.S. Senate seats were up for grabs in Tennessee during the same election year. It is very unusual for that to happen, and it was a result of Al Gore's ascension to the vice presidency in 1993. Therefore, a special election was being held for his seat, along with the GOP challenge to Tennessee's other senator, eighteen-year veteran Democratic

Senator Jim Sasser.

For Gore's open seat, both parties had already chosen their nominees. The GOP tapped Fred Thompson, Hollywood actor and and current presidential wannabe, and the Democrats chose respected moderate Congressman Jim Cooper, a competent guy with zero charisma.

For the other Senate seat, the Republican "six-pack" (the six Republicans running in the GOP primary) faced Democratic veteran Senator Jim Sasser, chosen at the time to be the Senate majority leader after the elections. (Little did anyone know at the time that, after the 1994 elections, there would be no Democratic majority leader anymore; nor would there be a Senator Sasser.)

I wanted so badly to be a press secretary, and I finally got the opportunity. Since I had briefly lived in Nashville during the early 1990s, I was very familiar with the state's politics. I finally took the job of press secretary with one of the six-pack candidates, right-winger Steve Wilson of Memphis, as soon as the position was offered. From the first minute of my interviews with both Steve and his terrific campaign manager, Bob Bibee of Chattanooga, we all hit it off great. I knew immediately I was with the right campaign. Wilson eventually came in third place in the six-way race, badly outspent by the eventual winner, political novice and Vanderbilt doctor-par-excellence (and later Senate Majority Leader) Bill Frist. But while working as press secretary for Steve Wilson, I learned, as I had with the Giuliani campaign, about opposition research—and how to use it by leaking damaging info to the press.

In primaries like this one, the front-runner is always being attacked, which in this case meant Bill Frist. In press conferences

I organized in which my candidate, Steve Wilson, would get endorsements from pro-life groups, it was fun pointing out that Bill First was neither pro-life nor pro-choice but "multiple choice," as he flip-flopped all over the map on the abortion issue. Since the majority of Frist's new worth was from HCA stock—HCA being the medical consortium created by his father and at that time run by his brother—we also broadcast the fact that HCA hospitals made millions on abortions. As a result, despite winning the primary, Frist didn't do so well with the evangelical vote.

I also saw how bad opposition research could backfire. Former Chattanooga mayor Bob Corker, the eventual second place finisher (who like Frist, would also spend millions of his own money on the race), ran an ad in the closing weeks of the campaign attacking Frist for not serving in Vietnam, with video footage of war protesters in the background. This was absurd, since Frist was never a war protester, and had avoided the draft with a college deferment. The voters saw through the attack ad for the nonsense it was, and Frist went on to an easy primary victory after Corker was called "pond scum" by Frist's campaign consultant, Tom Perdue. As I learned later as Oppo Man, and go into detail later in this book, negative advertising only works when the negative charge against the candidate is believable. In this case, the Corker ad against Frist was not believable. It was absurd. Ironically, when Bill Frist retired in 2006 after honoring his 1994 campaign pledge to serve only two terms, his successor in the U.S. Senate would be none other than his old nemesis, Bob Corker. Frist, showing immense class and integrity, not only honored his self-imposed pledge to serve only two terms in the Senate, he also graciously and wholeheartedly supported his old foe Corker in 2006 to take his place in the Senate.

That 1994 campaign was my first contact with Christian evangelicals, who to my way of thinking were firmly divided into two camps. The first camp was the vast majority of evangelicals, "legitimate" Christians, who not only talked the talk, but walked the walk and lived their lives in conjunction with their faith. The second camp was in the minority, the "phony" Christians, who took the concept of "grace" to such an absurd degree that they believed there was absolutely no connection between their faith and their actions as human beings. It's these "phony" Christians that I believe give so many good evangelicals a bad name.

Steve Wilson was a great guy; an evangelical who was a true Christian in the finest sense. But his faith turned out to be a major weakness, in my opinion, because I believe he was given bad advice and led astray by certain Christian advisors. Steve appeared to be conned fairly often by these "Christians" who advised him during the campaign but, as far as I know, had little, if any, campaign experience. It was a disaster.

As the campaign wore on, campaign manager Bob Bibee and I formed an alliance as Bibee tried to convince Steve that the sycophants surrounding him were ignoramuses. But Bibee and I lost our influence with Steve, who would always defer to his "Christian" sycophants.

For instance, when I scored a major coup by cajoling then-President of the Christian Coalition Ralph Reed to have a personal sit-down with Steve, Steve was convinced by his sycophants to snub Reed, instead making a campaign stop at a church that day. While the Christian Coalition as a charitable organization could not legally support any political candidate, Ralph Reed could *personally* endorse a candidate, as many evangelical leaders endorsed Jimmy Carter in 1976 and later endorsed Ronald Reagan in 1980 and 1984. A personal sit-down with Ralph Reed, resulting in his possible endorsement of Wilson, would have been front-page news, and a huge political boost for Wilson.

But Wilson instead spent the day at a campaign stop in a Tennessee church where he may have gained one hundred votes at best. A Ralph Reed endorsement in the *Tennesseean*, the newspaper serving "The Buckle of the Bible Belt," may have won Wilson tens of thousands of votes. But it didn't happen. However, Steve was still a strong enough candidate to finish third against two extremely rich opponents, Frist and Corker, both of whom spent millions of their own money.

However, the experience with incompetent political hacks was very helpful, as Oppo Man would later deal with the massive incompetence of many campaigns he worked for and against.

Having said that, it would be derelict if I did not mention that, despite the problems I encountered with "phony" Christians, the vast majority of Evangelicals I personally encountered during that 1994 race (and later on in my travels throughout America as Oppo Man) are the salt of the earth; great folks who use their faith to make this country and world a better place.

This is why it makes me sick to my stomach that these fine Americans are represented politically by such people as Pat Robertson, who believes 9/11 occurred because of "the abortionists and the feminists and the gays," and who said Ariel

Sharon suffered a stroke brought on by God because Sharon advocated the Israeli withdrawal from Gaza in order to make peace with the Palestinians. (The fact that Sharon was dangerously overweight and pushing eighty was apparently lost on Mr. Robertson.) I now sadly and fearfully realize that if Robertson and his ilk ever gain political power in America (he did run for president in 1988, claiming he didn't really want to but God told him to), they would do everything in their power to turn America into a theocracy.

First of all, they appear to be thrilled every time there is war, death, and turmoil in the Middle East, believing it's all part of Biblical prophesy. During the first gulf war it was Saddam who was the Anti-Christ; now it's bin Laden and/or Hezbollah.

However, none of the evangelical's outrageous extremism is nearly as offensive to me as their reaction—nonreaction, really—to the Scott Peterson conviction. For the first time since *Roe v. Wade*, evangelicals had a legal precedent that a fetus (baby Connor Peterson) was a human being, reinforced by a double-murder conviction. However, are the evangelicals, who have attempted every legal maneuver imaginable since 1973 to overturn *Roe*, using this legal precedent that's been handed to them on a silver platter?

No, because they refuse to make the case against abortion if it is not a religiously driven argument. The Scott Peterson conviction, and the legal precedent that a fetus is a human being, was not a *religious* decision by the California courts, but a moral one. Since it wasn't a religious-based decision, the evangelicals won't use it.

* * *

So much for the evangelicals.

Despite Steve Wilson's loss to Bill Frist, I was feeling great. I was confident that I could succeed in this business and that I had good political instincts. I felt I had a future as a political press secretary, and, after the Wilson experience, I was convinced that I was far more intelligent than most political hacks.

The day after the primary, I was glad to learn that Beth Fortune—the press secretary for then-Congressman Don Sundquist, who was the Republican nominee for governor of Tennessee—was looking for an assistant press secretary.

Sundquist was running against Nashville mayor (and today current Tennessee governor) Phil Bredesen. The race was looking to be close, and I knew Sundquist had a great shot to win. I also felt I had a good chance of getting the job, since, as Steve Wilson's press secretary, I personally knew the important members of the press throughout the state of Tennessee and was familiar with the majority of Tennessee's ninety-five counties, having traveled to most of them during the Wilson campaign. So the day after the primary, I went in, applied for the job, and had a good interview.

I was feeling good about the interview when I got home. Then I received a phone message that would change my life. It was the huge break I'd been waiting for and it came at the most unexpected time.

Richard Billmire, the "Research Director" from the National Republican Congressional Committee in DC, had left a message for me to call him back. As mentioned earlier, I had met Richard briefly earlier that year in DC, but never had a formal interview. Just a friendly chat.

When I returned Richard's call, he told me he had just been given funding to hire three researchers to do "field research" for open congressional seats (seats where there is no into the opposing candidate's district to dig up whatever dirt you can. Since I was already in Tennessee, Billmire offered me the job to do the field research in the Southern seats they were keying on. These were all congressional seats held by retiring Democrats that the Republicans had a shot of picking up, because polls in those districts indicated voters' massive dislike for then-President Clinton.

I told Richard I'd call him the next day with my answer. I wasn't sure which was the better job—digging up dirt in small Southern cities against Democratic congressional candidates, or possibly being the more respectable and serious "assistant press secretary" for the likely next governor of Tennessee, Don Sundquist. But it was an easy decision; so easy that I didn't even bother to follow up on my interview with Sundquist's office. Even if I was offered the job with Sundquist, and he became governor, I would probably wind up with a job in his press office, which meant living in Nashville, the state capital. However, if I took the "research" job with the NRCC, that was my ticket to Washington, DC, after the election.

Washington, DC—that beautiful city I had visited so many times, with the terrible disconnect between its physical beauty and my repeated failures during all my interviews there. Now, after all those months of failed interviews, Billmire was offering me a job without having ever interviewed me. How strange indeed. And the timing was eerie; Billmire received the funding to hire me and called me exactly one day after Steve Wilson's loss to Frist, my first day of unemployment. Believing that I was fated for the nation's capitol, I called Billmire and told him I'd accept the job.

But, of course, before I could make any possible move to Washington, I had to spend the rest of that 1994 election cycle going to all the Southern cities where I was now being assigned to dig up dirt on Democratic congressional candidates.

Without even interviewing me for the job, Billmire simply and casually explained to me over the telephone what to do. We had a great rapport from the beginning. Not only did I figure out how to do the job pretty quickly, I was also very good at it. Like I said so many times earlier, I had a great political antenna, meaning a good sense of what negative issues could be effectively used against the candidates I was researching. But as good a student as I may have been when it came to learning opposition research, I was lucky to have had the best teacher and mentor, Richard Billmire. I could have never done it without him.

My first stop was Chattanooga, Tennessee, only 100 miles down I-24 from Nashville. But it was 100 miles that would bring the biggest change in my life without my even knowing it: "Oppo Man" was being born.

✳ ✳ ✳

Upon arriving in Chattanooga, I immediately met Republican nominee Zach Wamp, my first Republican congressional candidate and the man on whose opponent I would be digging up dirt. I immediately hit it off with Wamp, who happened to be exactly the same age as me, and his campaign manager, Andrew Blaylock, with whom I became good friends after the election when we both moved to the nation's capitol.

Wamp's life was a fascinating and compelling one. A real estate broker and former Tennessee Republican Party regional director, he had narrowly lost the same congressional seat two years prior to Democratic incumbent Marilyn Lloyd. On the last weekend before the 1992 election (these elections always fall on a Tuesday), the Lloyd campaign pulled one of the greatest opposition research ploys I'd ever heard of—sending out a damaging mailing against Wamp just before the election. This meant that Wamp didn't have time to respond with a mailing or TV ad of his own. Adding to the brilliance of this ploy was the fact that the attack ad was unanswerable.

A recovered cocaine addict, Wamp had admirably turned his life around by defeating drugs through rehab, becoming a true "born-again-Christian," and finding a beautiful wife with whom he raised a beautiful family. But none of that mattered the weekend before the 1992 election, when a direct-mail piece came to the homes of all likely voters in the district, showing Zach's mug shot when he been arrested years earlier, while still in the throes of his drug addiction. It cost Wamp the 1992 election. He was slightly ahead of Congresswoman Lloyd before the weekend, but after the piece hit the mail, Wamp wound up losing the race, 51 percent to 49 percent.

It was now two years later. Lloyd knew she had no chance of pulling off the same miracle, since the drug story was now old news and most voters in the district knew Wamp had beaten his cocaine addiction. In addition, Lloyd knew it was shaping up to be a big Republican year (how big, we had no idea at the time). So, in 1994, Lloyd retired and Wamp won the Republican primary. He was now lucky to be facing what appeared to be a weak Democratic candidate in Randy Button, Roane County property assessor.

After meeting with the Wamp campaign, I was given my first assignment: dig up all the dirt I could on Randy Button. I was good at the job from the start—and lucky, too. Mostly through Richard Billmire's guidance, and somewhat though my own experience from some former investigative reporting I had done, I knew exactly where to look.

The congressional district they were vying for was one of those weirdly gerrymandered districts that zigzagged from Wamp's hometown of Chattanooga, in the southeast part of the state bordering Georgia, all the way up to central east Tennessee, where Button's home town of Kingston (near Knoxville) is located. My first stop was the libraries in Roane County (where Button was from) and in Hamilton County (where Wamp was from), reading from all the papers that covered Button's victory in the Democratic primary.

As a general rule, during primaries the Democrats run to the left and the Republicans run to the right. Then, in the general election, they both jockey for the political center. In most cases, especially in the South, Democratic primary candidates take liberal positions that come back to bite them in the general elections on hot-button issues such as crime, welfare, taxes, and abortion. Going though the papers from the three months before the primary, I studied all of Button's statements to the press, all of his remarks at political events, and all the positions he took during debates. It was a treasure trove of opposition research, as Button was forced to take usual liberal positions on the different issues. Unfortunately for him, those liberal positions wouldn't play well in this mostly Democratic but conservative district.

Back in 1994, I had yet to encounter Nexis (the online newspaper database), which was in its infancy then. Instead, I had to go though microfilm of the news articles in the libraries. Most folks would find this boring, but not me. I loved reading through old newspapers searching for dirt. Also, since my teenage years, I had always read one or two newspapers per day, a habit I picked up from my father, who now reads about ten newspapers per day online.

My next stop was the courthouse, which is another standard component of all opposition research. In the county, federal, and municipal courthouses, records of residents' having lawsuits or liens filed against candidates, delinquent property taxes, divorces, as well as deeds, mortgages, and business filings, are all public record for anyone off the street to see.

Again, I got lucky; this time, *really* lucky. Going though Button's deeds and mortgages, I found that he had sold his house to a key financial supporter, and at the same time purchased the house of the person to whom he had just sold his house. This house swap looked fishy for one key reason: Right afterwards, Randy Button put a much-needed infusion of campaign cash into his campaign, via a $54,000 loan to the campaign from himself. The infusion of cash came at the critical period right before the Democratic primary, which Button won in an upset. The money was almost to the dollar the amount of his profit from the controversial house swap.

How convenient.

And subject to serious question, since the person with whom he swapped houses was a campaign contributor from whom he possibly had, during the swap, received more money for the sale of his home than what the house was worth.

All the information regarding Button loaning his campaign the much-needed dough was also a public record with the Federal Election Commission (FEC). FEC records are also a key part of opposition research because they show all campaign contributions, who they come from, how campaign dollars are spent, and, in this case, a controversial infusion [loan] into the campaign by the candidate himself at a critical time.

While it's fairly common for candidates to loan money to their campaigns, this loan looked shady since the money came from the controversial house swap between the candidate and a key financial supporter.

I couldn't believe how lucky I was on my first job as "Oppo Man," finding something that could badly hurt Button's candidacy. And I couldn't believe how much fun "oppo" was. Instead of having to watch every word I said and write as a press secretary, and feel under the constant pressure of the campaign, I now had a job where I worked alone and set my own hours, as long as I got the work done. Despite how much I had wanted the job of press secretary, actually having been one never felt completely comfortable to me. Having to watch every word I uttered to the press, and always having to think before I spoke never came naturally to me. On the other hand, after one week on the job as "Oppo Man" it all came so naturally to me, and I was good at it. Completely by accident, I had found my niche.

However, even though I had done a good job finding this "research" it seemed at the time that what I found wouldn't even be used. As a general rule in all political campaigns, if your candidate is up by at least ten to fifteen points, you do *not* go negative or attack your opponent. It's counterproductive if you're way ahead, since as a general rule, you want your candidate to appear above the fray if he or she is that far ahead. But of course you still need the research just in case your candidate's lead dwindles or disappears altogether.

That is what happened here.

Throughout this race, Wamp's pollster *par excellence* Ed Goetz, one of the best in the country, showed Wamp far ahead during most of the general election campaign. Hence, none of my research was likely to be needed. At least that's what we thought.

But Button was slowly chipping away at Wamp's lead with his attacks, mostly old rehashes of Wamp's prior drug problems. Wamp's twenty-five-point lead dropped to twenty, then to fifteen, then in the closing two weeks, Zach was only ahead by seven to ten points. Finally, the Wamp campaign fired back and went negative. My research was used in a last-minute attack ad against Button during the campaign's final week. In the attack ad, Button was hit on several issues, including the controversial house sale. Wamp held on to win, 52 percent to 47 percent.

On election night I felt great knowing I'd helped Zach win. My belief that I had also helped many other Republican candidates as well as Wamp, leading to the historical 1994 takeover of congress, confirmed what I always believed to be true: that I was destined for a career in politics, and that I did the right thing by not giving up during all those bad interviews earlier that year. I was finally doing something with my life that I believed was constructive and important.

Besides the Wamp/Button race, I had done the same work researching the Democratic opponents of congressional campaigns of South Carolina Republicans Mark Sanford and Lindsay Graham; JC Watts of Oklahoma; Roger Wicker of Mississippi; and Sue Kelly and Dan Frisa of New York. All of these seats were critical since they all had been previously held by retiring Democrats, and were all eventually won by Republicans. These seats were to become part of the fifty-one-seat nationwide gain that the Republicans made in the House in 1994, resulting in Republican control of the House for the first time in forty years. Ironically, in 2002, Sanford would become South Carolina's governor, and Graham would become the state's U.S. Senator, replacing the retiring, one-hundred-year-old Strom Thurmond.

The Democratic opponents of Sanford and Graham were very easy to research because both Robert Barber, Jr., and James Bryan served for many years in the South Carolina State Legislature. Every state capital has a "state library" that is a treasure trove for opposition researchers. Every bad vote made by any state legislator can be found there.

Going through Barber's and Bryan's votes as state legislators, it wasn't long before I found bad vote after bad vote (which, in superconservative South Carolina, means liberal votes). I went through thousands of pages of state legislative minutes in order to get the goods. This kind of research would certainly bore the living daylights out of most people, but for Oppo Man, it was "Oppo Heaven."

Both Sanford and Graham won easily.

J. C. Watts' race in Norman, Oklahoma was also fascinating. The soon-to-be GOP-star Congressman Watts was a former University of Oklahoma stud quarterback who had led the Sooners to Orange Bowl victories in 1979 and 1980. Watts had had a successful career in the Canadian Football League before moving back to Oklahoma, where he was a commissioner on the State Corporation Council as well as a youth minister. He was now running for Congress in an all-white Oklahoma district.

David Perryman, Watt's dull, nondescript opponent from Chickasaw, Oklahoma, didn't appear to have much of a record to research, but it didn't matter. Oppo Man found that Perryman had served on the Chickasaw school board that had supported some off-the-wall (at least most parents in Oklahoma thought so) education agenda items dealing with homosexuality, condoms, and the like.

With the help of my research, Watts easily won his 1994 race. But a bigger factor in his strong victory was an attack counterproductive ad against Watts that backfired because it was considered racist. The ad came on the heels of a whispering campaign against Watts, who as a young man had fathered two illegitimate children with two different women. The charge proved to be true, but it never really damaged Watts. The voters saw that Watts' kids were born (as opposed to aborted) and were brought up by J. C.'s parents. J. C. was now happily married with five children, and was a very nice guy.

So, when that issue went nowhere, the Perryman campaign got desperate and ran the controversial ad against Watts. The ad is considered to this day, one of the worst in the history of political ads, boomeranging badly against Perryman. The voice-over in the ad was accompanied by a photo of Watts circa 1974, when he sported a huge Afro. It was believed by the Perryman campaign that in the South, a photo of a threatening looking black man with a huge afro would generally scare people. But this was J.C. Watts, hometown hero. Every viewer saw through this ad for the crap it was, because, by 1994, *everyone* knew the 1970s was a fashion and hairstyles wasteland. Not only that, every football fan in Oklahoma (which means 90 percent of the state) was familiar with J. C.'s afro from the 1970s because it was during that time that he led the state's beloved Sooners to those two Orange Bowl championships.

After seeing the ad, my first instinct was to figure the Perryman campaign was just plain stupid. But then again, it's more likely it was late in the campaign, they were far behind and about to go down to a terrible defeat, and they just figured "Hey, we got nothing to lose. What the hell. Let's take a shot."

Final Results: Watts 52 percent, Perryman 43 percent

Another interesting race occurred in New York, where Republican Sue Kelly from Westchester County, the old-money suburb of New York City, was running against Hamilton Fish Jr. Fish's father and grandfather had represented the district in Congress for generations. So why wasn't Fish Jr. elected to follow in their footsteps? Because Oppo Man found that Fish Jr. was an editor of *The Nation* magazine at a time, during the Reagan and Bush years in the 1980s, when the magazine flat-out supported Communist efforts against America. They even sponsored "Peace Trips" to Communist Cuba and then-Communist Nicaragua.

Fish was such a radical that his own father, the retiring congressman, told voters not to vote for him, especially since he was deliberately trying to confuse and fool the voters into believing they were voting for his dad. (They both technically had the same name, Hamilton Fish "Jr.") In the end the voters weren't fooled, since Fish's dad and granddad were both Republican icons, whereas this particular "Jr." was obviously not and was running as a Democrat. Final result: Kelly 52 percent, Fish 36 percent.

Of all the races I ever worked on, this was one of the most fun. Can you imagine poring through all those issues of *The Nation* and its communist propaganda, and thinking in disbelief, "This guy's running for Congress? In America?"

Finally, there was my work on behalf of Republican congressional candidates Dan Frisa from Long Island, who easily beat Democrat Phil Schiliro, and Roger Wicker of Mississippi, who easily defeated Democrat Bill Wheeler, 63 percent to 37 percent.

For the record, after the election, only two of the above-mentioned candidates I helped to elect thanked me. While in DC for their orientation after the election but before their swearing in, Zach Wamp of Tennessee and Mark Sanford of South Carolina came to my office at the NRCC to personally thank me.

Chapter Five

PERKS OF THE JOB

I t felt great to finally spend time in my beloved Washington, DC, with all its splendor, not as some schnook struggling through bad interview after bad interview, but as a paid employee for the Republican Party, doing (I believed) great things for America. You could say I was living the life of Riley.

But there was another special perk of becoming "Oppo Man." Different women in every city I visited. In the courthouses. In the libraries. In the hotels. In the restaurants and bars. In the streets. It was crazy.

I discovered quickly during my first oppo job for Zach Wamp's campaign in Tennessee that, just as men from the North find women with a southern accent attractive, even sexy, the flip side of that equation is also true. A guy like me with a New York accent is such a novelty in parts of the South (the rural parts in particular) that it's not difficult to get a woman's attention simply by speaking. And the way we dress and look is also different than most southerners, and that adds to the allure for many southern women.

Wamp's Tennessee congressional district was primarily rural, with the pretty city of Chattanooga thrown in for good measure. In that part of the state, as well as in much of rural America, there are few restaurants to choose from. That's where I first encountered one of the great staples of the South, the Waffle House.

Small, blue-collar, somewhere between a diner and a coffee shop specializing in breakfast food, Waffle Houses are located right off exits of federal interstate highways throughout the south. Being from the north, I had never tasted such delicious fare in my life. I got especially hooked on the hash browns. Sure, I had eaten hash browns at places like IHOP and Shoneys, but they never tasted anything like the hash browns at the Waffle House. Do you know why? The food is so greasy.

There's always action at the Waffle House. Since they're open 24/7, it's not unusual to see some post-barroom brawls after the bars have closed. Sometimes the girls take swings at the guys too, or start scratching their guy's car parked in the parking lot after he gets caught with another woman. One time when I was there (I swear to God this is true), a car came careening right through the glass window of the Waffle House and crashed right into the juke box. Fortunately, no one was hurt.

In the big-city Waffle Houses, the waitresses are usually blue-collar women. It's their regular job. But when you go out into the hinterlands, the Waffle House usually employs high school and college age girls, many of them beautiful.

That's where I met Courtney.

Back in 1994, as I was beginning my career as Oppo Man,

I saw Courtney at a Waffle House in Kingston, Tennessee, a small town near Knoxville. It was right smack in the middle of Zack Wamp's congressional district and late at night; there was literally nowhere else to go. She was nineteen, and I don't remember if she was working there or was there as a patron.

I had always lived in urban environments, and had never dated a small-town girl before. I was thirty-seven at the time, and I had dated primarily professional women and divorcees my entire adult life. Never anyone like Courtney.

Courtney lived with her divorced mom in a small house in rural Johnson City, Tennessee, right on the Tennessee/Virginia border, sort of in the middle of nowhere. She had a forty-five-minute drive into work every day. She was poor and going to college part time. She was beautiful and sweet.

After meeting Courtney at the Waffle House, I immediately asked her out. A day or two later we had dinner. Despite never having been with a young country girl like Courtney, I felt confident. After all, I was Oppo Man—I could do no wrong.

After dinner, I drove her home. We were right outside the front of the house and I was kissing her goodnight. As we kept kissing, I asked Courtney, "What if your mother sees us? The light is still on in the house and we're in a car right in the driveway." Courtney explained to me that it was okay since she had already told her mother about me and her mother encouraged her to see me. She already liked me. "Without even meeting me?" I asked Courtney.

So she brought me inside to meet her mother. Her mother loved me, and after some idle banter, she left Courtney and me alone. Then it finally hit me what was going on. Her mother *wanted* the relationship to advance with Courtney. She knew how difficult it was for her daughter to meet a decent guy in her environment. And me, coming into her house, I didn't look like the typical guy from that part of town. My clothing and accent were attractive to both Courtney *and* her mother.

I had unwittingly brought the two of them hope for Courtney in a life that is often bleak. Courtney's father had left them right after Courtney was born, forsaking her mother to an adult life full of hopelessness.

During my years as Oppo Man, I would meet women all over America in the same state of hopelessness: single mothers forced to live in small towns because that's where their children go to school, or because the child's father lives there and has visitation rights. In most of small-town America, it's very difficult for these single moms to meet the right man, since they are so stuck and isolated, where they know every bar, club, and single man in a fifty- to one-hundred-mile radius. The Internet now makes it easier for women in these situations to meet men, but for the most part it's a hopeless situation.

Although I hadn't yet learned this when I first met Courtney, I know now that to both mother and daughter, I was Courtney's possible ticket out of the difficult lifestyle that her mother had suffered through for twenty years. Courtney's mom wanted so badly for Courtney not to suffer the same fate. The fact that I was eighteen years older than her daughter (and not too far off in age from her mother) didn't matter.

I saw Courtney one more time before I had to leave Tennessee for other Southern states where I had to research other political candidates. She asked me if she could stay with me at my hotel that night. Her mother told her it was okay.

At the time I didn't realize it, but Courtney was very special. When we were intimate, I did feel real love for her. She probably feared it would be our last time together (and, of course, it was) so she was more loving than any woman I had ever been with up to that point in my life. All through the night, she kept saying "I love you," to which I would always give the obligatory reply, "I love you, too." Not that I didn't feel it at the time. I did. But the seriousness of those words and how real they were for Courtney didn't hit me until the next morning when I had to go.

Courtney began to cry and asked me to please not leave her. When I told her I had to go, she asked me to take her with me. She and her mother had even discussed it. At that time, I had no idea how commonplace this situation is, but I would learn the hard way. People in bad situations will often meet someone they believe can take them out of that situation, whether it's a bad marriage or the hopelessness I previously described. And they will take off with someone the first or second time they met them. It happens all the time. I didn't know it at the time, but during the next twelve years as Oppo Man, this scene would repeat itself many times. Not only with young women like Courtney, but with single mothers like her mom; even with married women in bad marriages.

So I just did the best I could with Courtney, trying to extricate myself in one piece, while at the same time trying to make Courtney feel good. Or, at least, not feel so bad. Promising her over and over again that I loved her, too, and would be back to see her again. And in my mind I believed my own bullshit. I really thought I'd see her again.

I never did.

I did tell her the truth, that I had to leave Tennessee, but I also told her that I would come back soon to see her again. The same pathetic scene would play out for Oppo Man over the next twelve years, as he met and left women in city after city. Not that he didn't see some of them again. He did. But only when it was convenient for Oppo Man. Basically, only if and when he had to be back in that city again sometime later would he see the women again.

But with Courtney, it was the first time I went through this awkward dance. I could be forgiven this time, because I was indeed sincere in wanting to see her again, and in believing that I would. But years later, I was pulling the same bullshit with other women, when surely I knew it was bullshit. The fact was, with each woman, I really had no idea whether or not I would see her again.

In retrospect, knowing what I know now, I should have taken Courtney with me when we first met. At least I should have given it a chance. It may have worked out and it may not have. If it had worked out between us, I would not only have saved Courtney from hopelessness, but I would have also saved myself from what was to become the hopelessness in my own personal life over the next twelve years, going from woman to woman with no clue as to what I was doing.

After I left Courtney and Tennessee, my next stop was Tupelo, Mississippi, to research the Democratic opponent of Republican congressional candidate Roger Wicker. In Tupelo, I had an experience with a woman I met there different from my experience with Courtney, but also an experience that would be played out over and over again for Oppo Man.

Tupelo is also a nice small city, pure blue-collar and cigarette-smoking. It had three or four clubs, and once I walked inside one of them, I knew I was going to be okay. Most of the guys were locals, and the women looked at me a little differently. So I got lucky there.

Except this time the young lady, unlike Courtney, had no illusions. She was older, probably about thirty or so, and she knew the score. I was leaving in a few days. No promises. No broken hearts.

I wish they all could have been that simple.

Chapter Six

BUSH VERSUS CHILES: THE 1994 FLORIDA GUBERNATORIAL RACE

I t was mid-October 1994, only a couple of weeks before the election on November 8, and most of my work as Oppo Man for the 1994 election cycle was winding down. The traveling part of my job (or what we refer to as "field research") was pretty much done, so I was spending the closing weeks of the campaign in the Washington, DC, office of the NRCC, just a block away from the Capitol.

Our offices were on the second floor, whereas our counterparts at the RNC were on the ground floor. As I entered work one day, nature called, so instead of immediately going up to our second-floor offices, I bolted into the first-floor men's room.

As I stood at the urinal, in walked Chris Hennick, at the time the director of the Republican Governor's Association (RGA), an arm of the RNC. Chris later served in the White House as deputy chief of staff to Karl Rove and as deputy assistant to President George W. Bush. He also was Bush's contact man to New York Mayor Rudy Giuliani on 9/11. Chris eventually left the White House for a job with Giuliani Partners, the ex-mayor's consulting firm. As of this writing, he's with Giuliani's presidential campaign.

The moment Chris saw me, a look of relief came over his face, but I didn't know why. "Are you still doing oppo up there?" he asked, meaning on the second floor where I worked. "Yeah, why?" I responded. Chris, as head of the RGA, was in charge of all the gubernatorial races across the country. He explained that Jeb Bush, who was running in his first campaign for governor in Florida (as was his brother George simultaneously in Texas) had a problem.

Since his press secretary had to travel full-time with the candidate, they needed another press person to field calls at the campaign's headquarters in Tallahassee. "How would you like to spend the rest of the campaign out of this crappy weather and down in sunny Florida?" Chris asked, a big grin on his face.

Chris remembered that I had been a press secretary before becoming Oppo Man. At that point, I still believed that after the election was over I might go back to being a press secretary. How could I in my right mind pass up a trip to Florida in late-October? This was action!

So Chris asked my boss, NRCC "Research Director" Richard Billmire, if the RGA and the Jeb Bush campaign could borrow me for the remainder of the election season, since my oppo work was for the most part done. Billmire, a friend of Chris' didn't give it a moment's thought and graciously let me go. The next thing I knew I was on a plane to Tallahassee, studying the campaign material provided me by the RGA so I could quickly bone up on a race with which I was totally unfamiliar.

After reading the material, I realized that the campaign had gotten itself into a mess. As the campaign was winding down, the Bush campaign was losing ground fast, despite greatly outspending the incumbent Democratic governor, Lawton Chiles, despite liberal incumbent Democrats like Chiles dropping like flies in 1994 (especially in the South), despite 1994 having the most Republican-friendly political climate of any year in the twentieth century, and, finally, despite previously having a ten-point lead in polls. As I was touching down in Florida, "Walkin' Lawton" Chiles had big momentum and had actually pulled ahead of Jeb.

Apparently the one issue that brought Chiles' campaign back from the dead, and that now was putting the nail in Bush's coffin, had arisen around a notorious TV ad and its immediate aftermath. In the ad, the Bush campaign made a critical mistake based, ironically, on *bad* opposition research.

In the ad, the mother of a murdered young girl implied that Governor Chiles was responsible for the fact that her daughter's killer hadn't yet been executed, despite having been on Death Row for fourteen years. The ad implied that Chiles was dragging his feet signing the death warrants of convicted murderers. Except there was one problem with the ad: There was nothing the Florida governor could do to speed up Death Row executions. Making matters worse, Jeb Bush acknowledged after the ad came out that there was nothing Chiles could have done to speed up the execution, in effect acknowledging that his own ad attacking Chiles was based on an untruth (at best) or a lie (at worst).

In addition, while many Floridians may not have agreed with all of Governor Chiles' political views, the man's folksy, regular-guy manner and integrity were beyond reproach and were by far his greatest political assets. During the TV-ad fiasco and its aftermath, the fact that Bush appeared to be lying about Chiles caused Bush big problems.

I was met at the airport by a Bush campaign aide and immediately taken to a hotel room provided for me. The next day, I met the campaign's press secretary, Cory Tilley, who was great towards me. He didn't have much time to spend with me since he had to catch a flight to wherever Jeb Bush was at that time, but he showed me my "office" and warned me about the hundred-plus press calls per day I would have to answer. The next thing I knew I was dropping him off at the airport and he was gone. I never saw Cory again until that historic election night, November 8, 1994.

The job was fun. I have to admit I enjoyed the break from living in the shadows of "Oppoland." And I enjoyed having normal contact with normal people, in this case members of the media.

Can you imagine media folks seeming "normal" to me at the time? But in fact they really were. They were, for the most part, totally unpretentious, polite, and professional—exactly as the press had been in Tennessee when I was working as press secretary for Steve Wilson. Believe it or not, the vast majority of my experience with the press (even the national press in DC) has been very positive.

Ninety percent of my job was simply sitting for hours with the telephone attached to my ear, answering press inquiries. I really enjoyed talking openly with people again. I know it may seem difficult to believe a press secretary would feel he's talking "openly" with the press, but compared to the way I had to talk to other folks as Oppo Man, talking to the press seemed easy at the time.

I was also surprised at how enthusiastically accepted I was by the Tallahassee Bush staffers. In most campaigns, when anyone from DC is sent to "parts unknown," the campaign staffers are usually suspicious (at best) and hostile (at worst) towards the "outsider" in their midst, particularly if he's from Washington, where no one is trusted. However, the Bush staffers, mostly young and highly motivated, accepted me unconditionally, never once questioning anything I said to the press. Whether it was returning each day from lunch, when I would always be handed a stack of press messages, or just coming into my office to shoot the breeze, every single staffer in that Tallahassee office made my job enjoyable. And since the regular press secretary and campaign manager were never there (having to travel with the candidate every day as the campaign wound down), I was never even once told what to do. They didn't even know me, yet trusted me implicitly and unconditionally to do my job—not the normal campaign environment with its usual back-stabbing and office politics.

The polls never moved while I was in Florida, with the election being too close to call (with a very slight lead for Chiles within the margin of error) until Election Night. The night before the election, I was the only one left at the office working late, making sure I was prepared for the trip the next day to Miami for Election Night. Before leaving for the night, I put on CNN and listened to all the talking heads agree that despite his campaign's late issues, Jeb Bush was going to win in Florida, while George W. was going to lose to Anne Richards in Texas.

As I was leaving the building around 11:00 PM, the phone rang. Figuring it was either something important and campaign-related or an important press call, I answered the phone. It was Mary Matalin, Republican political hack-extraordinaire and wife of the eccentric, brilliant, and passionate James Carville. Having never met her before, I introduced myself. She asked if her friend, Jeb Bush Campaign Manager Sally Harrell, was there. I told her Sally was in Miami with the candidate and figured that would be the end of the conversation. But Mary just kept talking. About the race. About the Bush/Richards race in Texas. About the GOP taking over Congress. About everything. We talked for an hour or so and she was such a political junkie that no subject could be left untouched, even with me, a total stranger. And I thought *I* was addicted to this stuff. But Mary was ten times the junkie I was and lots of fun to talk to.

Finally, I woke up on November 8, 1994. After spending some of the day fielding a flurry of last-second press calls, I went, in the late afternoon, with the rest of the Tallahassee staffers to the airport for the short flight to Miami.

The Crowne Plaza Hotel was a madhouse, as I expected it would be. As day turned to evening, I was finally reunited with Corey Tilley. He told me to be on call and be available to him that night, since he was handling the press. I didn't really have much to do, so I spent most of the evening at the buffet table, occasionally meeting a press person with whom I had spoken on the phone from Tallahassee but was now meeting in person for the first time.

While invading the buffet table, some of the press folks would ask me if I knew anything regarding exit polls or early results coming out, but I said I didn't.

But there actually was one thing I did know at the time: Every time I asked Corey if I could do anything for him, he appeared distracted and not in his usually good mood. I didn't know him well enough—and had too much respect for him—to ask him flat-out if the numbers coming in were bad. But I soon found out, and was asked not to say anything to anyone—not to the press, not to staffers, not to anyone. But that didn't last long, as I soon saw female staffers crying and hugging each other.

I couldn't handle it. While I had worked with the campaign so briefly, most of the other Bush staffers had been working 24/7 for at least the past year, waiting for this fateful night. I couldn't stand there watching these good folks hurting so much. I went downstairs.

When I got there, the Bush supporters who had come into the hotel to join the festivities were all standing in front of television sets, screaming and yelling wildly in ecstasy. I started thinking in a million directions. *Could I have been given wrong information upstairs? Did the Jebster actually pull if off and win?*

I ran to the crowd in front of one of the TVs and saw what all the commotion was about: Newt Gingrich's smiling face was everywhere. The networks were making it official: The Republicans were going to win control of *both* houses of Congress for the first time in generations. Although everyone knew fully well what was going to happen in the Senate (since the polls the night before were all crystal clear in the key Senate races), what happened in the House was a complete shock.

All the press and all the political folks I had worked with had previously agreed with the conventional wisdom—the GOP would pick up anywhere between ten and twenty-five seats in the House. A few wildmen I worked with predicted thirty, but that's about as high as any prediction got. But fifty-one seats? Taking control of the House? This was not only unheard of, it was *unthought* of as early as twenty-four hours prior. Despite the knowledge that Bill Clinton's popularity was in the tank, and that Hillary's health care debacle was going to take down many Democrats, no one, not even the smartest Republican operatives had any idea of the level of hatred America was feeling towards the Clintons on November 8, 1994.

This wild scene of Republicans celebrating downstairs was a surreal disconnect with what was going on upstairs. Everyone was crying. Chiles 51 percent to Bush 49 percent. I couldn't take it, so I walked over to the phones and called my co-workers in DC. It was a madhouse on the phone, too, everyone screaming and celebrating like crazy. Back to reality and the second floor. Everyone crying again.

I was fully aware of what was happening across the country, but I couldn't feel it. I was with one of the very few key losing Republican campaigns of 1994. I briefly saw Corey Tilley, Jeb, and Mrs. Bush down the hall. I felt an initial impulse to walk over and offer my condolences, but just couldn't do it. I later did give Corey whatever words of encouragement I could muster, but I never met Jeb. It just didn't seem appropriate. Having been with the campaign so briefly, I didn't feel worthy of saying anything to the man in his hour of personal grief. So I didn't, and never met Jeb personally.

Ironically, as I write this in Fort Lauderdale, Jeb Bush is finishing his second successful term as governor, unable to run again because of term limits. So, in the end, it worked out for him. After Lawton Chiles' unfortunate, untimely death in 1997, Jeb was easily elected governor in 1998. And despite being the most polarizing politician in America after the 2000 presidential recount, he went on to crush his Democratic opponent in 2002. He left office in 2006 with a sky-high approval rating, popular even among Democrats and Independents.

What accounts for his popularity? Florida today enjoys the highest rate of job creation and is the fastest-growing Eastern state.

Job well done, Jebster.

* * *

Little did I know that this "press" job for Jeb Bush's *losing* 1994 campaign would ironically teach me one of the most valuable lessons about opposition research that I would ever learn. Jeb Bush blew a 10-point lead and lost the election largely because of a research snafu, when he accused Chiles of something he wasn't responsible for. And if you don't know what the word "snafu" means, it's an acronym for "Situation Normal All Fucked Up," which is the best way to describe what happened to that campaign.

Not only did Jeb Bush lose because of bad research, the counter-attack from Chiles accusing Jeb of lying was what put the nail into Jeb's coffin. Meaning that Chiles won the election not because of anything positive regarding himself, but because of something negative regarding Bush. As I will keep repeating throughout this book, most elections and most of American politics is driven by the negative, not the positive.

There was a major irony of those 1994 elections that is rarely discussed. As mentioned earlier, the night before the elections, many of the "experts" were predicting Jeb Bush would defeat Lawton Chiles in Florida, and that George W. Bush would lose to Anne Richards in Texas.

In retrospect, we now know, of course, that the exact opposite happened. Which leads to two interesting hypothetical question no one I know of has ever addressed:

What would have happened to America had the pundits been right, had Jeb *won* and George W. *lost*?

What would have happened had they both won? Which brother would have run for president in 2000?

In answer to question #1, I believe Jeb Bush would have been elected president in 2000 by a very wide margin over Al Gore. In answer to question #2, in my opinion, it's the same answer: Jeb.

Anyone who has ever seen Jeb Bush enter a room knows what I'm talking about. Unlike his president brother and ex-president dad, Jeb has rock-star presence when he enters a room, not too different from JFK, Reagan, or Clinton. It's an intangible thing that neither his brother nor dad have, for some reason.

But as we know, history turned out differently. It's still amazing that in 1994 George W. Bush could have beaten Anne Richards by ten points despite Richards having a high approval rating as governor. How did he do it? Here's my admittedly unscientific opinion which I've also never heard addressed before.

On Election Day 1994, as the GOP took over both houses of Congress for the first time in generations, it was due to one and only one reason: dissatisfaction with the Clintons. In Texas, it wasn't dissatisfaction they felt towards Bill and

Hillary, it was *hatred* (this was shown in exit polls). However, what was *never* polled in exit polls in the Texas gubernatorial race is was what I firmly believe: Texans were not only angry at Clinton for the way he governed in 1993 and 1994, but they were *doubly* angry at the fact that Clinton had become president by defeating their native son George Bush I in 1992.

Texans were still seething at this fact on Election Day 1994, and this was a great way to make it up to the old man: elect his son governor.

Chapter Seven

GUNNING FOR GEPHARDT

The 1994 Republican juggernaut had created a new Speaker of the House, Newt Gingrich. My stint with the National Republican Congressional Committee was supposed to end January 1, 1995, as the new Republican-controlled Congress was sworn in. However, as soon as the new Congress swung into action, I was summoned to do a "sensitive" research project regarding the new speaker's Democratic counterpart, Richard Gephardt of Missouri.

This seemed a little odd. I had been told that Gingrich and Gephardt had always enjoyed a good personal relationship before the 1994 election. Now I was being told that this particular job of digging up dirt on Gephardt was coming directly from the Speaker himself, although I never knew for certain if that was true. If it were true that the two men had a good working relationship, it didn't make sense that Gingrich would now be suddenly going after Gephardt, unless he believed

Gephardt was a threat to his new political agenda and the GOP's "Contract with America," which was to be passed in the new Congress' first hundred days.

What was also strange was that my paychecks for this job no longer came from the NRCC, but from an "independent" group I'd never heard of. I don't even remember the name of the group, only that it was the type of usual generic name most "independent" groups (now called 527 groups) use to hide their true identities and agendas, something along the lines of "Citizens for a Better America" or some such drivel.

I hadn't been poking through Gephardt's records very long before I found something very unusual. It pertained to his second home in the ultra-chic Outer Banks of North Carolina, in a city called Duck, far from his native St. Louis. Two things stuck out in regard to this property, which was, in fact, a mansion.

On his personal financial disclosure (PFD) statement, a form all members of Congress are required to fill out, Gephardt had listed the property at different times as a "rental property," a "second home," and a "vacation home. But there was a problem with that. Gephardt had received a generous tax break known as "The Starker Amendment," which comes into play when two parties swap properties, allowing them to avoid paying taxes on the exchange, including capital gains taxes. But the Starker Amendment applies only when "investment" properties are swapped, it does not apply to vacation homes, second homes, or rental properties. Yet Gephardt took advantage of the massive tax break nonetheless—the same Gephardt who, throughout his entire political career, belligerently insisted that any tax cut of *any* type proposed by the Republicans was benefiting "only the rich." He was now taking advantage of a tax break designed *solely* for the rich—without actually qualifying for it. This was damning material.

The next thing I discovered was that Gephardt had all kinds of regulations in his mortgage forbidding the property to be used for "rental" purposes. Again, Gephardt acknowledged he used his property for rental purposes on his own government financial filings. Thus, the government filings don't jibe with his own IRS filings, and they didn't jibe with his own mortgage documents.

The IRS and federal banking law violations weren't the half of it. I found that as soon as Gephardt made this questionable house swap, he started holding frequent fundraisers for the high rollers who contributed big bucks to his leadership PAC, which he called the "Effective Government Committee PAC. Except there was a problem: While the high rollers did indeed attend the fundraisers, and while they did indeed fork out big bucks, the fundraisers themselves didn't raise any money! Why not, you ask? Because the money was instead going primarily to the *overhead* for these very same "fundraisers," largely to cover catering and lodging costs. An estimated $70,000 for catering and lodging went to a group of companies owned, in part or in whole, by Richard A. Brindley and Associates. Besides the catering-related firms, Brindley and/or his family also owned Outer Banks Ventures, the company that developed the real estate subdivision Corolla Light. And where was Gephardt's new house? You guessed it. Corolla Light. Therefore, much of the overhead was being paid to the man who held the note on Gephardt's mansion.

Outer Banks Ventures is also the firm that provided Gephardt an initial $304,205 loan to buy a premier lot worth $375,000, where he later would erect his "Northern Star" home at an estimated cost of about $300,000, according to local builders. Brindley also appears to have provided Gephardt with a generous extension of nearly six months past the due date of the original note. In his government financial filings, I noticed Gephardt did not disclose this information as either a debt or a gift—another violation of federal law.

I submitted my findings to my superiors at the NRCC and, as ordered, we shared information with Paul Rodriguez at the *Washington Times,* who coincidentally was also researching the story.

When confronted by the press regarding fundraisers that didn't raise any funds, Gephardt lamely replied that the events in question weren't really "fundraisers" but rather "outreach" for his financial benefactors (sound familiar, Al Gore?). And believe it or not, while it appeared that Gephardt had violated IRS and federal banking laws with his "Starker Amendment" manipulations and had violated the terms of his mortgage, the Gephardt "fundraisers" were completely legal under Federal Election Commission (FEC) laws. Gephardt had every legal right to spend the money he raised from these events in any manner he chose, as long as the cash didn't wind up in his own pocket (more proof that the FEC is a joke).

After the facts were in, I assumed the Republicans would immediately take action against Gephardt. Except the craziest thing happened: For some strange reason, no Republican in Congress wanted to file a complaint against Gephardt with the House Ethics Committee, which was the logical place to take the research. Over a year went by before Congresswoman Jennifer Dunn finally filed a formal complaint against Gephardt with the House Ethics Committee. Finally Gephardt would be held accountable. Or so I thought.

When confronted with the charges by the committee, Gephardt lamely responded that he would never "knowingly" violate the laws, and that the laws are "very technical matters." Can you believe the stones on this guy? Serious violations of IRS and FEC laws are mere "technical violations?" Or a "mere bag of shells" as Jackie Gleason used to say.

The next day, the ethics panel's five Republicans and five Democrats agreed to dismiss allegations against him. And although the Ethics Committee was headed by Republican Nancy Johnson from Connecticut, the committee nonetheless gave Gephardt what amounted to a pass. Even Gingrich himself, who I was told ordered the research against Gephardt in the first place, was strangely quiet

Why was no action taken against the highest-ranking Democrat in the House of Representatives? Did the Ethics Committee chairman and/or members have skeletons in their own closets? And why in the world did Newt suddenly go silent? Could it have been related to ethical indiscretions by the Speaker himself—indiscretions involving his two marriages that would later become so publicly humiliating for Gingrich?

What makes this episode especially galling to me is that, whatever you may think of Newt Gingrich, all the actions taken (not to mention all the yelling and screaming by the liberals) against Newt later on regarding his book deal were ridiculous considering that virtually no action was taken against Gephardt for his far more egregious chicanery. Despite all the hoopla surrounding the money Gingrich made from his book deal, he had done nothing wrong. No one cared a whit when Hillary Clinton and Colin Powell received similarly huge advances from book publishers, yet Newt was nonetheless raked over the coals while his Democratic counterpart Dick Gephardt was given less than a slap-on-the-wrist by the GOP-controlled House Ethics Committee.

When I asked some insiders what was going on, I was told that Gephardt was basically a nice guy who got along well with Democrats and Republicans alike. Whether or not that was the reason Gephardt was given a pass I'll never know. However, what we do know is that there is absolutely no doubt that Gingrich was not well-liked by many of his colleagues, including many Republicans, as we saw during the failed coup attempt by fellow Republicans against him in 1998. He was particularly despised by members of his own party. For instance, the one-time congressional star Republican Susan Molinari had this to say about Gingrich: "He's an emotionally unstable egocentric who wakes up every day thinking he is Napoleon Bonaparte in the saddle at Waterloo."

It's not surprising that there's a double standard of how politicians are treated by their peers based on personality. That's kind of the way it works in all walks of life. However, these are public officials supposedly held to higher standards. So this double standard appears to be a violation of the people's trust.

What makes the Gephardt case even more appalling is that, since Congress is exempt from open records laws (a major outrage in itself), the Ethics Committee records of this matter are also not public and therefore are being de-facto censored from the American public.

This was a very frustrating episode for Oppo Man. I gave the Republicans the goods, and they apparently were either too cowardly or too frightened by the thought of their *own* unethical behavior coming to light to take any action against Mr. Gephardt. After having seen first-hand how my oppo work from 1994 was used so aggressively, brilliantly, and successfully, the Gephardt experience was a bitter pill to swallow.

As 1994 rolled into 1995, Oppo Man had received his first hard lesson regarding how naïve he had been to actually believe the political system would always work exactly the way he thought it should. It was also my first inkling that Newt Gingrich and the "Republican Revolution" were not what they'd been cracked up to be. It was in fact entirely likely that these Republicans had skeletons of their own!

Chapter Eight

THE BUCHANAN PRESIDENTIAL CAMPAIGNS: THE WORST SIDES OF AMERICAN POLITICS

My one political job in DC that was *not* supposed to involve opposition research ironically turned into the most incredible opposition research project I could ever imagine.

In May 1995, after finishing up my work for the NRCC digging up dirt on Dick Gephardt, I left the NCCC and joined Pat Buchanan's 1996 presidential campaign. Working for Buchanan proved to be a fateful decision—one that subsequently led to my writing an exposé on questionable financial dealings within Buchanan's campaign for *Penthouse* magazine and filing a formal complaint with the Federal Election Commission (FEC). In both cases I detailed the illegal and what I believed were *immoral* goings-on of the campaign—charges that led to an FEC investigation confirming my allegations.

This eye-opening experience brought opposition research to a new level for me, as I connected the dots that exposed money laundering, repeated financial chicanery, and repeated lawbreaking.

* * *

I know what you're thinking: "What in the world would a nice boy from Brooklyn be doing working for *Pat Buchanan?*"

During my work researching Dick Gephardt in early 1995, I began thinking that the only thing I really wanted to do in 1995 and 1996 was work on the 1996 presidential campaign, the one campaign level I hadn't yet reached. That would be the ultimate; working to defeat Bill Clinton.

Like lots of folks on Capitol Hill, I was waiting with bated breath for Colin Powell to run. Polls showed that Powell was the only candidate who could easily defeat President Clinton in a general election by splitting the black vote in the big states as well as splitting the traditional democratic base of women, Hispanics, Jews, northeastern "Reagan Democrats," union members, and so on. But as we know, Powell decided not to run, so we were left with the weakest GOP field of presidential candidates in my lifetime. As President Clinton said at the time (and he was right), "Dole is the only one of those clowns who's qualified to be president."

I decided to try to get a job with the Dole campaign. In the meantime I was told through the political grapevine that Pat Buchanan had scored a major coup by hiring Guy Rodgers to be his campaign manager, and Rodgers was looking for an assistant. Rodgers' reputation as the national field director for the Christian Coalition was stellar. He had a network of right-wing Republicans in all fifty states that, if mobilized, could make Buchanan dangerous in the primaries. I was also told Rodgers' assistant would help him coordinate the efforts nationwide, which sounded like fun since I loved to travel. It would also be an interesting change of pace from opposition research.

The problem was that Buchanan still was a long shot, and I still really wanted to work for Dole, since he was obviously the only Republican who had a chance of defeating Bill Clinton. So I spoke to Maryanne Carter, Dole's research director, whom I knew from Tennessee in 1994 when I was working for Steve Wilson. Maryanne at that time was doing opposition research for Fred Thompson in his Tennessee Senate race (which he won). I told Maryanne I'd be interested in a position on her team.

But then a strange thing happened: she advised me that since it was only April 1995, very early in the campaign, it would be smarter for me to try to get the job with Buchanan. When I asked her why, she told me that Dole wasn't hiring any researchers for several months. If I worked for Buchanan first, then, after Dole knocked Buchanan out of the race in 1996, I would have a better chance getting hired by Dole because I was a good researcher who had the advantage of knowing where to find all the Buchanan supporters that Dole would need in the general election. It made sense to me.

Next thing I knew I was in Pat Buchanan's campaign head-quarters in McClain, Virginia, a beautiful, old-money suburb of Washington, DC. The first thing I saw upon entering was a huge picture of Pat Buchanan hanging on the wall, staring right at me. I admit I thought for a second "What am I doing here?" but then I was met by an exotic and beautiful young lady who asked if she could help me. I asked to see Campaign Manager Guy Rodgers.

Rodgers and I hit it off immediately, and I was offered a position as his assistant. My initial duties would be two-fold. The first was learning the different electoral procedures and requirements in each of the primary and caucus states, to make sure Buchanan got on the ballot in each state. The second was coordinating our campaign workers in various states nationwide. This entailed screening and organizing potential Buchanan staffers across America, who would eventually be hired by Rodgers to become our state, county, and district chairmen. (In many states at that point Buchanan had little or no organization.)

My first day on the job for the Buchanan campaign was on my thirty-eighth birthday, May 7, 1995. I was excited when I started, as I believed it would be an interesting job with a terrific boss in Guy Rodgers. And it was.

For two weeks.

✳ ✳ ✳

Two weeks into the job, I was just getting into the swing of things. One afternoon Rodgers called me from out of town. He told me to take the call in his office and to shut the door. I could tell immediately something was wrong. Rodgers got straight to the point: he was resigning from the campaign because of "differences" with Angela "Bay" Buchanan, the campaign chairman and sister of the candidate.

Rodgers, a gentleman and team player to the end, never said a negative word about Bay, nor about his exact reasons for resigning. But everything became crystal clear once I lost Guy as my buffer and had to begin dealing directly with Ms. Bay.

Unlike normal campaigns, where the campaign manager runs the day-to-day operations and the campaign chairman is more of a figurehead, in this campaign, "Chairman" Bay totally ran the show, as Guy Rodgers and I learned too late. A formidable woman, she had previously served as the campaign treasurer for the 1980 and 1984 Reagan presidential campaigns, and as national treasurer for President Reagan from 1981 to 1983. As Pat's sister, and now his campaign chairman, she exercised complete authority and tolerated no dissent.

With Rodgers gone, Bay's top political assistant became Tim Haley, a former employee of Perdue Chicken who appeared to have little if any professional campaign experience. With Guy Rodgers gone, I now had to report directly to Bay and Haley. I never hit it off with either of them. Both had contempt for me and the feeling was mutual. So I was demoted to working the phone banks, calling supporters and urging them to attend campaign events. I was stunned. It was one of the lowest jobs in the campaign, and I knew I would have to quit, sooner rather than later.

Not long after, I was summoned along with some other staffers into Bay's office, which for me was like entering "The Twilight Zone." We sat around a big oval conference table, with Bay holding court. After perfunctory remarks, Bay got right to the point. She stood up and looked down at me. Tall, with Pat's great smiling face, but none of his likability, she was quite intimidating. Bay proceeded to tell me how useless my work was.

"Stephen," Bay said sternly, without shouting, and swiveling her body around to face Haley, who sat there smug and confident, looking like the cat that just ate the canary. Imitating Bay, he sat with his arms crossed. Bay then pointed to Haley: "Stephen, there is so much, so much you can learn from this man," she said. Then she told me I would be canned if I didn't shape up.

I didn't know whether to laugh or cry. All I knew at that point was I had to get out, soon.

Many terrific staffers had already done so, due to problems with Bay and/or Haley. This included two state coordinators in Iowa and New Hampshire, and one of the campaign's legal counsels. One former key state coordinator told me, "I gave my life to them and even moved to a different state for the Buchanan campaign." This individual, a respected and savvy political operative with successful presidential-campaign experience, went directly to Pat Buchanan concerning a dispute she had had with Haley, but to no avail. Pat predictably sided with Haley and Bay. The following day the state coordinator left the campaign.

After being demoted to working the telephone banks and being berated in the meeting, I was about to quit. But suddenly I noticed a lot of strange goings-on at the other end of the campaign, the part we call "Treasury," which deals with the campaign's fundraising. "Treasury" and "Political" staffers got along well, and we all hung out with each other to see what the other side was doing.

Despite everything that happened at the political end of the campaign, and despite my differences with Bay, I *never* saw any lawbreaking. You know why? At the political end there were no laws to break, but the treasury end dealt with the one thing sure to bring down the force of the law: *money.* That's where the action was.

Buchanan was running his campaign on these main points:

- Cut government waste
- Stand up for the little guy against the wealthy and powerful
- Bring morality and ethics back to government

What I saw in the treasury group was a campaign being run in the exact opposite manner of everything Pat Buchanan said he stood for in his campaign. Before too long I saw not only FEC laws broken, but other multiple laws being broken by the campaign as well. I also saw, just as I had in the political end, an ethical atmosphere somewhere between the toilet and the sewer.

After the shock of seeing what was actually going on at the Buchanan campaign wore off, I actually got a rush watching all this lawbreaking. I decided not to quit the campaign, but to stay awhile and document all the financial chicanery, corruption, and unethical behavior I was witnessing and go public with it. Oppo Man was back in action! Even though I stayed with the campaign only three months, what I discovered was mind-boggling.

* * *

Before I describe the litany of lawbreaking and unethical behavior, I am obligated to say two things about Pat and Bay Buchanan. First, Pat Buchanan *never* had anything to do with any of what I'm about to reveal, and as far as I know never made an illegal or unethical dime off the campaign. That was the purview of his sister Bay, which this chapter will discuss in great detail.

Secondly, regarding both Pat and Bay, I'm also obligated to state here that despite what Pat's opponents always said to try to attack him, I saw zero evidence that either one of them is anti-Semitic. True, Pat's isolationist foreign policy views may show great paranoia towards Israel, but I'm convinced that he is *not* a bigot; nor is his sister. I heard him in a telephone conference with Bay speak of his Jewish supporters (primarily orthodox Jews) with great affection, and not in any way patronizing. Same for Bay.

Pat was an absentee boss, always on the road campaigning and hardly ever in the campaign headquarters, entrusting the campaign lock, stock, and barrel to his sister. I never got to know Pat, meeting him only once and chatting for about a minute, but I believe strongly that after some wild younger years, he's a straight-arrow, honest, good guy. The media folks I know all have the same opinion.

However, I believe Buchanan would have made a *terrible* president for one basic reason: He would have been an absentee figurehead president, with Bay Buchanan probably running the country—a bad scenario indeed.

However, he is still ultimately responsible. His hands-off leadership style kept him totally isolated from the day-to-day operations of the 1996 campaign. This, coupled with his unconditional trust in his sister, led to the immoral behavior that permeated that campaign, behavior made all the more inexcusable considering that 1996 was Pat's second presidential run. The Buchanans couldn't use the excuse that they were inexperienced and didn't know what they were doing.

✳ ✳ ✳

Pat Buchanan was right about one thing. His campaigns were not "politics as usual"; they were much worse. A large part of Pat Buchanan's appeal as a candidate was his championing of the American worker and the "little guy" against the greedy and powerful. While with the campaign, I quickly discovered this to be so much hypocrisy. I was told by some staffers earning as little as $7 an hour that the campaign flatly refused to properly compensate them for overtime.

One staffer decided to fight back. Robin Hatfield, a single mom who was forced to work up to seventy hours a week without overtime, filed a formal complaint with the U.S. Department of Labor while still working for the campaign, and subsequently filed a lawsuit against the campaign in the U.S. Federal District Court in Fairfax, Virginia. The campaign finally settled the suit in June 1998 for $5,000, more than three years after Hatfield's original complaint to the Labor Department.

Shortly after I left the campaign, I tried to help the hourly paid staffers by bringing their situation to the attention of Terry Jeffrey, a close friend of Pat's and the only senior staffer I believed to be principled. I told Jeffrey how these workers were being cheated, and even quoted to him the applicable provisions of the Fair Labor Standards Act. He thanked me profusely for informing me of the problem and assured me the situation would be rectified. But nothing changed; the staffers continued to be cheated. Jeffrey, now the editor of *Human Events*, was a good and honest guy, but in reality, what could he do? Take on Bay? He wasn't that stupid. He knew blood was thicker than water.

I then checked out courthouse records and found that low-paid staffers weren't the only "little guys" the Buchanan campaign was cheating. The campaign was also notoriously delinquent when it came to paying small businesses like office suppliers, printers, and temp agencies.

But according to their own FEC records, the campaign had plenty of money to pay Bay Buchanan and the firms she controlled. In fact, Bay was raking in her largest monthly checks during the same period the campaign was ignoring a nine-month-delinquent $1,300 bill from Miller's Office Supplies of Springfield, Virginia (which led to a lawsuit, subsequently settled out of court), and ignoring Robin Hatfield's complaint to the Labor Department.

According to FEC and IRS records, I could see that Bay Buchanan earned roughly $100,000 to $120,000 in 1992 for her work on her brother's first campaign, and continued to reap six-figure annual salaries during 1993 and 1994, the years between campaigns. In that two-year period, Bay received $113,000 from the 1992 campaign committee (which had forfeited its lawful right to conduct business in Virginia in September 1993) and another $127,500 from Pat's nonprofit foundations, The American Cause and the Coalition for the American Cause.

Between January 1995 and September 1996, when Bay left the second campaign to pursue a career in television, she took home roughly $130,000 in net salary from the 1996 Buchanan campaign, which suggests that her gross salary during this period was close to $200,000. (Press reports during this period cited Bay's "annual salary" as $120,000.) Although her annual salary was not unusually high for her position in the campaign, what was peculiar was Bay continuing to draw a regular salary for two full years after the 1992 election. (Pat's 1996 campaign didn't get underway until early 1995.)

"It's not unusual to see a campaign manager earn a salary for four or five months after a presidential campaign is over," Charles Black, former campaign manager for both George Bush and Phil Gramm, told me in my *Penthouse* expose. "But collecting a salary for two more years after the election is unusual." Apparently Bay Buchanan saw nothing irregular about the arrangement. Questioned about these off-year campaign earnings by the *Wall Street Journal* in March 1996, she responded, "I earned every bit."

An even worse controversy erupted in March 1996 when the press discovered that Bay Buchanan, despite her handsome earnings as a campaign chairman, had found a creative way to supplement her income even further, through her creation of a media-buying company, WTS, Inc. Instead of the normal practice of hiring a professional outfit to purchase and place television and radio commercials, Bay Buchanan formed WTS in December 1994 to place media buys for her brother's 1996 campaign. WTS reportedly received eight-percent commissions on these media buys. According to FEC records, the 1996 Buchanan campaign spent close to $4 million on commercials through WTS, meaning commissions would have totaled more than $300,000. Bay was the firm's sole owner, and she hired one of her friends, Carolyn Melby, to place the media buys. Melby's Maryland condominium was listed as the firm's business address.

The flap over WTS began when Carolyn Melby, in response to queries from the *Wall Street Journal*, claimed that she was the owner of WTS, adding that WTS was derived from the initials of three "relatives of mine." Confronted with corporation papers identifying Bay Buchanan as the real owner, Melby and Bay both admitted the truth, acknowledging that WTS, in fact, was named from the initials of Bay's three sons.

When questioned about WTS's profits by the *Washington Times* in April 1996, Bay responded that the firm had to make a profit in order to remain legal, but she wouldn't specify which law backed up this dubious claim. Bay and Melby also appear to have made conflicting statements regarding the financial compensation Bay personally received from WTS, whose commissions would have equaled half the entire payroll of the campaign's one hundred paid staffers during the first quarter of 1996, according to the *Washington Times*. In a letter to the editor of that newspaper in May 1996, Bay stated, "I have not received, nor will I receive, any fees, commissions, or income from WTS." Yet Melby had previously told the *Wall Street Journal* that "profits will go to me, and hopefully Bay." Adding to the controversy, a Prince George's County (Maryland) spokesperson stated that the use of Melby's home as an office violated a county zoning ordinance prohibiting condominiums to be used for business purposes.

The controversy died down after Bay had been hammered in the press. Instead of continuing to respond to the media and repeatedly putting her foot in her mouth, Bay got smart and flatly refused to answer further questions regarding WTS. Since her brother was no longer a viable candidate by mid-1996, the press let the matter drop. How much of WTS's $300,000-plus in revenues went to Bay Buchanan is still a mystery, since the company's records are not public. Could you imagine if Hillary Clinton or Laura Bush had made a killing on media buys? The press would have crucified them.

(I feel compelled here to note that Carolyn Melby was a wonderful woman with whom I personally worked at the campaign. She was a Howard University professor and long-time friend of Bay. In my opinion, Carolyn was just doing what Bay told her to do. I would bet my life that she didn't rake in the hundreds of thousands of dollars Bay may have from WTS. I believe strongly that she was simply used by Bay, who needed cover on WTS.)

Around the same time as the WTS imbroglio, another bit of Pat Buchanan flim-flammery caught the eye of Beltway insiders. Instead of formally dropping out of the race once Bob Dole clinched the nomination, he "suspended" his campaign in April 1996, not formally endorsing Dole until the GOP convention in July. This enabled him to continue raising millions of dollars in campaign contributions, much of it coming as the result of an April fundraising letter, sent out to 140,000 supporters, which implied that Pat was considering a third-party run.

Was this letter simply a ruse to solicit money, raising false hopes among those who desperately wanted Pat to run as an Independent? Even political pundits challenged Buchanan on the matter. In an interview on his television show "One-on-One," John McLaughlin repeatedly asked Pat whether or not the fundraising letter was a "charade," finally cornering him by asking whether the response to the letter would be the determining factor deciding whether or not Pat would run as a third-party candidate. Buchanan, clearly on the defensive, could only respond lamely, "We're going to take those views into consideration." As it turned out, of course, Pat did *not* run as an Independent in 1996 (as he did in 2000), nor was any of the money raised by this letter returned.

Then there was the FEC audit I saw in 1995 of the 1992 Buchanan campaign, the finances of which had been controlled by Bay Buchanan and Campaign Treasurer Scott Mackenzie. What I read in that audit set off alarms in my head. The FEC ruled that the campaign committee illegally used campaign money for "nonqualified campaign expenses," which included nearly $8,000 in start-up costs for Buchanan's nonprofit foundation, The American Cause. The audit stated that campaign dollars were also improperly used to cover payroll-tax penalties and parking tickets. In addition, the 1992 Buchanan campaign committee was fined $20,000 for accepting improper campaign contributions, including more than $50,000 from individuals who exceeded the $1,000-per-person contribution limit.

These violations appeared so flagrant that I began to wonder about the involvement of Bay, and also wondered if this sort of activity was still going on in the 1996 campaign. It would appear that my concerns were valid. In January 1999, the FEC released its audit of the 1996 Buchanan campaign, finding it, too, guilty of "apparent nonqualified campaign expenses." One such was an $8,213 trip to Paris and London taken by Pat, his wife, Shelley, and an unspecified aide in June

1996, apparently paid for with campaign cash. The travel agency that booked the trip signed an affidavit stating it was not paid for with campaign funds, but the FEC was not impressed.

The FEC audit explained why: "The cost of the tickets was listed in the (*travel agency's*) June 1996 statement for the (*Buchanan campaign*) Committee's account. The September 1996 (*travel agency*) statement indicated that all but $825 of the costs of these tickets had been paid (*by the campaign committee*). The (*Buchanan campaign*) Committee did not provide any additional evidence in the form of the copy of a canceled check or account statement detailing the payment (other than by campaign funds) for this travel" (italics mine).

These unqualified campaign expenses paled beside a far more serious violation of federal election laws that I saw while still working for the campaign: laundering money to fraudulently obtain federal matching funds.

During presidential elections, when campaigns receive certain types of contributions, the federal government gives the campaigns a "matching" contribution of the same amount, up to $250 per contributor. Certain types of campaign contributions to presidential candidates do *not* qualify for federal matching funds. Cash contributions do not qualify. What did the Buchanan campaign do when they received ineligible cash contributions? They simply converted the money into contributions that *were* eligible, according to former staffer Robin Hatfield, who told me this personally. Robin worked as a data-entry supervisor.

According to Hatfield, the campaign used cash contributions to purchase money orders, and, in turn asked campaign staffers like herself to sign the money orders. She personally signed one such money order for $450 in June 1996. The signed money orders were then endorsed to the Buchanan campaign as campaign contributions, ostensibly from staffers. These money orders, unlike cash contributions, were eligible for federal matching funds.

Indeed, a close examination of FEC records reveals that Hatfield and other Buchanan staffers made contributions to the campaign, some via money orders, of at least $200 apiece.

It's a bit of a stretch to believe that all these staffers, many in low-paid jobs, were making such contributions to the campaign. It's even more of a stretch to believe that Robin Hatfield, who had already filed a complaint against the Buchanan campaign with the U.S. Department of Labor for unpaid overtime wages, and would later successfully sue campaign officials in federal court (more on this later), would contribute $450 to Buchanan out of the goodness of her heart. The FEC acknowledged these abuses only after I filed a formal complaint, including a loose-leaf binder full of evidence showing that my allegations were true. According to Justice Department spokesman John Russell, the Buchanan campaign's crime would violate the anti-fraud provision of the Presidential Primary Matching Fund Act and would be punishable by up to five years in federal prison and/or a $250,000 fine. Despite this, the FEC took no action against the Buchanan campaign.

Furthermore, after looking through corporation records in Richmond, Virginia (the estate capital), I found that both Buchanan campaigns and their nonprofit foundation, The American Cause, conducted business and raised millions of dollars despite having had their lawful rights to do business revoked by the state of Virginia owing to multiple failures to pay registration fees and failure to file annual financial reports.

According to records from the Virginia Corporation Commission, Buchanan's 1992 presidential campaign, Buchanan for President, Inc., forfeited its lawful right to conduct business in September 1993 for failure to file an annual registration fee. This campaign nevertheless continued to do business until its campaign committee was closed by the FEC in December 1998. As a corporation, its right to conduct business was never reinstated, which means the campaign committee raised money and operated illegally for more than five years. This violation could be a misdemeanor punishable by up to one year in jail and/or a $2,500 fine, according to Section13.1-768 of the Code of Virginia.

Apparently unconcerned about such legal niceties, Buchanan's second campaign, whose corporate name was BFP, Inc., also had its lawful right to conduct business revoked in Virginia in 1996 for failure to pay an annual registration fee. According to the FEC, this 1996 campaign committee was still open until 1999—which means it was operating illegally for nearly three years.

Buchanan's tax-exempt foundation, The American Cause, incorporated in February 1993, and a spin-off, The American Quest, incorporated the following month, *also* forfeited their rights to "transact business in Virginia" in September 1996 for failure to pay annual registration fees. The American Cause's rights were reinstated in April 1998—but the foundation had continued to raise money during the nearly two years its charter was revoked. The American Quest never had its charter reinstated.

This pattern of revoked business charters seems to have rubbed off on Pat Buchanan personally. According to the District of Columbia's Department of Consumer and Regulatory Affairs, PJB Enterprises, Inc., which has handled Pat's television and journalistic pursuits since the 1970s, had its Articles of Incorporation revoked in September 1998 for failure to file annual financial reports for 1997 and 1998. This firm, which lists Pat as its "President" and "Vice President," as well as its "Secretary" and "Treasurer," had its articles revoked once before, in September 1993, for failure to file annual financial reports in 1992 and 1993. Those articles were reinstated in July 1994.

If Pat Buchanan had conducted any business affairs through this firm since the September 1998 revocation, or between September 1993 and August 1994, it could have also be a misdemeanor, punishable by up to one year in prison and a $500 fine, according to Title 29-399.25 of the DC Code.

Through more investigation, I also learned that Buchanan campaign-related corporations were guilty of repeated tax delinquencies. The American Cause was late paying its Virginia state franchise taxes in 1995, 1996, and 1997, and American Quest was late in 1995.

When the 1996 Buchanan campaign ended, Bay Buchanan began a television career on CNBC's "Equal Time" whilst continuing as president of The American Cause. Perhaps not surprisingly, this Buchanan-controlled operation has also attracted scrutiny and lawsuits.

In September 1997, I also found that The American Cause, a foundation created by Bay in February 1993 as a "think tank" for conservative political issues, was sued by Connecticut Attorney General Richard Blumenthal in

Connecticut Superior Court in Hartford. The suit alleged that The American Cause violated the state's Unfair Trade Practices Act by "willfully" failing to file annual financial reports in 1994, 1995, and 1996. The complaint asked for an injunction barring The American Cause from soliciting funds until these reports were filed properly, and also sought $15,000 in civil penalties.

According to court documents, an "Agreement of Stipulation of Judgment" was signed by both parties in October 1998, with The American Cause agreeing to file the proper financial reports and pay fines. David Ormstedt of the Connecticut Attorney General's office has since told me that, while the fines were paid as agreed to, the annual financial reports have not been filed despite the stipulation's agreement that this be done no later than November 15, 1998.

In yet another lawsuit I found filed in March 1999 in Fairfax County (Virginia) Circuit Court, the foundation's lobbying arm, which is called the Coalition for The American Cause, was sued by Right Concepts, Inc., a Chantilly, Virginia, direct-mail-marketing firm, for more than $1 million for breach of contract and civil fraud. The suit claimed that the Buchanan foundation fraudulently misrepresented itself as a 501(C)(4) tax-exempt organization, entitled to a discount postage rate. The lawsuit further claimed that Right Concepts suffered financial loss as a result of sending out fundraising letters for the Coalition for The American Cause based on false claims of having a tax-exempt permit. The lawsuit was settled.

IRS documents appeared to support Right Concepts. The documents indicated that the Coalition for The American Cause claimed tax-exempt status on its application for discounted postal rates five months before actually applying for tax-exempt status. According to Justice Department officials, this action could constitute the felony of mail fraud and/or filing false statements on a federal document for the purpose of financial gain, in this case discounted postage rates.

Upon closer examination of the organization's application to the IRS, it appeared that the Coalition for The American Cause further falsely stated, "The above Directors do not receive any compensation for their work for the Coalition for The American Cause." This contradicts the coalition's 1994 IRS filing, which indicates $26,000 in "consulting fees" paid to director and president Bay Buchanan.

If you think Bay Buchanan can't possibly top everything you've read so far, I have a surprise for you. Going all the way back to the *late 1970s*, Bay Buchanan was executive vice chairman of "Citizens for the Republic," a California-based political action committee (PAC) that grew out of Ronald Reagan's first race for president in 1976, and that raised money for his 1980 victory over Jimmy Carter.

Well after President Reagan's 1980 victory, the PAC was still paying Bay during 1992, when Pat Buchanan made his initial run for president. In 1991, Ms. Bay received hefty consulting fees along with her cohort in Citizens for the Republic, former Reagan press secretary and aide Lynn Nofziger. FEC records show that in 1991, Bay was paid $58,500 and Nofziger $43,500. When the group's treasurer, Carolyn Robertson, was asked by the press what Bay and Nofziger did to earn that money, she said: "That's a good question. You've got me on that."

* * *

I quit the Buchanan campaign after three months. After the 1996 campaign ended, I decided that I had to at least do my part by putting everything I saw and knew on the record regarding the corruption of Pat Buchanan's 1996 campaign. I filed a formal complaint with the FEC, including hundreds of pages of back-up documents proving my charges. I documented a paper trail and a money trail to prove my allegations. Not unexpectedly, the FEC agreed with me and found the Buchanan campaign guilty of multiple illegalities, including money laundering. What did the tough strict FEC do about it? The same thing they usually do. Nothing.

In their report after investigating my allegations, the FEC first outlined the litany of laws broken by the Buchanan campaign, including the most serious charge of money laundering. They then went on to state that they didn't have the time or the resources to continue investigating the campaign. Despite acknowledging all the lawbreaking by the Buchanan campaign, no penalties were assessed, and the matter was dismissed. The FEC also pointed out that Bay Buchanan had not cooperated with them. Despite proof of several violations, the FEC conceded defeat to the Buchanans.

Shocked and frustrated, I decided to put the truth on the record in a different way, one sure to gain more attention than the FEC could generate. I wrote an exposé about the Buchanan campaigns for *Penthouse* in the fall of 1999.

Unfortunately, the timing of the article wasn't the greatest. Buchanan had already declared as a Republican candidate for president in 2000, but the press wasn't taking him seriously and the big story of his bolting the GOP for the Reform Party was yet to come. At the time of the article's release, interest in Buchanan was low.

I had documented Buchanan campaign corruption to the federal government's supposedly most powerful agency regulating political campaigns, the Federal Election Committee. I had also documented the corruption for the public with my 6,000-plus-word exposé in one of America's most well-read (albeit not one of its most respected) publications. Lastly, I had exposed the corruption to the campaign itself.

In short, I had done my part. What else could I do? Oppo Man was no match for a corrupt campaign and an inept federal agency refusing to do anything about its lawbreaking. It was a tough pill for me to swallow.

* * *

However, this was not the end of my involvement with Buchanan. After the end of the 1996 campaign, most political observers (including myself) thought they had seen the last of Pat Buchanan's political career. But, unbelievably, in March 1999, Buchanan announced he was running again in his third straight presidential election. I thought the 2000 race could not possibly match up to the chicanery, double-dealing, and overall debauchery of the earlier campaigns.

Wrong again.

Buchanan's 2000 campaign was the most mysterious and craziest of them all. When Buchanan bolted the Republican Party to run for the nomination of the Reform Party, the campaign had its eyes on the big prize: the $13 million the Reform Party nominee would receive in matching funds based on Ross Perot's strong performances in 1996 and 1992. When the 2000 campaign began in 1999, Pat claimed that sister Bay would *not* be in charge this time, but would only be "an adviser."

I found this difficult to believe, but I was open-minded enough to check it out. So I took a look at Buchanan's 1999 first quarterly filing with the FEC. Bay Buchanan was the first person listed under "Payroll," having received a $2,376.68 check in net pay for the first pay period, higher than any other employee, as well as checks totaling more than $4,500 for reimbursed expenses.

Bay's not having the title of "Campaign Chairman" may have had something to do with the fact that she was still trying to launch a television career (she was eventually let go from the role as co-host of "Equal Time" due to poor ratings). It would have looked ridiculous to have Bay running the campaign while she was hosting a TV show. So, on paper, the campaign manager was Jay Townsend, a well-respected veteran New York political operative who once worked with Dick Morris. Townsend left in mid-campaign—and guess who became Pat Buchanan's new campaign manager? No, not Bay Buchanan. It was Tim Haley. Unbelievable.

As Pat was fighting his way into becoming the Reform Party nominee in 2000, another strange thing happened. I was contacted by the Associated Press' DC news editor Jonathan Salant and his sidekick, journalist Jon Solomon. They said they were interested in the FEC complaint I had filed and wanted a copy of it.

They took me to lunch at a Chinese restaurant close to the AP offices in DC. It's common for reporters and political hacks like me to barter information, so I didn't know if I was there to get some information in return for the information I was giving them, or if this was just a thank-you lunch for my intel. It didn't matter to me, since I really liked these guys, both professional journalists and, as far as I could tell, totally honest.

Midway through lunch they got to the point. They told me that they were about to run a story about Pat Buchanan where my material would be used, but there was really a much *bigger* story there. Then one of them causally asked me, "I take it you know about Pat Buchanan's alleged illegitimate daughter?"

I did, including her name and the city she lived in, but I never talked about it since I couldn't prove it.

Solomon and Salant told me that the alleged daughter of Pat Buchanan had originally agreed to tell them *everything*, then, at the last moment, changed her mind. They added that the big bosses at the AP were intimidated by Bay Buchanan and the Buchanans' high-priced DC lawyers. According to Bay and her lawyers, one negative word about Pat Buchanan would spell financial doom for AP.

Solomon and Salant asked me, "Do you know anything new, or know of any document [birth certificate or letter, for instance] that could help us prove the allegation without her admission?" Unfortunately, I did not. I knew only what they knew. The woman was allegedly fathered by Buchanan while he was an undergrad at Georgetown, and that she was at that time in her forties and lived in Midlothian, Virginia, a suburb of Richmond. Neither we nor any of the beltway's other top reporters (some of whom I would later learn had been working this story for *years,* including E. J. Dionne of the *New York Times* and Michael Isikoff, probably the best investigative reporter in America) were able to prove the allegation.

After meeting the AP guys, I began swapping intel with the other reporters I knew who had worked the story. It was a waste of time. We all knew the same facts, but it was all circumstantial evidence. There was no smoking gun, but this made me more determined than ever to find one. I decided to look at the one place I still had access that none of the reporters working this story could utilize: former Buchanan staffers.

One person I wanted to speak to, whom I believed might have known something, was Pat and Bay's right-hand man for over twenty years, Campaign Treasurer Scott MacKenzie. He was Bay's closest confidant, going back to the early 1980s when she was Ronald Reagan's campaign treasurer but had mysteriously left the Buchanan campaign. Hoping he'd had a falling out with the Buchanans and might talk to me, I tried to find him, but to no avail. He was gone.

Whenever Oppo Man can't find someone, he has one basic rule: hit the courthouse of their home county. After about ten minutes in the Fairfax County Courthouse, I found out why McKenzie left the campaign. There were two ongoing lawsuits. The first one had Mackenzie suing the Buchanan campaign for allegedly stiffing him out of $250,000. The second lawsuit was a counter-suit by the campaign that was so ridiculous I couldn't stop laughing as I read it. It accused Scott of every single criminal misdeed except for violating sodomy laws. Suddenly I felt bad for Scott. The Buchanans were using tough, high-priced lawyers to try to pummel him into the ground and/or scare him into dropping his lawsuit against them

The way the Buchanans were paying Scott back for his lifetime of loyalty made me want to vomit. I liked Scott a lot. A dead-ringer for a forty-year-old Jack Nicholson, with the same mischievous smile, Scott was the guy at the Buchanan campaign that all the women were after. He was charming and a lot of fun to be around—not only because of his great personality, but because he was the only guy in the campaign who could match me on music trivia. I was glad to see from later court documents that the lawsuits were settled and Scott came out okay.

But still no sign of him.

The story of Pat's alleged illegitimate daughter seemed dead, and it was for four years. A perusal of the Nexis news database shows a total of zero stories in the news relating to Pat Buchanan's alleged illegitimate child. *Zero.* This is amazing considering the fact that "rumors" are reported all the time in the media, especially in Washington.

Then, suddenly, in mid-2004, the story came back from the dead. Out of the blue, I was contacted by the *Village Voice*, the major alternative newspaper in New York known for their excellent investigative reporting. The *Village Voice* was going to break the story of Pat's alleged illegitimate daughter. After some back and forth conversation with Jesse Singer of the *Voice*, I realized that we both had much of the same information regarding the illegitimate daughter. Neither of us had a smoking gun.

The *Voice* has always been flagrantly ultra-liberal in their politics, except when it comes to investigating political wrongdoing. The *Voice* has exposed political wrongdoing over the years *equally* between Democrats and Republicans, as I mentioned earlier how their fine investigative reporting in 1989 almost cost David Dinkins his election against Rudy Giuliani.

I was told by Ms. Singer that she and the *Voice's* investigative reporter-extraordinaire Wayne Barrett, although not having any new information, were going to run an exposé on the "rumor" of Buchanan's illegitimate daughter and the circumstantial evidence behind it.

The *Voice* would now become the only publication to release this story to the public. The *Voice* reporters asked me to fax a copy of my *Penthouse* piece, since it was unavailable at the time (*Penthouse* was out of business), as well as a copy of my FEC complaint. I also gladly told the *Voice* reporters everything I knew, which they told me pretty much confirmed what their other sources told them.

Thus, it all finally came out in the press, if only as a rumor. Even though they didn't have a smoking gun, the *Voice* nonetheless ran the story (mentioning me and other former Buchanan staffers as having been contacted by other members of the press who were chasing this story as well).

The *Voice* reported the rumors about Pat's alleged daughter with a new wrinkle: the alleged involvement of "hush money." While Pat having an illegitimate daughter may have been a salacious story, there didn't appear to be any lawbreaking involved. The involvement of reported hush money was another story.

According to the story, sources had told the *Village Voice* that the Buchanans had made hush money payments to Buchanan's illegitimate daughter through an attorney in 1992 as Buchanan was gearing up for his first presidential run. While the Buchanans admitted making payments to the attorney, they denied it had anything to do with hush money. Well, sort of denied. While Bay's response was a flat denial, Pat couched his words more carefully; in fact, he sounded quite Clintonesque: "I'm not going to go into that. I don't know the details of anything. It deals with a private matter."

* * *

For years I was obsessed with the Buchanan illegitimate daughter story. But one evening, after a few belts of Black Jack, for some inexplicable reason I began for the first time to re-think the entire matter. I asked myself, "If the story was true, what did Pat Buchanan do that was so terrible that it warranted this much attention from me and from the media?" Pat apparently dated a girl at Georgetown and got her pregnant. The girl did not have an abortion, but gave birth to the child. Subsequently Pat and his girlfriend put the child up for adoption. In the meantime, Pat apparently helped his daughter financially until she was an adult. So what was the big deal? Pat did all the honorable things after the fact. Was this all so salacious only because it involved Pat Buchanan, probably the most controversial figure in American politics at that time? Or maybe because Pat had always worn his "Family Values" on his sleeve?

Finally I realized that my search for Pat Buchanan's alleged daughter had nothing to do with Pat Buchanan, and had nothing to do with finding the truth. It had *everything* to do with only one thing: my utter contempt for Pat's sister, Bay Buchanan. I couldn't believe that I had put so much time and energy into chasing the Buchanan illegitimate daughter story all for the wrong reasons.

My contempt for Bay had become personal, especially after the two of us debated my *Penthouse* piece on the FOX News program *FOX & Friends*. It was the first time I was ever on TV, and I have to admit that Bay (a seasoned public speaker with lots of TV experience under her belt) totally crushed me. However, during this debate, she never addressed any of the charges I had made regarding the Buchanan campaign's corruption, but instead used the common debate tactic of changing the subject with repeated name-calling. She kept saying "Mr. Marks is a fraud. Mr. Marks is a FRAUD!" In retrospect, I could have successfully sued her for slander and defamation of character by asking one question: "How can I be a fraud if one of the most respected and talented attorneys in America, Victor Kovner, fact-checked every word of my exposé?"

After realizing that I was chasing the illegitimate daughter for all the wrong reasons, did my sudden act of conscience stop me from being Oppo Man on the story at that point? Of course not. I had to play out my hand, just for the sake of due diligence.

Oppo Man visited Midlothian, Virginia, in a last-ditch attempt to find the woman in question and sweet talk her into giving me a smoking gun. I failed, as had so many members of the media who had chased this story before me. But for all those media folks chasing the story, it wasn't personal, just business. For me it was personal.

I did the best I could, but in the end Bay Buchanan and Pat Buchanan pulled it off and got away with everything.

Or did they?

After the 2000 election, I simply chalked up Buchanan's poor showing to what I believed was just the typical incompetence of Bay Buchanan and Tim Haley.

Wayne Barrett of the *Voice* had other ideas. He first pointed out the following strange-but-true facts:

- Pat raised $7.1 million before he received the $13 million in matching funds after wrestling away the Reform Party nomination in the summer of 2000. From that point on, Buchanan raised a grand total of only a half-million dollars. This didn't make sense, since Pat received tons of publicity during the wild fight for the Reform Party nomination, which certainly would have excited his financial supporters. Inexplicably, Pat's fundraising *and* campaigning after the convention was pretty much nonexistent.

- In the closing weeks of the campaign, Buchanan dumped $10 million in campaign funds for media buys to a totally unknown firm in Texas that was known for selling mattresses and had no political experience. Strange indeed, but not as strange as the fact that few folks can remember seeing any Buchanan TV ads during this period.

- During those closing weeks of the wild 2000 campaign, Buchanan spent very little, if any, time campaigning in the battleground states, including Florida, where Pat has some very strong support in the northern part of the state.

What does all this mean?

According to Wayne Barrett of the *Village Voice*, there's only one way to connect the dots so that all these mysterious facts make sense. If George W. Bush's campaign had "the goods" or a "smoking gun" on Buchanan regarding his alleged illegitimate daughter, they could have blackmailed Buchanan, promising to not release the information to the press if Buchanan would agree not to campaign seriously after his Reform Party nomination.

At first I thought it was just a very interesting theory. Then I remembered something even more interesting: During the 1996 campaign, Pat's support, unlike any candidate I'd ever seen, was not better or worse in any specific geographic part (or parts) of America. Pat had the same exact hardcore 20 to 30 percent of GOP voters in most states across America, due to his positions on immigration and his anti-NAFTA economic message to blue-collar workers. It was amazing how he had the same appeal in every state.

What happened to all these voters in 2000? Buchanan's name and notoriety alone should have given him many more votes than the feeble 0.4 percent of the vote he earned, compared to Ralph Nader's 2.7 percent of the vote.

Then I remembered something else: the mighty impressive sight of Buchanan's mailing list of supporters across America that I saw in 1996. During the 1996 campaign, Buchanan had *more* individual contributors than either Bob Dole or Bill Clinton. This sounds unbelievable, until you consider that Pat's average contribution was about $20, whereas Dole and Clinton mostly received $1,000 contributions, the legal limit at that time. Buchanan didn't get as much money from his supporters, but still had as many if not more hardcore loyal supporters as Dole and Clinton. Bottom line: $20 Buchanan contributor or $1,000 Bush/Gore contributor, each contributor can only vote once.

So what in the world happened to all those Buchanan voters on Election Day 2000?

For now it continues to be a mystery puzzle—which seems to be the case with so many things involving Pat Buchanan. Did the Bush campaign have a superior Oppo Man or Oppo Woman who got the goods the rest of us failed to get?

Great question.

Chapter Nine

PROOF THAT NEGATIVE CAMPAIGNING LEADS TO ELECTORAL VICTORY

Y ou may be thinking, is negative campaigning really all that effective? Doesn't it turn off voters more than win them over? Quite the opposite. To see how opposition research and negative campaigning are the major reasons why political campaigns are won and lost, let's simply take a look at the seven presidential races since 1980.

2004

Let's begin with the most recent, 2004—Bush versus Kerry. There were, of course, many reasons why Kerry lost this close race, but if you had to choose *one reason alone* it would have to be that negative ads effectively destroyed him. Of course, I'm referring primarily to the incredibly effective "Swiftboat" ads that blunted any momentum he may have had after the Democratic Convention.

The "independent" 527 ads showed Kerry being verbally attacked by his fellow soldiers from Vietnam. What made the

"Swiftboat" ads doubly effective was the fact that they hit Kerry right at the heart of his major strengths: his heroism in Vietnam and the plain fact that he served in the war and George W. Bush did not.

While the effective "Swiftboat" ads against John Kerry got all the attention, another negative ad damaged Kerry badly as well. The Bush campaign's "Wolf" ad was effective in putting doubts into voters' minds about Kerry's ability to lead the country through the war on terror. Featuring a pack of wolves on the prowl for food, a female narrator ominously warned that Kerry would be weak in the face of terrorism. **Therefore it was Kerry's negatives, more than Bush's positives, that decided this election.**

2000

One major negative attack, which was relatively under the radar, lost the election for Al Gore. It was also the reason why Gore lost normally Democratic (blue) states he had no business losing, such as West Virginia, Iowa, and Missouri—not to mention his own home state of Tennessee and Clinton's home state of Arkansas. Gore also had to spend precious time and resources in Democratic states he should have won easily, but which instead were close, such as Pennsylvania, Michigan, and Minnesota.

The reason for Gore's disappointing showings in all these states can be summed up in one word: guns. All those Democratic-leaning states that should have easily gone to Gore were a problem because the vast majority of folks in those states are gun owners. To most gun owners, the issue of gun rights transcends political parties and affiliations. Gore's support for the Brady Bill was all the ammo the NRA needed to send out the most damaging negative direct mail piece of that campaign. The Gore campaign had no idea what had hit them until the final ten days or so before Election Day, and by then it was too late.

The NRA sent out the scariest mailer ever sent to gun owners. Signed by Charlton Heston, the mailer implied that if Gore was elected president, all guns would be confiscated. Of course, this was ridiculous. But ridiculous or not, it worked, as normally Democrat voters turned against Gore, and for George W. Bush, on this single issue. The direct mail piece was based on a statement by Clinton Administration officials that the Second Amendment didn't protect an *individual* right to keep and bear arms. Very clever.

And once again, it was Gore's negatives (which also included his infantile behavior during the presidential debates), more than Bush's positives, that decided this election.

1996

1996 was a bizarre election year. Coming off the 1994 "Republican Revolution," Bill Clinton looked as if he had zero chance of being re-elected in 1996. In late 1995, Clinton's approval ratings had improved but were still in the low forties, and he was definitely beatable. So how did he win—and win easily—in 1996? Not by convincing the voters how great *he* was, but how *awful* the Republicans were. It was again effective negative campaigning that won Clinton re-election, not any great love of the American people for Clinton.

Clinton aide Dick Morris convinced Clinton to begin raising money immediately after the 1994 debacle and to run negative ads against the Republicans a year before they normally would begin to do so. The ads were not against Bob Dole in particular (it still wasn't known for certain who would win the GOP nomination), but against the Republicans in general.

The ads were not nationally televised and, like the NRA ads of 2000, were under the national media's radar because they were aired locally across America. At the time, the Republican Party believed this to be a massive blunder, thinking the American public wasn't paying attention that early, more than a year-and-a-half before the 1996 election. But the public was indeed paying attention, and the Democratic ads quite efficiently attacked Republican attempts to cut spending on such popular programs as Medicare, student loans, and the school lunch program. The ads also attacked legislation that was passed in the Republican House of Representatives that cut government programs for *legal* aliens, as well as legislation that allowed big corporations to pollute at will. It didn't matter that these types of crazy legislation never became law. The mere fact that these abominations were passed by the Republicans in the House was damaging. In addition, a renegade group of Republican House members were responsible for the government shut-down in the closing weeks of 1995. Those demented Republicans gave that powerful issue to Clinton on a silver platter.

These anti-GOP attack ads continued nonstop, with zero response from the GOP. Haley Barbour and the geniuses at the Republican National Committee bought into the conventional wisdom that the ads were being aired too early and would have little effect. Despite having far more money to spend than the Democrats, the Republicans nonetheless decided not to spend any money responding to the ads until it was way too late. By the time they reacted, Clinton had built up an insurmountable lead over Bob Dole that fluctuated anywhere between ten and twenty points, a lead Clinton never relinquished. The anti-Republican message had been embedded into the minds of the voters, and had solidified into stone. **Once again, negative campaigning ruled the day.**

1992

In 1992, the race was again won on negative issues. In this case the Clinton campaign was given great opposition research by none other than George Bush I himself, with his now-infamous "Read my lips, no new taxes" remark. The footage of Bush saying this from his 1988 convention acceptance speech was all the Clinton campaign needed to cripple Bush. Add in the quasi-recession in the country at the time, and the huge budget deficit, and the voting public wanted change. Bush was toast.

Breaking his "Read my lips" pledge also thoroughly destroyed another one of Bush's great political assets up until that point: his integrity, which until then had never been questioned. Raising taxes was not only bad policy (stunting the country's economy) but bad politics as well, as Bush's popularity went down the drain. **Once again, negative issues decided this election.**

1988

Of course, in 1988 George Bush I had the advantage of running as if it was for a third term of the popular, outgoing

Ronald Reagan. However, he still was reported to be as much as eighteen points behind Michael Dukakis after the Democratic Convention in the summer of 1998. How did Bush make up the deficit and go on to an easy 54 percent to 46 percent victory while winning forty out of fifty states? Very simply—by going negative.

There's a great story here about how the opposition researchers for Bush brought file cabinets full of anti-Dukakis research to Bush's Campaign Manager, the late Lee Atwater. Atwater's response was simple: Please get rid of all these file cabinets and bring me just *one* index card with three simple hits to be used against Dukakis.

And indeed they did:

- Willie Horton
- The Pledge of Allegiance
- Boston Harbor

With these three hits, Dukakis was finished. The public learned first about the absurd furlough program in Massachusetts that allowed convicted murderers to "get out of jail free" for a weekend, and that one convict, Willie Horton, raped a woman and violently pistol-whipped and knifed her fiancé while on furlough.

Number two on the Dukakis hit parade was the fact that, as governor, he had opposed public school children reciting the Pledge of Allegiance. It's easy to press buttons with that one.

And finally came the *coup de grace*, hit number three: Dukakis's claim that he had "cleaned up" Boston Harbor was exposed as a farce. Graphic photos and video footage on TV showed all the nation that the "luxurious" Boston Harbor was a dump.

There was no love for the winner in 1988, George Bush I—he possibly could have been beaten by the right Democrat, maybe someone like Bill Clinton. But not an ultraliberal Democrat from an ultraliberal state with a record such as Dukakis had as governor.

1984

1984 was the *only* presidential election since 1980 that was won for positive reasons instead of the usual negative issues, due to the massive popularity of Ronald Reagan. But what crushed Mondale into oblivion, causing him to lose as badly as he did (winning only one state, his home state of Minnesota, and barely winning that one) was negative research against Mondale gleaned from Mondale's own mouth while he gave his acceptance speech at the Democratic Convention.

Just as George Bush I gave the Clinton 1992 campaign all they needed on a silver platter with "Read my lips," Mondale did the same, but in the opposite way: He opened his convention speech by boldly and loudly proclaiming to America that if elected, he was going to raise taxes. It's true that Reagan would have won easily without this amazingly stupid campaign blunder by Mondale—but probably not by the 49-1 state margin. Reagan won on his popularity and on his record as president. But the trouncing Mondale took was due to something negative against him, right out of his own mouth. I have to admire Mondale's integrity and for being so brutally honest, but his political smarts were another story altogether.

1980

In 1980, Jimmy Carter was the incumbent president, and as was the case in 1992, the voters simply wanted change. Remember: This was 1980, not 1984, and Reagan was not yet the popular man he would become. He won in 1980 with only 50.7 percent of the vote (admittedly, this low percentage was partly due to votes siphoned off from third-party candidate John Anderson). It was not a mandate *for* Reagan, but a mandate *against* Carter.

Recession plus inflation plus high unemployment plus high interest rates plus our hostages still in Iran plus Afghanistan plus long gas lines plus malaise equaled doom for the hapless Carter. And all Reagan had to do to win the presidency in 1980 was to go negative in his closing statement during their sole presidential debate, exactly one week before the election. It was vintage Reagan: After listing all the negatives above against Carter, Reagan summed it up thusly: "Before you go into the voting booth next Tuesday, ask yourself one question; are you better off or worse off than you were four years ago?"

That was the ultimate and most effective negative campaign attack line in my lifetime. Just one sentence said it all, and Carter was done. **And the negative prevails once again.**

Chapter Ten

JESSE HELMS VERSUS HARVEY GANTT

A fter leaving the Buchanan campaign, I spent the rest of 1995 working on three races, the guberna-torial campaign in Illinois, the gubernatorial campaign in Indiana, and the senatorial campaign in Alabama. Ironically, all three of my client's candidates lost, and all the candidates I researched won.

These races featured Al Salvi defeating Bob Kustra for the Republican gubernatorial nomination in Illinois (Salvi would eventually lose to current U.S. Senator Richard Durbin); Indianapolis Mayor Stephen Goldsmith defeating Rex Early for the Republican gubernatorial nomination in Indiana (Goldsmith would eventually lose to then-Lieutenant Governor Frank O'Bannon); and Jeff Sessions defeating Sid McDonald for the Republican senatorial nomination in Alabama (Sessions would go on to defeat Roger Bedford and continues to hold that Senate seat today).

In 1996, one of my clients was the National Republican

Senatorial Committee (NRSC). Oppo Man was hired to dig up dirt on U.S. Senate candidates in the same manner in which he had worked in 1994 and 1995 for the National Republican Congressional Committee.

My first campaign was in North Carolina, where the controversial Jesse Helms was once again being targeted by the Democrats. It was Oppo Man's job to check out Helms' Democratic opponents. We knew at the time that Helms was vulnerable, but one must look at his prior victories in 1984 and 1990 to truly understand *how* vulnerable—and the context of this 1996 race.

Throughout his Senate career, all of Helms' races were close. Since he was such a polarizing figure, he equally moti- vated voters on both the left and the right, never garnering more than 54 percent of the vote, usually ending up in the 52 to 53 percent range. In his last two races for re-election, Helms had defeated then-popular Democratic Governor Jim Hunt 52 percent to 48 percent in 1984, and then defeated former Charlotte Mayor Harvey Gantt 52 percent to 47 percent in 1990.

The 1984 race against Hunt was a dogfight, and a nasty one at that. Hunt was a moderate Democrat and a fine governor. The race was dead even, but once the voters saw that Hunt was accepting big dough from the Hollywood and New York liberal elite (not to mention from gay groups that despised Helms), Hunt's poll numbers went south and he lost. (Good oppo work in 1990 by Helms' Oppo Men no doubt picked up those tidbits.)

The 1990 race against Gantt was very similar, very close throughout until the end, when the Helms campaign lowered the boom—a television ad regarding affirmative action. This ad, produced by GOP TV guru Alex Castellanos, is either one of the most brilliant ads ever created, or one of the dirtiest, depending on your point of view. During the final week of that campaign, the ad showed a pair of white hands crumpling a job rejection notice. The narrator of the ad said that the job had been given to a minority candidate and that Gantt supported quotas in hiring. (Gantt was himself black, adding to the emotion on both sides.)

The ad put the final nail in Gantt's coffin. Many white voters, including many registered Democrats, had friends, relatives, and acquaintances who were either passed over for jobs because they were white or whose children were passed over for college admissions and scholarships in favor of black students.

It was a political issue that became personal for white voters. And it was a winning issue politically with no downside for Helms' campaign, since black voters were going to vote 90 percent Democratic anyway. There was zero risk in running such an ad, which would certainly win votes from white Democrats and Independents.

Of course, the liberal response was that the ad was racist. The fact that the ad may have appealed to some white racists is beyond dispute. But that's not the point. The point is that the ad depicted a very real scenario that had been playing out in thousands of white homes throughout North Carolina.

It's a terrible dichotomy: On the one hand, there's no doubt that affirmative action has been a good thing for America because it has brought so many good, hardworking African American folks into the American middle class. However, just as true is the fact that white, middle-class, blue-collar folks have been hurt, and continue to be hurt, as a result of American racism for which they are not in any way personally responsible.

So regardless of what you think of the ad, this much I believe to be true:

- Was the ad highly negative and inflammatory? Yes.
- Was it dirty? Maybe.
- Was a legitimate issue being brought to the voters' attention? Absolutely.

Nevertheless, the ad incensed Helms's opponents. So, in 1996, the liberals were out for blood. There were two men running in the Democratic primary for the opportunity to face Helms in the 1996 November general election. Harvey Gantt, the former mayor of Charlotte, was running again, knowing that, if nominated, another close race was inevitable. This time, Gantt believed he would learn from the mistakes of 1990, that the affirmative action issue would be "old news," and that, with just a little luck, he could pull it out. Charles Sanders, CEO of North Carolina pharmaceutical giant Glaxo-Wellcome, was also in the race.

Oppo Man was told to immediately get the goods on Sanders. Since Sanders had never run for office, and had no liberal positions to attack (as Harvey Gantt did), Sanders was considered by the NRSC to be the tougher opponent against Helms in the general election. And considering how close Gantt came in 1990, the thought of an even *tougher* opponent than Gantt was truly scary to the Helms campaign and to the NRSC.

Sanders was a tougher opponent because (unlike Gantt) he was white *and* rich. Couple this with all the money Sanders would be certain to raise from North Carolina's "Research Triangle," including all the hospitals and medical interests and Sanders would certainly have made a formidable opponent.

However, digging up dirt against Sanders was one of the easiest jobs in "Oppo Man's" career. Much of the dirt was in Glaxo-Wellcome's own annual reports.

Here are some of the highlights:

- Price gouging, which especially hurt the elderly
- Massive layoffs, while Sanders and his cronies were jacking up their salaries into the Ken Lay range
- One section in each Annual Report, entitled "Ongoing Lawsuits" or "Ongoing Litigation," included the same company line, something along the lines of "Lawsuits are expected to be settled without any adverse affects on the firm . . ." This casual response to lawsuits from the families of patients who had either died or were severely injured by faulty Glaxo drugs sickened me.

Helms ran TV ads attacking both Sanders and Gantt, trying to paint them with the same broad liberal brush. Then suddenly in April 1996, I began hearing about ads attacking Sanders, using much of the material I had gleaned against Sanders and Glaxo. I found it strange that the Helms campaign would be using these attacks against Sanders so early; it didn't make any sense.

But I had it all wrong. The attack ads against Sanders were not coming from the Helms campaign. They were coming from Harvey Gantt! Was the NRSC or the Helms campaign leaking my material to the Gantt campaign, wanting Gantt to win since all polls showed Sanders would be the tougher opponent against Helms? If so, it made perfect sense—and it was brilliant: get rid of your most feared opponents by having someone else do the dirty work. Of course it's also possible the Gantt campaign found the same research I did on their own.

✶ ✶ ✶

The primary was held on May 7, 1996. Everything worked as planned: Gantt 52 percent to Sanders 42 percent.

The general election campaign was much the same as 1990 (almost a repeat), with Helms accusing Gantt of being too liberal for North Carolina. The general election was, as expected, tight, with polls showing the race too close to call just days before the election. Some polls even had Gantt ahead by a point or two. But in the end, Helms won.

Some of you might be thinking: *Isn't that dirty politics, leaking dirt to your opponent because he would make a weaker challenger than his primary opponent?* I don't have the answer to that one; except to say that dirty or not, it's brilliant politics, and such things have been going on long before I arrived in this world.

Deceptive? Absolutely. But dirty? I don't know. I would probably tend to lean towards "no" to that question. How can it be dirty when the person who will be your general election opponent is in cahoots with you in this alleged dirty trick? And how is it dirty when the material being leaked is all true?

Ever more food for thought . . .

Chapter Eleven

JOHN KERRY VERSUS
BILL WELD

I t was being billed by the press as the "Battle of the Titans," and the "marquee" U.S. Senate race of 1996: the popular U.S. Senator John Kerry versus just-as-popular Governor William Weld of Massachusetts.

Just two years before, in 1994, Weld had easily won reelection, drubbing Democrat Mark Roosevelt 71 percent to 28 percent. This was unusual for a Republican in Massachusetts. To be *that* popular in such a liberal state? Weld did it by staying liberal on key social issues such as abortion, gay rights, and affirmative action. But on other key issues, important to Massachusetts voters, Weld was to the right of Attila the Hun. On the issues of taxes, welfare, and crime, Massachusetts voters were with Weld. Therefore, the Weld campaign believed they would win if they could keep the campaign against Kerry focused on those three issues, where Kerry had taken opposing liberal positions.

Oppo Man spent more time in 1996 working for the

National Republican Senatorial Committee on the Kerry/Weld race than any other, and spent more time in the state of Massachusetts researching John Kerry than in any other state that year. In Washington, he also toiled through every one of John Kerry's Senate votes, as well as his statements on the Senate floor. The research against Kerry was time-consuming but lots of fun.

Kerry's votes on taxes, crime, and welfare were plentiful, and many of them very bad—votes for more taxes; votes for more criminals being let out onto the street; and votes for more welfare spending. These old-shoe liberal views had even been discredited by then-President Bill Clinton. But it didn't matter, Kerry was so far to the left it was ridiculous. As an example, whilst perusing the *Congressional Record* in the Library of Congress, I discovered that the Senate was debating a bill that would require welfare mothers to work ten hours per week in government jobs to receive their benefits. Kerry, on the Senate floor, called this bill "inhumane."

In addition, while going through Kerry's financial and real estate records, I discovered he was broke (not yet having married his future wife, Theresa Heinz) and was paying one-tenth the market rate for rental of a beautiful condo on the water, courtesy of close friend and campaign Finance Director Wesley Finch (who was forced to resign from the position as Kerry's chief fundraiser after the press revealed what appeared to be financial misuse of government-subsidized housing that Kerry may have helped him acquire). The cut-rate rent for Kerry's condo was also considered an illegal campaign contribution or gift.

Then there was the minor matter of Kerry's receiving campaign cash from Duvan Arboleda and Harry A. Falk, both indicted as members of the Cali drug cartel. Kerry claimed in 1996 that he had no idea about their involvement in a multi-billion-dollar money-laundering operation, despite it's being front-page news in the *Boston Globe* in 1991. All this at the same time that Kerry was chairman of a Senate panel investigating international drug smugglers and money laundering.

As opposed to all this dirt on Kerry in 1996, there didn't seem to be much to attack Weld on as governor, since he took the same liberal positions as Kerry on issues that had voter approval. Weld took conservative positions on taxes, welfare, and crime, all issues where Kerry took the liberal positions and was politically vulnerable.

The only area in which Weld appeared to be vulnerable was in his hundreds of vetoes. Oppo Man had to look though each and every one of them so we knew where Weld would be attacked with the usual claims that "This veto hurt the elderly," "This veto hurt the children," and the like. You know, the usual liberal mantra against *any* government spending cuts.

So the race looked winnable for Weld, at least on paper. And the polls all were hopeful, with the race being dubbed a "toss-up" by every reputable pollster. Between all the campaign turmoil and the eight debates between Weld and Kerry, Oppo Man was on call year-round, going to Massachusetts throughout the year at a moment's notice.

The race was for the most part civil—until the end. In the final weeks, all hell broke loose and I was glad to see Weld finally coming out of his shell. He was never comfortable (as was Kerry) showing emotion or going on the attack on television, but in the seventh debate, on October 20, he let Kerry have it. After Weld brought up Oppo Man's research on Kerry's low-rent payments on his high-rent condo, Kerry's response was lame: "Since I was living in Washington most of the time, I was only in the Boston apartment for a small portion of each month. Therefore, we pro-rated the rent to reflect that."

Can you believe it? That would be like you telling your landlord, "Hey, Moby, since I was traveling in South Kenya during the months of September and October, and therefore wasn't here, I'm not paying rent for those two months. And as for the five days I took off for Thanksgiving, I'm going to pro-rate the rent so I only pay for twenty-five days in November." Weld also pointed out during the debate that Kerry pulled the same nonsense in DC while he was also broke, receiving free or cut-rate housing while living there, too, as a U.S. senator.

Whenever Weld directed a totally factual charge against Kerry—for instance, that he was opposed to welfare mothers being forced to work ten hours a week—Kerry would look Weld straight in the eye, and with an angry look wave his finger back and forth at Weld, like a teacher reprimanding a schoolboy: "Governor, you ought to be ashamed of yourself for saying such a vicious lie. That's a lie and you know it's a lie." Meanwhile, Weld had already retrieved the document in question from the congressional record proving the charge against Kerry was true, and waved it back at Kerry, who nonetheless continued shaking his head, and continued repeating, "Governor, you ought to be ashamed of yourself for saying such a vicious lie. That's a lie and you know it's a lie."

Watching this, I just couldn't believe Kerry's audacity in lying so flagrantly, even with Weld waving the evidence straight in his face. It would be as if Mike Dukakis had said in 1988 "I never furloughed convicted murderers! That's a lie! A vicious lie! And you ought to be ashamed of yourself for saying such a vicious lie!" or Lyndon Johnson saying, "I never sent more troops to Vietnam. That's a vicious lie!"

But during that final debate, in response to Weld's attacks, Kerry was just as good at dishing out the dirt. He accused Weld of being responsible for the deaths of two young children in foster care and of using funds designated for hiring social workers to pay for an election-year tax cut.

But the one moment that proved most clearly that Kerry had *no shame* and would say anything to win and/or fool the voters, came in his response to Weld's bragging about his historic tax cuts. Kerry responded that the tax cut implemented by Weld was really to be credited to Mike Dukakis. Weld could hardly contain his laughter as he responded, "Senator, if you say Mike Dukakis is responsible for my tax cuts, you're simply hallucinating."

But in the campaign's final week, the poll numbers, which had been steady for almost a year, finally began to move for Kerry, and in a big way. And I knew why.

You had two very popular politicians running against each other, one in the U.S. Senate and one in the governor's mansion. If Weld won, the voters would lose their extremely popular governor (who would go on to be senator) *and* their extremely popular senator being voted out at the same time. On the other hand, if Kerry won, the voters would get to keep them both where they were, and where the voters liked them.

I knew this could happen because of what happened in 1982 in New York State when I lived there. Ed Koch had just been re-elected mayor of New York in 1981 with a record 76 percent of the vote. (After his first term, he was so incredibly popular that the Democrats *and* Republicans both nominated him for re-election). After that strong 1981 mayoral re-election, subsequent polls showed Koch would easily win the 1982 Democratic gubernatorial race against then-Lieutenant Governor Mario Cuomo (then-Governor Hugh Carey chose not to run for re-election). The polls showed Koch ahead of Cuomo in almost every county, and Koch held steady with a ten-point lead over Cuomo throughout most of the campaign, moving down to a seven-point poll lead on Election Day.

Then a funny thing happened, a precursor to Massachusetts in 1996. During the campaign's final debates, Cuomo would say, "Ed Koch is a great mayor. Vote for him for governor and you will lose him as mayor. Vote for me and you get us both." The polls may have said one thing, but those last words by Mario Cuomo were still resonating in the ears of many voters on Election Day, voters who woke up that morning honestly believing they would vote for Koch entered the election booth and realized that they didn't want to lose Koch as mayor. And while they preferred Koch, Mario Cuomo wasn't such a bad guy, was he? Certainly no slouch. *Let's keep them both.* The voters decided it in September 1982: Cuomo 53 percent to Koch 47 percent.

The fate of Ed Koch in 1982 was exactly the fate that befell William Weld in 1996. This is certainly not to say Kerry would have lost to Weld had this one factor not been in play. But Kerry certainly wouldn't have beaten Weld as easily as he did. There was no other reason for the numbers to spike so quickly in Kerry's favor in the last week of the campaign. No scandal. No last-second surprises.

The result: Kerry 52 percent to Weld 45 percent.

Because of the "*You can keep us both*" problem Weld faced in 1996, I believe the only chance Weld had of winning and completely negating the issue was to simply resign as governor before the race began. This would have forced the voters to make a straight-up choice between the two, without the "Weld is still governor" fallback. But Weld *didn't* resign as governor, and subsequently lost.

But then Weld did the craziest thing: He resigned anyway *after* the election. On July 30, 1997, only eight months after being beaten by Kerry he resigned to accept the post of ambassador to Mexico, having been nominated by Bill Clinton. Ironically, Weld would never get the post, as the nomination was destroyed by none other than Jesse Helms who, as Chairman of the Senate Foreign Relations Committee, had the ultimate power through the Senate's arcane rules to decide if Weld would get the job. The fact that Weld's wife had supported Helms' opponent Harvey Gantt at the same time in 1996 as both men were running as Republican for the U.S. Senate in tough races didn't score any points with Helms. That—plus the fact that, during that same 1996 campaign, Weld refused to acknowledge, that if elected to the Senate he would support Helms as Chairman of the Armed Services Committee—spelled Weld's doom. Weld never made it through Helms' committee. The full Senate (who would have easily approved Weld for the job) therefore never got to vote on Weld's fate.

Weld went on to briefly run for governor of New York in 2006, but dropped out early in the race. Kerry, on the other hand, almost became president in 2004.

One of the obvious questions regarding all the dirt on Kerry was why it was never brought out during the 2004 presidential election. Everyone remembers that race as having been nasty and negative, but the nastiness was deceiving. All the dirty stuff came not from the Bush or Kerry campaigns, but from the 527 groups MoveOn.org. and Swiftboat Veterans. Even Oppo Man had a nasty 527 ad about Kerry as a private attorney securing parole for a man who pled guilty to trying to kill a police officer.

On the other hand, the Bush and Kerry campaigns stayed above the fray. You rarely heard either candidate say a nasty word about his opponent. This could explain why none of the negative issues mentioned above from 1996 ever surfaced in 2004. Perhaps there was a "gentleman's agreement" between Bush and Kerry to let their 527 surrogates do the dirty work. But again, I'll never know for sure.

* * *

All throughout that election year of 1996, the John Kerry I saw was polished, poised, strong, and able to express anger in a subtle, inoffensive way. And one more thing: He always looked *very* senatorial. Even *presidential.* It was obvious to all who saw him during those debates that he would someday run for president.

Having lived though that 1996 campaign, which featured John Kerry at his best, his 2004 presidential campaign remains an enigma to me. Against George W. Bush, Kerry's surrogates (including George Soros, Kerry's very rude wife, the Hollywood elite, etc.) may have been aggressive in their tone against W., but Kerry never was.

Now, I agree that for Kerry to have personally attacked a sitting president during wartime would have been sticky. But Kerry just never had the "fire in the belly" I saw so clearly in 1996.

Just as Bob Dole failed miserably in 1996 at distinguishing himself in any way against President Clinton, eight years later Kerry did the exact same thing: He never clearly articulated to the voters how and why he was different from President Bush, nor how and why he would make a better president. His answers always seemed along the lines of "I agree with what the president is doing, I'll just do it better."

Kerry showed zero vision. His "Reporting for Duty" theme was amateur hour at best, and was completely neutralized by the Swiftboat controversy. Still, Kerry was given every opportunity to show America how and why he was different from Bush—how and why he was *better* than Bush.

He never did.

He clearly showed himself to be a decent man, and to be personally likeable. But the spark I saw from John Kerry in 1996 was never there in 2004. What happened? Why did Kerry play everything so close to the vest? For instance, why did he not appear on Bill O'Reilly's "*The O'Reilly Factor*" show, with its millions of viewers? Yes, O'Reilly would have asked tough questions, but he wouldn't have sandbagged Kerry. In fact, I believe he would have been so honored to have Kerry on his show he would have very respectful towards him. During the general election, O'Reilly repeatedly invited Kerry to come on his show, (as had President Bush), but Kerry inexplicably never did.

The only excuse Kerry would have for not having appeared would be if his internal polls had him easily winning the election, and he thought he could just run out the clock, thereby making any high-profile interview risky. But I can't imagine that was the case. All the polls showed the race was too close to call at best, and at worst Kerry was slightly behind. An interview on O'Reilly would have garnered so much publicity beforehand that it would have attracted untold numbers of undecided voters, including God-knows-how-many in Ohio.

So why did the Kerry campaign hold everything so close to the vest in the waning moments of that 2004 presidential campaign? The 1996 John Kerry would have been fearless. He would have gone on O'Reilly with *relish*. He would have believed in himself, and in retrospect, he may have moved those 65,000 votes in Ohio, which would have won the election. All he had to do was to tell those voters who he was!

The 1996 John Kerry would have

Chapter Twelve

DIRTY TRICKS: THE RISE AND FALL OF GEORGIA SENATOR MAX CLELAND

I n the summer of 1996, I received a strange call from the National Republican Senatorial Committee (NRSC). They asked me to go to Worcester, Massachusetts, to find a specific piece of research to be used against Democrat Max Cleland, who was then running for the U.S. Senate in Georgia.

That Senate race in Georgia had gone crazy. Democratic icon Sam Nunn was retiring from the U.S. Senate. The race was considered extremely important because it would indicate whether the Republican steamroller across the South would continue, or if the Democrats still had the ability to win statewide in the deep South.

Cleland was one of the most fascinating figures I've ever encountered in American politics. During the Vietnam war, he had lost both legs and one of his arms when he reached down to pick up a live grenade. After the war, Cleland came back to America as a war hero and entered politics in his home state of Georgia.

In 1996, Cleland was the secretary of state of Georgia and a popular political figure. His Republican opponent was Guy Millner, a wealthy, right-wing businessman. Before getting the phone call from the NRSC, I had paid only cursory attention to the race. But the mudslinging going on in Georgia between Cleland and Millner was already national news. Cleland was being attacked relentlessly by Millner for writing a letter on behalf of a murderer seeking parole. The murderer was indeed paroled and went out and committed another murder. It was Willie Horton all over again.

Cleland was also being attacked because of a lawsuit in which a black woman, fired by Cleland, won a $200,000 settlement from the state, and because a Cleland employee had retired with a pension after being investigated for sexual harassment. These were all truthful attacks, as was Cleland's attack of Millner for his eight-year membership in a Florida club that excluded blacks and Jews.

The attacks against Cleland were orchestrated by Millner's political guru, GOP campaign strategist extraordinaire Tom Perdue. I had remembered Perdue from two years prior in 1994 when I was working as the press secretary for Steve Wilson, who lost to Bill Frist in the Tennessee Republican primary for the U.S. Senate. Perdue had run Frist's campaign that year, and he was smart and tough. His personal attacks were as vicious as his political attacks—as mentioned earlier, he once referred to Republican opponent Bob Corker as "pond scum."

The 1996 race in Georgia was a dead heat. The negative attacks by Perdue and Millner against Cleland intensified as they tried to tie Cleland to the poster boy of hated northern liberalism, Ted Kennedy. That's where Oppo Man came in.

I was told that the campaign received a rumor that there had been a newspaper story in the Worcester, Massachusetts, press that featured a photo of Max Cleland together with Ted Kennedy's nephew Michael, who was also Ted's campaign manager. Cleland had made a stop at a center for veterans in Worcester, Massachusetts, to support Kennedy for re-election in 1994, citing Kennedy's strong support for veterans. I was given a rough timeframe of the article in question and told to go to the library in Worcester and find the picture in the newspaper's archival microfilm.

This was not the normal research, where Oppo Man decided what dirt to look for. This was a specific order telling me to look for a certain item. Oppo Man did as he was told.

I was at that moment in Albany, New York, and Worcester, Massachusetts, wasn't that far away. So I just packed a few things for what I figured would be a short, one-day trip, and got in the car.

The next morning, I was in the Worcester library, going through the microfilm tray to find the offending photo of Max Cleland and Michael Kennedy. Well, I quickly found the article, but not the picture. The article only made reference to the picture, which was not actually in the article. The photo was located in a local center for veterans. How was I going to get that photo?

The only way was to request a copy of it from the lodge. And the only way to get them to do so would be to misrepresent myself.

So I made my way down to the lodge and casually sauntered inside. Before anyone even noticed me, I spotted the picture hanging on the wall—a framed photo of several men all smiling for the camera, including Max Cleland and Michael Kennedy.

The next thing I knew, a friendly blue-collar gent walked over and smiled at me. "Hi," was all he said. I stuck out my hand and introduced myself with some bogus name. Then I pointed to the picture, put my finger on one of the anonymous faces in it, and said, "See this guy? Do you know who he is?" As soon as he said "No," I knew I was in.

"That's my uncle Chester. What a great picture. I was told you might have this photo. Do you have any copies of it?"

I knew he didn't, but I figured he'd offer to let me photo-copy the picture, which would have been good enough for what my client needed. But this fine fellow gave me even more than expected: "You know what?" he said. "Take the photo down the street to the photo shop. They can make you a professional copy of it." I couldn't believe my luck.

So that's what I did. I went down the street, made a copy of the photo, had the copy blown up to 8" x 11" and sent the copy via FedEx to Tom Perdue at the Millner campaign. No concern whatsoever about the fact that I had misrepresented myself to get the photo. An oppo man cannot do anything so brazen when getting official records from a courthouse or government office, since lying about your identity in those cases is against the law. But lying to a private citizen? No problem.

I was elated, and I was proud of myself; regardless of what I personally thought of the absurdity of this so-called "hit." I was *so* creative (albeit admittedly ethically challenged) in getting what I wanted. I was Oppo Man!

The race ended with Cleland eking out a 49 to 48 percent victory over Millner. And he only won because a third-party

Libertarian candidate siphoned off 81,000 votes from Millner, when Cleland won by less than 30,000 votes. Whether or not the picture of Cleland and Ted Kennedy Jr. moved any votes one way or the other, there's no sure way of knowing.

*　*　*

After being elected to the U.S. Senate, Cleland became an instant national celebrity, in part due to the novelty of his being a one-armed, legless senator in a wheelchair. But his stay in the Senate was a short one. In 2002, Tom Perdue finally got even with Cleland.

This time running the campaign of Cleland's new opponent, GOP Congressman Saxbe Chambliss, Perdue again used vicious and relentless attack ads against Cleland, this time focusing on the fact that Cleland had repeatedly voted against President Bush's war on terrorism initiatives. Cleland not only voted against the bill creating the Department of Homeland Security, but cast ten other votes against Bush regarding the war on terrorism and national security.

Perdue's ads against Cleland were even more vicious than those of 1996. The 2002 ads featured pictures of Cleland along with pictures of Osama bin Laden and Sadaam Hussein. Remember, this was in 2002, only a year after 9/11, when Bush was at the top of his popularity ratings. We hadn't yet gone into Iraq.

Liberals and Democrats shouted, "How can you question this man's patriotism? A man who lost three of his four limbs fighting for his country?" But the howls of protest missed the point; Cleland's service in Vietnam and the tragedy he suffered were not in question. What *was* in question was his judgment concerning the war on terror and how he voted as a U.S. senator. No one questioned his patriotism. Only his judgment.

The voters agreed, as Chambliss easily defeated Cleland 53 to 46 percent.

During that 1996 election cycle I also got to work for the NRSC on three other key Senate races, all eventual Republican winners:

- Colorado Senator Wayne Allard, digging up dirt on Democrat opponent Tom Strickland
- Oregon Senator Gordon Smith, digging up dirt on Democrat opponent Tom Bruggere
- Idaho Senator Larry Craig, digging up dirt on Democrat Walt Minnick

The Oregon and Idaho races were fairly uneventful, with Gordon Smith coming back from a narrow defeat at the hands of Democratic Senator Ron Wyden just the year before to defeat Bruggere. But Oppo Man did have one fine moment in the Allard/Strickland race, which helped the Republican Allard to victory.

Traveling to Colorado, I spent several days in the beautiful Rocky Mountains, which I hadn't seen in person since I was fifteen years old. In between my sight-seeing tours, I managed to stumble upon a strange lawsuit in the federal courthouse in Denver.

Democrat Strickland was slightly ahead in the polls at that time and his biggest strength was being one of the most influential environmental attorneys in the most environmentally conscious state in America. He seemed to always be fighting polluters and doing his best to keep Colorado beautiful.

Except for one problem: I found a case in the federal courthouse where Strickland defended one of the worst polluters in the state's history. Strickland and his client lost the case, which resulted in his client receiving one of the largest environmental fine in the state's history. That was what we call a great hit!

Final results: Allard 51 percent, Strickland 46 percent.

Chapter Thirteen

DOLE VERSUS CLINTON

As I wrote earlier, after leaving the Buchanan campaign, my goal was to eventually work for the Dole campaign, since I believed in 1995 that Dole had a chance of defeating Clinton. But it was not to be: neither me working for Dole, nor Dole defeating Clinton. I never did any work for the 1996 Dole presidential campaign, instead getting tied up with the other political races mentioned previously as well as some corporate clients.

However, the 1996 Clinton-Dole race was a defining moment for Oppo Man, who was pondering the once-unthinkable: Who really deserved to win that 1996 presidential race, Dole or Clinton?

In the closing month of the election, with Dole way behind, it was obvious that his only chance to win was by going negative and attacking Clinton more aggressively, especially since there were plenty of good negative issues to be used against Clinton. Dole was so far behind, with some polls showing a twenty- to twenty-five-point deficit, that he *had* to go negative.

But he didn't. While being interviewed in the campaign's closing weeks, Dole was flatly asked why he wasn't attacking Clinton more forcefully. Dole's response was lamer than anything I had ever heard in any presidential campaign in my lifetime. He said, "I'd rather lose with dignity."

What that means is that Dole didn't have the political stomach to do what was necessary, the "down and dirty" presidential politics that he would have had to employ in order to have a chance to defeat Clinton.

It's like a boxing match where the boxer losing late in the fight can only win by going for the knockout, but to do so would require that boxer to get in close, where—win or lose—he would take a pounding. In order for Dole to win, he had to get bloodied in the process, as Clinton had successfully done four years prior in 1992, when he took every pounding imaginable (Gennifer Flowers, draft dodging, etc.). Whereas Clinton in 1992 kept taking the punches and simply continued to dust himself off and get right back up, Dole didn't have Clinton's stomach for the pounding he would have had to take should he go on the attack against Clinton in 1996.

Dole simply didn't have inner toughness. Clinton did.

I felt completely disillusioned. The Republican candidate for president didn't deserve to win. Bob Dole, while certainly a decent man and lifelong, selfless public servant, campaigned with zero passion as if he didn't really care whether he won or lost. On the other hand, Bill Clinton left no stone unturned and did anything, including raising every campaign dollar (legal or illegal), to get re-elected.

Whereas Dole had no passion, Clinton cared and was deeply passionate about being president, getting re-elected, and doing what he believed was "the people's work."

Suddenly I was actually thinking the unthinkable. Only two years after coming to Washington to become Oppo Man for the sole purpose of defeating Democrats and removing Bill Clinton from the presidency (after the GOP took over Congress), I now realized sadly that Clinton deserved to win this race. Not only did he care more than Dole did, but his record was pretty impressive; as he rebounded incredibly from his disastrous 1993–1994 with a great 1995–1996; creating a booming economy; passing NAFTA, which helped boom the economy; cutting the federal deficit in half; and most incredibly, getting rid of America's worst social issue headache by passing welfare reform.

So as 1996 came to a close, I found myself in a weird place politically, as cracks began to appear in my Republican armor. I was crumbling bit by bit; it would be years before I broke down altogether. Part of the breakdown was political, part of the breakdown was moral (discussed in great detail later in the chapter "Sex, Lies, and Republican Hypocrisy"), and part of it was finding out over and over again the hard way that I was not always working for the "good guys," as I had originally thought. Earlier I used the Jack Abramoff case to illustrate this point, but it began before that, as Oppo Man worked on behalf of clients outside the political world who were just as powerful, just as corrupt, and just as deeply tied to the Republican Party—corporations.

Chapter Fourteen

CORPORATE HITMAN: DIGGING DIRT FOR CORPORATIONS

A s in the Abramoff case, my counterpart Oppo Man often seems doomed to realize only after the fact that he was working for the bad guys. This was unfortunately also the case in 1996, when I was hired for my dirt-digging skills by a client working on behalf of a corporation instead of a politician. I was working on behalf of Koch Industries, the largest oil company in America no one has heard of ("Koch" is pronounced the same as "coke"). Koch is also one of the biggest Republican contributors in America, and I was brought in on behalf of the firm to investigate renegade family member William Koch.

Koch Industries is the largest privately held corporation in the world in terms of revenue (more than $80 billion annually). And the story I'm about to tell of Koch Industries is one you'd more likely see on a bad made-for-TV movie than in real life. But as I can once again strongly attest, fact is indeed far stranger than fiction.

After the death of founder Fred Koch, a twenty-year-long legal civil war broke out between three of his heirs, his sons Charles, David, and William (Bill). (A fourth brother, Fredrick, wanted nothing to do with the business.) Bill tried to take over the company but his power play failed, and Charles and David forced him out. Or, at least, he was out of the day-to-day dealings of the company; he was never *really* out, as he waged his twenty-year battle against his two brothers.

When I was brought into the picture in 1996, all I knew was that renegade brother Bill was trying to exert political influence in different parts of the country, and that the other family members were concerned. I was told the major worry of the other family members was that Bill might receive a high government appointment by then-Kansas Governor Joan Finney, who was a personal friend of Bill Koch. The company was a Kansas firm, founded in Wichita, and I was told of the family's fear that Bill Koch and then-Governor Finney could make trouble for Koch Industries.

Oppo Man was soon on a trek across all seven states (Kansas, Oklahoma, Texas, Louisiana, Florida, Minnesota, and Delaware) where Koch Industries *and* Bill Koch had done business, including political business—meaning campaign contributions. Koch industries wanted to know what Bill Koch had been up to politically and compare that to what Koch Industries was up to politically—just to make sure they had covered all bases and hadn't left out any politician with whom Bill Koch may have curried favor.

In each state, I was to research the following:

- To whom was Bill Koch contributing money?
- To whom was Koch Industries contributing money, including the individual Koch execs?
- What other business interests did Koch Industries and/or Bill Koch have in those states?
- Were there any lawsuits or anything else bad out there in any of those states against either Koch industries or Bill Koch?
- Was Koch industries guilty of environmental infractions in any of those states?

In retrospect, it was that last question about Koch's environmental violations that should have set off alarm bells in my head, but that alarm bell never went off.

The job was fun. PAC contributions from Koch Industries to dozens of the state legislators in Kansas, as well as many in the other states, were mind-boggling. Bill Koch's contributions were negligible. And it was easy to convince myself that Bill Koch was the bad guy, given all the lawsuits in his personal life, which rivaled that of Howard Hughes. Not only did he have three stormy marriages, but there was a bitter and vicious lawsuit between Bill and a mistress who refused to leave one of his homes, until he forced her eventual eviction from the premises. Bill was a wildman. Even his 1992 America's Cup victory against Ted Turner appeared to be nothing more than a distraction for a bored rich guy who had nothing to do. He won by simply hiring the world's best sailors, engineers, and so on.

At least that's how it appeared to me. Koch Industries, on the other hand, appeared to me to be one of America's great straight-arrow, buttoned-down corporations, the antithesis of playboy/yachtsman Bill Koch's image. Even after viewing all of Koch Industries environmental and EPA violations (there were dozens), I was still blind to what was really going on. Oppo Man was just too arrogant to believe he could be working for the wrong side.

However, I was finally forced to see the light, first in 1999, long after my work for them had ended, when the federal government ruled that Koch Industries was guilty of stealing oil, and again in May 2001, when the Koch family finally settled their legal differences. Here's what happened:

- In December 1999, a federal investigation found that Koch Industries had stolen oil from the public and lied about its purchases—24,000 times.
- Former EPA administrator Carol Browner announced in 2000 that she was hitting Koch Industries with the largest civil penalty in the history of the federal Clean Water Act: a $30-million fine. She said that Koch Industries spilled over 3 million gallons of crude oil in six states; the EPA complaint targeted more than three hundred oil spills, some poisoning fisheries and drinking water.
- In May 2001, after the Koch family members settled their differences in court, the agreement stipulated that Koch Industries would pay $25 million in penalties to the U.S. government for improperly taking (some would say stealing) more oil than it paid for from federal lands, such as natural forests owned by the public, and also from Indian lands.

It's important to mention that one-third of this settlement went to Bill Koch for bringing the case to court. Also, fifty former Koch employees testified against the company, some in videotaped depositions, attesting to their oil thefts. In the 1980s alone, Koch records show 300 million gallons of oil the company never paid for. It was pure profit.

Then there were lawsuits brought against Koch Industries by individuals blaming Koch for their children's deaths. In one documented case in Texas, a high-pressure pipeline started spewing butane, which sparked an explosion that killed two teenagers. The resulting investigation exposed a pattern of negligence and cover-up involving the pipeline, which was described as looking like Swiss cheese. Federal investigators blamed the explosion on Koch's failure to adequately protect the line, and in 1999, a jury found Koch Industries guilty of negligence and malice. And as if that weren't enough, Koch Petroleum Group was also fined $20 million after it released huge amounts of cancer-causing benzene from a Texas refinery and then tried to cover it up.

I couldn't believe I had worked for these guys—particularly since it was now clear I was working against the Koch brother who turned out to be the good guy in this fight. Making matters worse and even more disillusioning for me was the fact that Koch Industries was basically a Republican firm. Not only was the GOP the major benefactor of their corporate largesse, three of their major lobbyists on Capitol Hill were Republican lobbyists: LPI Consulting, The Policy & Taxation Group, and John Stinson.

So not only does Oppo Man help elect low-life politicians too incompetent to discuss with a straight face, he also helps guys like Jack Abramoff and companies like Koch Industries, just because they are connected to the Republican Party?

Makes sense to me.

Chapter Fifteen

ACTION IN TEXAS

October 1997 brought me to the state of Texas for the first time as a political hitman. Right away, I understood clearly why many Texans consider Texas to be a separate country. Because it is, sort of. In fact, it manages to feel both like a different country and totally American at the same time.

While the state is primarily flat, it does have its physical attributes. San Antonio is beautiful, as are Houston, Austin, and most of Dallas. The western half of the state, including the panhandle, brings Texas into the west, with the beautiful pristine air that rivals neighboring New Mexico and Colorado. Texas is so immense that the drive from the southwest corner of El Paso to the northeast corner of Texarkana is one thousand miles, longer than the distance from New York City to Florida. And of course there's another very special thing about Texas, the women. In my opinion, they are the best-looking women of any state in America.

While the state contains three big cities (Houston, Dallas, and San Antonio) and a handful of mid-sized cities, it is nonetheless primarily thousands of miles stretching in different directions encompassing hundreds upon hundreds of tiny cities, each one a population of ten thousand or less. In most of these cities, you won't find a chain hotel, but a mom-and-pop motel. You won't find a McDonalds or Burger King either, though you can generally stumble upon a Dairy Queen.

I entered the state for the first time in late 1997 and made my first stop in Austin, the state capital. I had my hands full getting ready for the key 1998 races about to get started, including the five key statewide races. First there was the race for governor, where first-term Governor George W. Bush needed a strong showing to convince the national media and Republicans nationwide that he had the broad appeal to run for president and win in 2000. The race for lieutenant governor was also key because if W. became president in 2000, the lieutenant governor would automatically become governor.

I was never asked to do any research involving Bush's opponent, possibly because all the polls indicated Governor Bush was going to easily defeat Democratic challenger (and retiring state Land Commissioner) Gary Mauro. However, the race for lieutenant governor was another story, where the *GQ*-handsome Republican Agriculture Secretary Rick Perry was facing the popular and well-respected Democratic State Comptroller John Sharp. I ended up spending a good chunk of late-1997 and 1998 researching this race, as well as the other statewide races for attorney general, state comptroller, and state land commissioner.

But most of the action was in the race for lieutenant governor. I realized immediately that, regardless of who won, the state was going to wind up with a fine lieutenant governor. In so many races I have worked on, the electorate has been forced to choose between the lesser of two evils. This race was the exact opposite and made me feel good about Texas, although, of course, Texas has had its share of dog politicians throughout its long and storied history.

Researching both candidates, I spent a lot of time in Rick Perry's hometown of Haskell, Texas, and Democratic opponent John Sharp's hometown of Victoria. It's always better for a campaign to research its own candidate as well as the opponent, to discover ahead of time what attacks to expect. The two men had a strange history and went a long way back together. They had been classmates at Texas A&M in College Station, Texas. After graduating college, where they both were average students at best, they went their separate ways, both returning to their hometowns. Sharp pursued a career in real estate, while Perry joined his father in running the family's financially successful farm.

The farmer and realtor were both subsequently elected to the state legislature from their respective hometowns in the same year, 1984, both as Democrats. In those days, just about any politician in Texas worth his salt was a Democrat, which, of course, has since been turned around 360 degrees by political guru Karl Rove. Both men moved up the political ladder at the same time when they ran for state office in 1990, Perry as Agriculture Commissioner (after switching parties and becoming a Republican), and Sharp as state comptroller (preceding Carole Rylander, referred to in this book's first chapter). The eerily similar career paths of the two former Aggie classmates were on an obvious collision course as they both won easy re-election in 1994 and were both term-limited out of their jobs in 1998, exactly when long-time Texas Lieutenant Governor Bob Bullock announced he was going to retire.

First stop: Haskell County Courthouse in Haskell, Texas, Rick Perry's hometown, a tiny dry city with a population of 4000 people, but a very pretty and friendly city nonetheless. The first step was the usual checking out of property records, possible lawsuits, liens, or anything else I could find in the county courthouse regarding Perry. While checking records in most county courthouses, when dealing with the clerks who help you find the material you're looking for, it's generally easy to remain anonymous. That's because much of the information is on computer databases, and when you do have to deal personally with a courthouse clerk, those folks are generally apolitical and have worked in the courthouse all their lives. However, the Haskell County Courthouse was one of those courthouses where it was impossible for me to remain anonymous. It's just too small a county, and at that time there was only one employee in the entire courthouse—and if it's just one guy in the whole place, he has to be politically connected.

As soon as I began poring through the county's real estate records to look at Rick Perry's property tax payments, the clerk demanded that I stand right across the counter from where he was standing, so he could see whose records I was looking at. Didn't bother me—until I saw Rick Perry's multiple late property tax payments. There were lots of them.

This could hurt Perry politically, since the vast majority of voters pay their property taxes on time and would have been mighty pissed to see this multi-millionaire with a repeated pattern of late tax payments.

And there was something even worse, and possibly very damaging should it become public. While Perry was still the Texas state Agriculture Secretary, he and his father were sued over a relatively small matter involving two elderly sisters, whose property next to the Perry farm had been trashed due to the negligence of the Perry family farm. But that wasn't the main problem—after the lawsuit was filed against the Perrys, complete with photographs proving their case, all the Perrys had to do to rectify the problem was to clean up the mess they made, and amicably settle the case out of court. Instead, for reasons unbeknownst to me, the Perrys decided to fight the charges. How could Perry let this case go to trial where all the details would become public record if he was planning to run for higher public office?

In the end the Perrys lost the case and had to make amends to the two elderly ladies. The combination of the late property taxes, and what looked to be a millionaire father-and-son tag team trying to screw over two old ladies of modest means, could be very damaging indeed.

I asked the clerk behind the desk for copies of all the documents I found that were so damaging to Perry. Now, when I suspect a clerk may be suspicious of what I'm looking for, it's usually pretty easy to throw him off by requesting copies of multiple documents, most of them junk, with the relevant documents thrown in and hopefully unnoticed. But not in Haskell. Maybe once every three years or so someone comes in asking to look at property tax records of the county's most prominent public official. And a guy with a Brooklyn accent? Maybe once every fifty years. Plus, the guy behind the counter had been keeping track of what I was looking at the entire time. He knew what I was doing.

As soon as he saw Rick Perry's name on the property tax records I had requested him to copy, any pretense of politeness disappeared. A scowl crossed his face as he leaned over the counter and feebly tried to intimidate me. "What is your name, sir?" he asked, which he had every legal right to ask. He knew he couldn't deny me the copies of the damaging records regarding Perry, and he wasn't so stupid as to deny me public records. But he was within his rights to ask me my name and to subsequently try to figure out who I was and what I'm doing there. He did all he could do—which was nothing—and walked away to make the copies I requested.

He was gone for about twenty minutes, far longer than it would take to make the copies. When he came back, he started sucking up to me so hard it was embarrassing. "Mr. Marks, here are your copies. Is there anything else I can do for you? Mr. Marks, are you sure you don't need anything else from me?" It was so hard not to start cracking up. He had obviously called either Rick Perry or someone close to him, asking if they knew who I was. And once he found out I was working for a client on behalf of the Perry campaign, not opposing Rick Perry, he was suddenly my best friend.

Then it was time to research Perry's opponent, John Sharp. It took just the first day of my research in the Victoria County Courthouse to realize that Rick Perry had nothing to worry about regarding his late taxes. Sharp had late taxes as well; even worse, some were delinquent. What's great about the record books in Victoria County is that they list, for each property, when the taxes were paid and whether or not they were late; if they were past thirty days late the property is stamped "DELINQUENT"—the perfect visual for a TV ad or direct-mail piece.

I found one more major "hit" against Sharp buried in an 800-page report he had issued during his time as state comp-troller entitled "Disturbing the Peace." The report was half monstrosity and bureaucratic mumbo-jumbo, and half mighty impressive document on how to streamline government. Some of the proposals were actually passed into law. But one thing stuck out in the report like a sore thumb: Despite his being for the most part a moderate Democrat, when it came to the report's views on crime, Sharp still appeared to be in the 1960s "sympathy-for-the-criminals" mindset that's so badly out of touch with Texas. The report's section on crime was chock full of "alternatives to prison," which would easily sink Sharp in a state with so many annual executions.

Now I'd found two major hits to be used against Sharp— the multiple delinquent property taxes, and a soft-on-crime record of proposals that have always been damaging and some-times even lethal in political races. After finishing my research against Sharp, the Perry campaign alerted me to a possible rumor they might want checked out.

In the end I had found great research on both candidates, but none of it was ever used by either campaign. This happens in political races from time to time, where neither side goes negative because the race is so close. The possibility of a backlash against the first one to go negative is just way too risky in a close race. There's also the possibility of MAD to deal with: mutually assured destruction. In these cases, once one attack is made, both sides pull out all their ammo and it becomes a bloodbath.

In Perry's case it was better to forego attacks, let the race end quietly, and hope that George W. Bush's coattails at the top of the ticket were long enough to pull him in—which is exactly what happened, and Perry rode W.'s coattails to a narrow victory, 52 percent to 48 percent.

My fondest memories of that Perry/Sharp race were how in Texas, despite being an outsider, I was nonetheless welcomed by the folks in the Perry campaign. During one staff meeting in Austin with all of Rick Perry's political staff in attendance, we were all sitting around a long legal table, going through some campaign talk, when into the room walked Rick Perry himself. It was the first time I ever saw him personally, and the last, except very briefly at a small party after he was inaugurated as lieutenant governor along with then Governor George W. Bush.

When the candidate just saunters into a campaign meeting in progress totally unannounced, and casually sits down without saying a word or looking at anyone—everyone in the room feels awkward but continues as if the candidate wasn't there, trying to act casual. At some point I said something, and Perry broke his silence and asked me "You're not from the South, are you?" I replied, "Yeah, South Brooklyn." It broke the ice and finally everyone had a good laugh.

Ultimately Rick Perry turned out to be a standup guy and has also turned out to be one of America's finest governors, having been easily re-elected twice since that 1998 race.

$\star$ $\star$ $\star$

In 1998, Oppo Man was picking up women left and right all over the great state of Texas, and particularly in Austin. And I usually did a pretty good job of keeping my work secretive. One young women I met in Austin, who I will refer to here as Samantha, seemed very nice, sweet, and, well, not crazy—until I went back to Washington. Unlike so many of the other women Oppo Man met across America, Samantha had no illusions (or so I thought) and understood from the get-go that I did not live in Texas and would eventually have to go back home to DC. I had made it clear to her that it would be very difficult for us to evolve into a serious relationship, although I really did like her. I never flat-out told her there was no chance of a long term relationship, which was a mistake—in her mind, I was somehow leading her on.

Before she went crazy on me, there was an incident that should have set off alarm bells about Samantha. One night, long after I had left Texas, she showed up unannounced around midnight at my DC apartment at the Watergate. I was shocked, but Samantha was acting sweet, so I was actually glad to see her. However, that changed quickly. Samantha somehow was able to obtain my cell phone records, which of course is completely illegal, and something even Oppo Man has never done. She called every single number on the bill (for the month right after the political campaign season). She was looking for other women, and any time a woman answered the phone, Samantha told her that Oppo Man was an ax murderer, pedophile, and too many other outrageous accusations to recount here. One woman in Tennessee, my friend Mendy

Caldwell who works for me (and is currently helping with this book), had to get police protection because Samantha showed up in Nashville, called her out of the blue, and asked to meet for lunch as if they were old friends. They had never met, except over the phone, when Samantha was telling her I was a psychopath.

I laughed off Samantha's calls to the other women, even when I was forced to file an FBI report against her to scare her into stopping the harassment. However, it was no joke when she saw a 512 (Austin) area code that I had called repeatedly during the billing cycle. Thinking it was another woman in Austin, Samantha instead was shocked when the Rick Perry campaign answered the phone. This of course made sense, since I had called the campaign almost daily during that final month of the campaign. The Perry campaign folks, up until that point, loved me and treated me like royalty during my visits to Austin. They appreciated the fact that I had been able to do so much good work under the radar. So it must have been quite a shock when the Perry campaign received a call from an obvious nut job, spewing awful, venomous lies about me. I have no idea to this day how many times she actually called the campaign. The entire episode must have baffled the Perry campaign, and I was too embarrassed to even talk to them about it after the incident.

Although I was not responsible for this woman illegally obtaining my telephone records, I was nonetheless still responsible for choosing what woman or women to spend my time with . . . and this was an obvious miscalculation. When you're an Oppo Man, you can't afford these kinds of transgressions—I was lucky that there were no long-term effects from Samantha's rampage.

★ ★ ★

That 1998 election cycle in Texas also found Oppo Man working for clients who hired me to dig up dirt on the Democratic nominees in three other statewide campaigns. These were the Democratic opponents of Republican attorney general candidate John Cornyn (now a U.S. Senator); Republican land commissioner candidate David Dewhurst (who won and is currently Texas' lieutenant governor); and Republican State Comptroller Carole Rylander (who won, and later became Carole Strayhorn while going on to lose a bizarre third-party-bid suicide challenge against Governor Rick Perry in 2006).

The Republicans won all those statewide races (as well as George W. Bush's easy re-election as governor, a race I did not work on). The sweep was historic; the first time that Republicans had total control of all statewide offices since Reconstruction. And this vision of a Republican Texas was single-handedly pulled off by Karl Rove, who went on to help President Bush get elected and re-elected, and later left the Bush administration in August 2007.

And while the Perry-Sharp campaign ended quietly, that isn't often the case in Texas. Texas politics is very similar to the New York politics I grew up in, for a unique reason—lots of "characters." That was the case in the race for state attorney general, which featured one of Texas's true characters, former Texas Attorney General and Democrat Jim Mattox running against Republican Supreme Court Judge and virtual unknown-at-the-time, John Cornyn. It was a race featuring some wild opposition research by Oppo Man.

Because of his huge advantage in name recognition over Cornyn, Mattox began the general election campaign with a big lead. That soon changed.

First, the basic research on Mattox refreshed the voters' memories as to why he lost his bid to be elected governor in 1990, being defeated by Anne Richards. Mattox wasn't the world's nicest guy. During that 1990 gubernatorial primary, he accused Richards of having been a cocaine user and alcoholic. Further hurting Mattox badly with women voters, the basic research reminded the electorate that Mattox had once referred to Senator Kay Bailey Hutchison as "a witch." But the *coup de grace* was not old rehashed research, but some very funny new material found by Oppo Man.

Checking through courthouse records in the Dallas area Mattox hailed from, the first strange thing I noticed was that Mattox, an attorney, had not been doing much, if any, legal work since leaving the state attorney general's office in 1991. Instead he was immersed in other businesses, mostly involving real estate. And his associates in these dealing were suspect, to say the least.

As the campaign drew into its final weeks, and Cornyn began closing in on Mattox, the Cornyn campaign used the research I dug up to run one of the most brilliant television ads I've ever seen. Several of Mattox' former business partners and associates were in prison for various criminal activities, so the ad showed these former business colleagues' mug shots. The ad invoked the Garth Brooks classic, referring to the men in the mug shots as Mattox's "friends in low places."

On Election Night, the results came in—Cornyn 55 percent; Mattox 44 percent.

I must also add here that while in Texas, except for my fluke encounter with Rick Perry during the staff meeting, John Cornyn was the only one of the Republican statewide candidates who made a point of meeting me during the campaign and thanking me for my work. This is unusual since most candidates in all races keep the oppo men and women at arm's length personally, with at least one or two layers of buffer or campaign hacks in between. But not John Cornyn. A perfect Southern gentleman, Cornyn has since been elected to the U.S. Senate in the wake of Phill Gramm's retirement, and has a fine future ahead of him.

Chapter Sixteen

SEX, LIES, AND REPUBLICAN HYPOCRISY: THE DOWNFALL OF THE GOP, 1994–2006

I
f you watch any of the popular shows on Fox News, you'll see former Speaker of the House Newt Gingrich fairly regularly opining on the news of the day. He comes across as highly intelligent (which he is) and level-headed (I'm not so sure about that one). In his current quasi-retirement, Newt has become a Republican elder statesman of sorts. He articulates Republican thinking better and more clearly than anyone I've seen since Ronald Reagan.

However, Newt is certainly far more complex than the glib, smiling, likeable fellow you see these days on Fox News. During my career as Oppo Man, I personally saw the rise and fall of the Republican Party up close, from its historic takeover of Congress in 1994 to its historic loss of Congress in 2006. If you need to understand and see clearly everything that was great about the Republican Party during that historic period, and everything that makes a good number of Americans want to vomit about the GOP at the same time, you need look no further than one man—ex-Speaker Gingrich.

Gingrich is personally and politically the perfect microcosm of the complex—good, bad, and ugly—of everything the Republican Party has been in this generation. His brains and visionary thinking brought the Republicans to power in 1994. However, at the same time, the combination of his bizarre personality and the flaws and hypocrisy in his personal life are also a microcosm of everything that ultimately brought down the Republican Party. Although the Republican Party's total collapse didn't occur until 2006 because of Iraq, by the time of Gingrich's humiliating resignation in November 1998, the die was cast. The GOP was being brought down by the weight of their own hypocrisy and ineptitude.

I first met Newt Gingrich twelve years before my rebirth as Oppo Man, when I ran for Congress in 1982. All Republican congressional candidates nationwide are invited by the National Republican Congressional Committee to Washington each election cycle for a one-day crash course in campaigning. So in the summer of 1982, I went there not knowing that, twelve years later, I would be there again, this time working for the same NRCC as Oppo Man.

All the congressional candidates (myself included) initially were led into an auditorium to listen to different speakers. Then we were split up into smaller groups based on geographic location and went to question-and-answer sessions with various Republican politicos. My group was fortunate enough to get to meet the young congressman from Georgia who had only served two terms in Congress but was already making a name for himself: Newt Gingrich.

The former school teacher had gained some notoriety by winning his bid for Congress on his third try in a southern congressional district that had not voted Republican in more than one hundred years. That was an incredible feat, especially considering he was elected two years *before* Ronald Reagan changed the political landscape and made it respectable for American southerners to vote Republican.

Fast-forward twelve years to December 1994. I was again in the nation's capital in the same exact building, listening to Newt Gingrich addressing all of us at the National Republican Congressional Committee, thanking us for our efforts in helping attain his dream of a Republican takeover of Congress that had become reality a month earlier. Except for the fact that he was now much greyer and heavier than he was back in 1982, he was the same Newt Gingrich: soft-spoken, articulate, and smart.

Standing next to him was Bob Michael of Illinois, the outgoing House Minority Leader who had decided earlier that year not to run for re-election, instead choosing to retire. Had Michael not made that fateful decision to retire, he would have become the Speaker, not Newt. Looking at Michael, I had to wonder what he was really feeling behind the smile on his face. Michael retired believing the Republicans had no chance to re-capture the House in his lifetime. Gingrich, on the other hand, was a true visionary who not only believed it could be done, but had a workable plan to make it happen. And he did it. He deserved to be Speaker.

Those were heady days for Republicans. I was a true believer. I believed that Newt would lead us to the Promised Land; that the Republican takeover of Congress would lead to honest men and women running Congress, instead of the "good-ol'-boy," corrupt Democratic machine that we had defeated. To me, it was crystal clear and black and white. We Republicans were the *good guys*, the Democrats were the villains. This Republican Congress would restore honesty and integrity to government. We *really* were different.

Yeah, right.

I failed miserably to see the initial warning signs that the Republicans, while maybe having a better political vision, were going to be no different than the Democrats when it came to abusing the trappings of power. The biggest warning signs came during that historic 104th Congress in 1995 and 1996, signs I ignored at the time that were heralding the GOP's undoing. Signs of hypocrisy far more flagrant and moral corruption far greater than anything the Democrats had reached while controlling Congress. Signs of a monumental disconnect between the Republican Party's so-called "family values" and how those Republican members of Congress actually behaved in their own personal lives. If you're going to talk the talk, you'd better walk the walk. If not, you will eventually go down.

The downfall of the Republican Party, which came from within, not from without, would also demonstrate, in no uncertain terms, that negativity drives American politics. This downfall, which finally made Oppo Man see the light about what was really going on within the Republican Party, came in four stages, all separate but interconnected. Each stage by itself is interesting, but only by understanding the context of the four stages together can we truly connect the dots.

Stage #1: Shortly after the historic 1994 takeover of Congress, cracks quickly appear in the "family values" charade as many newly elected "family values" Republican members of Congress see their marriages fall apart in 1995 due to their own philandering,

Stage #2: During the 1996 presidential campaign, the Republican presidential and vice presidential nominees are unable to effectively attack a very attackable and vulnerable President Clinton due to their own sordid histories of marital infidelity.

Stage #3: In 1998, in the wake of President Clinton's impeachment, the most prominent Republican of this generation and standard-bearer of the Republican Party since the 1994 congressional takeover, Speaker Newt Gingrich, is forced to resign from Congress amid his own flagrant marital infidelities. His replacement as speaker, Bob Livingston of Lousiana, lasts only three weeks on the job and is also forced to resign from Congress, again due to multiple marital infidelities.

Stage #4: After President Clinton is impeached, he survives removal in the Senate. He survives in large part by successfully warning the Republican senators who would decide his fate with the implicit threat to expose those Republican senators' own sexual and other ethical lapses if he is removed from office.

History has thus far recorded each of these stages in a vacuum. Although I have never seen anyone besides myself propose this, I believe these four stages worked together to bring about the downfall that concluded in 2006. Having worked for both the National Republican Congressional Committee and the National Republican Senatorial Committee during this critical time in American history gives me special insight.

First I will connect the dots, then I will explain each stage in morbid detail. Taken together, these stages reveal the ugly truth that was in large part responsible for my own political metamorphosis, one that began with the stranger-than-fiction tale of Congressman Jon Christensen.

* * *

Stage 1: Republican Philandering
The first sign of the level of hypocrisy and deceit within the Republican Party was one I should have seen coming, but ignored due to my blind allegiance to the party.

Republican congressman Jon Christensen and his wife, Meredith, were the golden couple of the freshmen class of 1994. Jon was tall, handsome, likeable, and an articulate, conservative Christian who appeared believable. Meredith was the prototypical political wife from Texas (although she had moved to Nebraska to marry Jon); blonde, friendly, and gorgeous.

I first met Meredith Christensen during the two-month period between the November 1994 election and the January 1995 swearing in of the new Congress. During that period, newly elected members of Congress were going through their "orientation" and spending a great deal of time at the NRCC, where I worked. Meredith was put in charge of organizing events for the wives of newly elected Republican members of the House. With her personality and looks, she was perfect for the job.

Some of the other guys in the office found her to be slightly flirtatious, but I didn't think so. Those guys hadn't spent too much time in the South (as I had) and didn't realize that is just the way most Southern women are by nature. At least that's what I thought until just a few months later, when I heard about an odd incident in the anteroom off the House floor.

According to press reports and one congressman, the six-foot-tall-plus Jon Christensen and another Republican, big, burly J. D. Hayworth of Arizona mixed it up with another Arizona congressman, the diminutive John Shadegg. Given the physical size of the three men, it certainly didn't appear to be a fair contest. The two big men heard that Shadegg had been fooling around with Meredith Christensen and threatened the also-married Shadegg to stay away from her or else they'd "gerrymander the districts of his face." (Pretty strong trash talk for a couple of "Conservative Christian" congressmen.)

Though all parties involved later denied everything, I immediately began hearing talk up on the Hill that Ms. Christensen was also fooling around with other Republican congressmen as well. Soon enough news stories began to pop up about Meredith Christensen. *New York Daily News* reports linked her to "a half-dozen different representatives, including one from New York." In November 1995 the couple announced their intention to divorce, with Meredith taking the blame, admitting that she had been unfaithful to her husband.

Jon Christensen later went on to run for governor of Nebraska in 1998, and believe it or not, his ex-wife Meredith had the gall to run for the congressional seat he was vacating. Both Christensens lost, with Jon coming in third in the GOP primary with just 28 percent of the vote, having been defeated by Mike Johanns, who went on to become governor and was appointed U.S. secretary of agriculture in 2005. Meredith's campaign was completely baffling. Only two months into her run, on November 18, 1997, she suddenly dropped out of the race. Her exit was as unexpected as her entrance into the race.

While the Christensen incident in 1995 was peculiar, it appeared to be an isolated incident at the time. But it wasn't. Several other high-profile "family values" type Republicans from that "Class of '94" were headed for divorce, including Senator Rod Grams of Minnesota, Jim Bunn of Oregon, Enid Waldholtz of Utah, Jim Nussle of Iowa, Rick White of Washington State, and Steve LaTourette of Ohio. In addition, James Longley of Maine and his wife separated. Former Democratic Congresswoman Pat Schroeder told the *Los Angeles Times* that some wags had dubbed the trend "Fornigate."

First, let's take a look at Congressman Bunn of Oregon. Bunn won his seat in 1994 against a liberal Democratic divorcee. He pulled ahead in a close race largely by portraying himself as a "deeply rooted family man" and stressing his conservative values. He was also elected in large part because of his support from the Christian Coalition.

After winning his congressional seat, Bunn immediately ditched his wife (and mother of his five children), and married a staffer (as did Republican "family values" Senator Tim Hutchinson of Arkansas, whose exploits are covered in detail in the following chapter). Bunn further had the gall to put his new wife on the state payroll for the unheard-of salary of $97,500.

Bunn was then mulling a Senate race in his home state of Oregon when his divorce complicated his political plans, causing him to opt out of a run for the senate or re-election to his House seat. Bunn blamed his divorce on having to work too hard as a congressman. Get a load of this crock from Bunn: "With all due respect to the leaders, there is nothing family-friendly about this Congress except the legislation," he said, blaming the long hours of work being responsible for the breakup of his family.

Now let's look at another "family values" type of guy, Congressman Rick White of Washington. Also elected in 1994, White was a strong critic of President Clinton in 1998 during the Monica Lewinski fiasco. It just so happened that White and his wife of fifteen years separated in 1997, and White sued his wife for divorce in 1998. Their divorce became messy when the couple couldn't agree on "spousal mainte-nance" for Vicki, who was unemployed and the primary care-giver to the couple's four children, while the congressman was earning a salary of $136,700. White paid the price that November, losing his congressional seat to Jay Inslee.

The next casualty of "family values" was Jim Nussle of Iowa, who had been a Republican member of the House since 1991. Nussle and his first wife, Leslie Jeanne, divorced in 1996 as he retired from Congress to run for governor, a race he lost. Then came James Longley of Maine. It only took a few months after gaining his congressional seat in 1994 for Longley and his wife Ann to separate. The congressman later contested his wife's divorce filing. Longley lasted only one term, being defeated in 1996 by Portland Mayor Tom Allen.

The situation with the "family values" Republicans had gotten so bad that the Republican Bible study group began praying for "protection against rumors" and support for members whose reputations had been sullied—as if it was all really rumors and they were all really innocent! The audacity!

The best dose of wisdom on this subject came from the wife of another "family values" Republican fraud. LaTourette's wife Susan complained that he had called to inform her by phone that he was involved with a lobbyist and wanted a divorce. Susan LaTourette hit the nail right on the head when she explained what happens to many so-called "family values" Republicans: "Washington corrupts people," she said. "He was a wonderful husband and father, the best I ever saw, until he went there. I told him I was trying to get him out of the dark side, all that power and greed and people kissing up to them all the time. Now he's one of them."

Here's what Mrs. LaTourette was talking about: These guys were one day just some schnook for the hinterlands, then they somehow got elected to Congress by the sheer flukery of Bill Clinton's stunning unpopularity in 1994. The next thing they knew they're hob-knobbing with the rich and the famous; presidents, congressional leaders, media bigwigs, high-powered lobbyists, etc. They're suddenly rock stars with women all over them, no different than the groupies of the real rock stars and professional athletes. These guys go in innocently with lots if idealism, and once they see the trappings of power (which includes more female action in one day than they've seen in their lifetime) they go crazy.

Unfortunately—or fortunately, depending on how you look at it—I went through a similar transition. Once in DC and on the road as Oppo Man, it was the same for me. A fantasyland with women everywhere, where you become so detached from reality that by time you wake up from the dream it's usually too late. While all this Republican family values hypocrisy was taking place, like Nero, I just kept playing the fiddle. I still never saw a pattern emerging here. I thought the above-mentioned cases were all aberrations.

* * *

Stage #2: The 1996 Presidential Election

The next stage of the Republican downfall came during the 1996 presidential race. As Bob Dole was going down to a crushing defeat, I couldn't understand why he never attacked Clinton regarding the multiple scandals that tainted the president at that time and made him politically vulnerable facing re-election. Then I heard about Bob Dole and *his* reported philandering.

In the September 1996 issue of *Vanity Fair*, Gail Sheehy reported:

Phyllis Holden was the first wife who tried to save Bob Dole. In the last year of their twenty-three-year marriage, Senator Dole had dinner with his wife and child only twice—on Christmas and Easter. One day in December 1970 he walked upstairs and announced simply, "I want out." . . . . *A former stewardess, Phyllis Wells, was employed by Senator Dole's office from August 1971 to April 1972 according to the Senate employee-locator service, as a press assistant. Her salary was about $500 a month. "She was his girlfriend before he hired her," asserts David Owen. "She was just absolutely gorgeous, and much younger. There's no question that he was seeing her prior to being divorced.*

Then there was Dole's running-mate, the also-married Jack
Kemp. The former conservative congressman had developed
quite a reputation as a womanizer. Even Pat Robertson and
Newsweek openly commented on it.

Between Dole's and Kemp's backgrounds and reputations
when it came to women, it was impossible for *either of the two*
to attack Clinton forcefully, as that would lead to a certain
counterattack in a classic MAD scenario.

As for Kemp, in most presidential campaigns, the vice
presidential candidate of the challenging party is usually the
"pit bull" while the presidential nominee tries to appear above
the fray. As 1996 rolled around, Dole, in a surprise move,
picked Kemp (who hadn't even supported Dole in the
Republican primaries, instead supporting Steve Forbes).
Everyone in the press assumed Kemp would be the appointed
attack dog against Clinton. After all, Kemp was a terrific and
aggressive speaker. But, as it turned out, nary a word of attack
was heard from the former football star. Not only did he never
attack Clinton, Kemp was turned into chopped liver in the
vice presidential debate by that great debater, Al Gore.

The Dole/Kemp situation made me, for the first time, think
about what was really going on in Washington. Was the entire
Republican "family values" issue a charade? Was it Jimmy
Swaggert and Jim Baker from the PTL Club all over again?

At this point in 1996, I thought it couldn't get any worse.
Wrong.

★ ★ ★

Stage #3: The Fall of Gingrich

The year of Monica, 1998, was the year Bill Clinton's presidency would go down in impeachment and scandal. But the Republican "family values" charade would go down, too, this time for good. When Clinton was impeached, he made sure he took most of the Republican Party down with him.

Like most true believers, I was one of the last to figure it out. And so it was fitting that it all came full circle in 1998 back to the same man—Newt Gingrich.

Gingrich was still the face of the Republican Party from 1995 through the end of 1998. But well before his sex life would destroy his political career in 1998, crack after crack began to show in Gingrich's armor.

- First came Gingrich's off-the-wall remark in late 1994 that President Clinton had become "irrelevant" implying that he, Newt Gingrich, was more powerful than the president.
- Shortly after came Gingrich's failure to drum up support for his almost-candidacy for the presidency in 1996.
- Next came the government shutdown resulting from the budget being stalled in Congress, when Gingrich's leadership in the House was openly defied for the first time by his fellow Republican troops. During this government shutdown, for the first time, Bill Clinton took a lead over Bob Dole in the polls. Dole was considered at that time the frontrunner for the GOP.
- Then came the "Keystone Cops" hour, as the Republican leadership of the House conspired to overthrow Gingrich as speaker, failing only when one of the key conspirators

(who bore a strong resemblance to Fred Flintstone) switched sides once he realized his co-conspirators were not going to name him to replace Gingrich.

Thus, as Ken Starr's investigation and Clinton's impeachment were unfolding throughout 1998, Gingrich's star was falling fast. And I noticed another very strange thing. Newt Gingrich, despite all his problems, was still the nation's most vocal and powerful Republican. But he was strangely *very quiet* regarding the entire Clinton scandal. In fact, so were most Republicans. Except for Congressman Bob Barr of Georgia, the Republicans didn't seem to be saying much.

This was the exact opposite of 1974, when every Democrat in America was kicking Nixon while he was down. In fact there were more Republicans back in 1974 attacking Nixon than there were Republicans attacking Clinton in 1998. Something strange was going on indeed.

Come Election Day 1998, things became even stranger: Unlike 1974, when Nixon's impeachment caused the Republicans to lose forty-nine House seats and three Senate seats, what happened in 1998 was exactly the opposite. The Democrats, despite Bill Clinton's impending impeachment, actually *gained* five seats in the House (six, if you include left-leaning Independent Bernie Sanders of Vermont) and failed to lose any in the Senate (with the fifty-five to forty-five spread not changing)! What made this even more unusual is the fact that, even without the Clinton scandal, the party in power inexplicably gained seats in the off-year election, the exact *opposite* of what usually happens, even with a popular president in office.

What was going on?

We soon found out. The day after the election, all hell broke loose. It was a chain of events that would result in the impeachment of President Bill Clinton while at the same time bring down the leadership of the Republican Party. (The complete collapse of the GOP as the majority in Congress would have to wait until 2006.)

Immediately after the 1998 election, on November 6, 1998, Newt Gingrich announced his retirement—not only as speaker, but from his congressional seat as well, effective immediately. This despite the fact that he had just been re-elected by a whopping 71 to 29 percent margin over his Democratic challenger days before.

The press and most of the beltway immediately chalked up Gingrich's resignation to the poor showing by Republicans during the mid-term election held the day before. But it wasn't long after Gingrich announced his resignation word began to spread across Washington that there was a different reason for Gingrich's resignation; Gingrich's wife Marianne was about to sue him for divorce. She was about to expose him for a fraud, while taking him to the cleaners at the same time.

It turned out that there was apparently a good reason why Gingrich was so quiet about impeachment and had little to say regarding Clinton during the Monica scandal. At that same exact time, while Newt's wife was living in Atlanta, Newt had been having an affair with Celesta Bisek, a former congressional aide who at thirty-three was twenty-three years younger than Gingrich. (Bisek is now Newt's third wife.)

I was in disbelief. My hero? The man who really made me believe that we Republicans were better than the Democrats—

not just better at running the county, but better human beings? We would bring honesty back to a county that had become jaded by Bill Clinton.

What a crock. We were no different than them.

I had already known (as had most people in DC) about Gingrich's Jerry Springer-type divorce from his first wife, Jackie (his former high school geometry teacher and seven years his senior), and the mother of his two children, while she was in the hospital recovering from uterine cancer surgery. The couple reportedly haggled over the divorce terms while Jackie was still in the hospital, and Newt also reportedly had to be pursued for adequate child support payments. They had been married for nineteen years. Gingrich at that time had lamely defended his actions during the divorce by saying, "Even if I had been sensitive, it would've been a mess."

I had also known about his winning his congressional seat in 1978 on the slogan "Let Our Family Represent Your Family," while he was reportedly cheating on Jackie at the same time. In 1995, an alleged mistress from that period, Anne Manning, told *Vanity Fair*'s Gail Sheehy: "We had oral sex. He prefers that modus operandi because then he can say, 'I never slept with her.'" (Newt apparently was way ahead of his time. It wasn't until years later that Bill Clinton would use the same warped "I never had sex with that woman" logic regarding Monica Lewinski.) But it was also reported in *Vanity Fair* that Gingrich would have won his 1974 failed congressional run "if we could have kept him out of the office, screwing her [volunteer Dot Crews] on the desk."

None of that stuff had previously bothered me; it was ancient history. But now it was November 1998 and it seemed like déjà vu all over again. Gingrich's new marital fiasco was no longer ancient history.

Maybe I'm naïve, but I was shocked that Gingrich would do something so flagrantly wrong on the "family values" front that it would most likely end his political career. When he became speaker, one of the first things Gingrich did was to pledge that he would make Congress a more "family friendly" place to work. "We're going to turn values into policy and not just leave them empty rhetoric," Gingrich told a new Republican majority elected on family-friendly themes. A special room in the capital was set aside where members and their families could spend time together, and a committee chaired by his second wife, Marianne, was established to shepherd further reforms. And she was about to take Newt to the cleaners! *What the hell was going on?*

Could he really be that arrogant and stupid? I couldn't believe it. His actions now appeared to be almost as dumb as those of Gary Hart, the Democratic frontrunner for president in 1988 who told reporters "Follow me" while denying he had a mistress, while then proceeding to lead the reporters who "followed him" to the airport, where he met his paramour. All Hart had to do was have his girlfriend (whom no one in Washington would recognize at the time) take a cab to his brownstone in DC. Instead, he chose to go to the airport himself, where as a U.S. senator running for president, he would be certain to be recognized picking up his new action. Everyone asked at the time, "Did he *want* to be caught?"

The answer is the same as it was with Gingrich, and for Bill Clinton as well: No, he didn't *expect* to be caught. All these men had gotten away with so much for so long they were in a fantasy world of pure arrogance where they actually believed they would never get caught. Unbelievable.

For the first time since becoming Oppo Man, I felt completely disillusioned. I had felt partially disillusioned after the 1996 elections after the thumping Bob Dole took from Clinton. But this was worse.

Ultimately, Gingrich learned nothing from what was happening to Bill Clinton in 1998. When asked during the Paula Jones deposition if he ever knew Monica Lewinski, all Clinton had to do was say, "It's none of your business." The judge would have never had the stones to hold him in contempt, and the Republicans (considering all the sexual skeletons in their closets) wouldn't have had the stones to do anything about it. The public would have supported Clinton, and it would have been a three-day news story. Instead it became a national scandal resulting in impeachment because Clinton chose to lie in a federal courthouse under oath.

Likewise, Gingrich could have avoided the same fate by simply leading his successful "Republican Revolution" on generic issues popular to the voters just like Ronald Reagan did in 1980, without the nonsensical "family values." Of course, individual Republican candidate could have made "family values" part of their platforms, but it had no place in the national debate.

All Gingrich and the Republicans had to do was be intellectually honest. But that was apparently not an option. They just couldn't help themselves. They just *had* to be just like the Democrats. It must be something encoded in their DNA, Democrat and Republican alike.

Gingrich's second divorce was right out of "The Twilight Zone." First, Newt called Marianne to declare that he wanted a divorce while she was attending a birthday party for her mother. Instead of being on the defensive, since it was he who was unfaithful and broke up the marriage, Newt instead played hardball with Marianne in court, despite admitting to a six-year extramarital affair with congressional aide Bisek.

Marianne's lawyers played hardball, and no one could figure out why Newt wouldn't settle instead of putting himself through this kind of humiliation. Finally, after more legal haggling, Gingrich finally worked out a divorce agreement with his second wife of eighteen years.

Gingrich went down, and with him the house of cards, beginning with the man chosen to succeed Gingrich as the new speaker, Bob Livingston of Louisiana. I believe that, just like Bill Clinton, Livingston was living in a fantasy world where he honestly believed (despite the sexually charged environment in DC) that none of his past indiscretions would ever become known. But he learned the hard way. Just six weeks after being named speaker, Livingston was forced into early retirement when he was about to be outed by none other than that paragon of virtue, Larry Flynt.

Flynt was obviously doing the Democrat's bidding, but he did have a point; the Republican hypocrisy he was exposing was legitimate. Flynt was able to prove that Livingston was not only an adulterer, but that he had had more than one affair. Even worse, Flynt suggested that those affairs involved lobbyists for whom Livingston favorably influenced legislation. Like Gingrich, Livingston not only stepped down as speaker, but resigned his congressional seat entirely.

With Livingston's outing, things spun ever more out of control. Events were forcing me—in no uncertain terms—to acknowledge what most of the American public had probably already known: When it came to family values, sex, and integrity, the Republicans were bigger hypocrites than Bill Clinton and the Democrats..

The Republicans now had to find a congressman without sexual baggage, or any other controversy for that matter. Dick Armey? Nope. Tom DeLay? Nope. But DeLay was able to do the next best thing to becoming speaker; he put in his right-hand man, the gym teacher from Illinois with no sexual baggage, Dennis Hastert.

There was one very interesting moment for me during that period, when the Republicans were looking for a replacement for Livingston. Congressman Dave Dreir of California was aggressively bucking for the job, making the rounds on all the TV talk shows. When one enterprising female reporter repeatedly asked Dreir if he had any "women" issues that could be a problem for him, the handsome congressman repeatedly dodged the question. Nothing was ever revealed that would support that he had any issues with women, but at that moment, it was obvious to me Dreier was not going to get the job.

* * *

Stage #4: The Clinton Impeachment

Things were getting hairy. People (myself included) began wondering if the Republicans in the House would have the guts to proceed with impeachment or would be paralyzed by their own collective sexual histories. It was hard to tell which way the Republicans go. Judiciary Committee Chairman Henry Hyde had made conflicting statements during 1998 as to whether or not he planned on going ahead with impeachment.

Then Salon.com outed the seventy-four-year-old Hyde regarding a five-year extramarital affair he had conducted in the 1960s. Hyde comically responded that the affair was a "youthful indiscretion" (he was in his forties while involved with Chicago hairstylist Cherie Snodgrass). If Salon.com thought the story would intimidate Hyde into dropping impeachment plans, they picked the wrong guy. Hitting him just weeks before the impeachment hearings were to begin was a mistake, and it boomeranged. Now that his affair was public, Hyde had nothing to lose by going forward with impeachment (plus, he was pissed).

There was another thing Salon.com obviously didn't know: Hyde was personally beloved by his colleagues in the Congress, including his Democratic Judiciary Committee partners that would hold the impeachment hearings with him. As soon as the hearings began, Democrats John Conyers of Michigan (the ranking Democrat on the committee) and Chuck Schumer (now a senator) from New York both went out of their way to praise Hyde and attack Salon.com. Hyde came through unscathed and looking like the victim. Especially considering he was a widower and the woman who Hyde cheated on was long deceased, Hyde in the end came out as a sympathetic figure and the impeachment proceeded. And the impeachment of Bill Clinton succeeded successfully, almost single handedly due to the testosterone of Henry Hyde and the "Hammer" of Tom DeLay.

True, outing Hyde didn't work as far as the House impeachment was concerned, but it nonetheless *did work* when you look at the big picture. It sent a strong warning shot across the bow of the Republican senators who would ultimately decide Clinton's fate should the House indeed vote to impeach. If *any* of them had any skeletons in their closet, sexual or otherwise, they had to think twice after the Hyde outing following the Livingston outing. Everyone was fair game, even Democrats. (Yes, I can assure you, many Democrats as well as Republicans were shaking in their boots.)

The gloves were off. Clinton would be protected by any means possible. It didn't matter if it was Larry Flynt, Salon.com, or the Clinton White House, the message was clear: Adulterers beware; vote against Clinton at your own peril!

Just in case the senators didn't get the message as they were about to decide Clinton's fate, Larry Flynt released a one-time, eighty-two-page publication called *The Flynt Report*. Both Flynt and the White House denied there was any corroboration between the two, but rumors persisted that James Carville, at the time a free agent no longer with the White House, was working in cahoots with Flynt on behalf of Clinton.

The Flynt Report added more fuel to the fire of Republican hypocrisy, and almost certainly struck fear into the hearts of the senators who would now decide whether or not to remove Clinton from office. Besides Livingston, the biggest target of the *Flynt Report* was then-Congressman Barr of Georgia, who had been by far Clinton's most vocal critic during *all* the Clinton scandals. The former federal prosecutor had called for Clinton's impeachment over Whitewater, Filegate, and Travelgate.

But now Flynt had the goods on Barr. The conservative, pro-life, "family values" Republican from Georgia who had also been one of the impeachment managers in the House, had divorced his second wife Gail while she was undergoing chemotherapy. He also asked his wife, who worked as his secretary, to arrange his lunch dates with his mistress, Jeri Dobbins, who became his third wife one month after his divorce from Gail. He also drove his wife to an abortion clinic and paid for her abortion—all while being rabidly "pro-life."

Also according to Flynt, Barr stood on the floor of Congress and said abortion was murder while at the same time letting his ex-wife have her abortion. Barr's divorce transcripts showed Barr and Dobbins responding to questions about their affair by repeating "I decline to answer" over and over like a pair of mob bosses. It was unbelievable.

Flynt had convinced Gail Barr to speak on the record, and it was nasty stuff. Mrs. Barr claimed her husband hadn't stood by her when she went to chemotherapy after discovering she had breast cancer. Instead he had urged her to help him campaign for a Senate seat (which he ultimately lost), saying it would "take her mind off her health problems," according to an affidavit she filed in their 1985 divorce. When Barr announced he was leaving her on Thanksgiving of that year, she pleaded with him to stay through the weekend for the sake of their two young sons, but he refused, she testified in divorce pleadings.

Adultery came up repeatedly in the affidavits, excerpted in *The Flynt Report*. When asked under oath in the divorce proceedings whether he had engaged in adultery before his marriage, Barr declined to answer, as did Ms. Dobbins. *The Flynt Report* suggests that they declined to answer instead of just saying no.

Flynt's report also rehashed some old stories that were no big deal *by themselves* but that, combined with all the other Republican debaucheries, did indeed create a pattern. This included Congressman Dan Burton from Indiana, another of Clinton's most vocal critics and chairman of the House Government Reform Committee. Burton had fathered an illegitimate child. And there was Congresswoman Helen Chenoweth from Idaho, another "family values" Republican, this time not an evangelical but a Mormon, who had a six-year sexual affair with a married man while she was single. Her confession followed a local newspaper story published after she ran campaign ads demanding Clinton resign over the Lewinsky affair.

Then there was Congressman Ken Calvert of California, who was arrested for soliciting a prostitute. Flynt's report referred to this episode as "Ken Calvert: Touched by a Hooker," and recounted the story first appearing in the *Riverside Press-Enterprise*, reporting that Calvert was caught with his pants down with a hooker in his car. Corona police reportedly found him with a prostitute's face "laying (sic) in the driver's lap" while the congressman "was placing his penis into his unzipped dress slacks and . . . trying to hide it with his untucked dress shirt." When asked his reasons for his conduct, he allegedly answered: "I was feeling intensely lonely."

Makes sense to me.

This was the political climate after the House impeached President Clinton and the Senate was about to decide his fate. Would he be removed from office or not? Would the Republicans have the stones to do the one thing that had to be done in order to have *any* chance of removing Clinton:

call live witnesses? This was key, since a live witness such as Clinton's secretary Betty Curry was *not* going to lie. If allowed to take the stand, Curry would no doubt have told the entire Senate the real story of what Clinton had said to her before she was questioned by the grand jury. The Senate would have then faced massive pressure—from the public, from much of the press, and from their own consciences (whichever members still had them) to remove Clinton from office had Betty Curry been allowed to speak before the Senate as a live witness.

The bottom line was this: Going into those Senate hearings, the Republicans had the votes and therefore the control to call live witnesses, which would have resulted in a good chance of President Clinton being removed from office. Calling live witnesses would have probably enabled the Republicans to pick off twelve Democratic senators (had they stuck together and voted as a block, as the Democrats did in 1974 against Nixon).

Democrat Senator Robert Byrd had already given Clinton a high-profile tongue lashing and looked like he would vote for impeachment if the evidence suggested Clinton was guilty. In response to reports that Clinton was preemptively making threats against certain senators, the then-eighty-one-year old Byrd warned—or should I say screamed—at Clinton on the Senate floor not to "tamper with this jury" referring to the Senate, which would now act as a jury to decide Clinton's fate. *"Don't tampahhh with this juuuureeeee!!!!!"* Byrd kept screaming on the Senate floor with arms flailing, taking his role as a Senator and the entire Senate for that matter, *very* seriously.

The thinking at the time was that if live witnesses were called, and the evidence showed that Clinton was guilty, Byrd would possibly defect, giving other Democratic senators the political cover to defect, too, since Byrd was so high-ranking in the Senate. Russ Feingold, the only Democratic Senator to vote against a motion to dismiss the charges against Clinton, was also thought of as a possible defector, as were several of the more honest Democrats, such as Joe Biden of Delaware, Paul Wellstone of Minnesota, Joe Lieberman of Connecticut, Daniel Patrick Moynihan of New York, Mary Landrieu and John Breaux of Louisiana, and Bob Gramm of Florida.

Would the Republicans in the Senate really try to remove Clinton from office? Or would they cave?

This was the true test for me as to whether there was even a modicum of truth to my belief that the Republican Party might be morally superior to the Democrats. For that to be true, the Republicans in the Senate would have to ignore all the threats, ignore all the Republicans already tainted by sex scandals, and, like Henry Hyde before them, take the heat and do the right thing. This meant calling live witnesses to ensure the Democrats would be forced into voting to remove Clinton.

Of course, we all know what happened next.

David Schippers, a Democratic lawyer hired by Henry Hyde to be the Judiciary's counsel during impeachment, goes into great detail, in his book, *Sellout*, on how the Republicans in the Senate went into the tank. Schippers believed "the ball-game was rigged before the first pitch was thrown," and intimates that the Clinton White House had the goods on Republican senators and blackmailed them.

Schippers told *Insight Magazine*:

And a lot of people may have had something in their background that they didn't want made public. Who knows? But everybody knew that if the president had it he would use it. There was always that sword of Damocles over their heads. Maybe that affected the way the senators voted.

Schippers believes some Senate Republicans caved under the implicit threat. "One of the things that always bothered me was why senators we thought might be willing to do the right thing and vote to convict Clinton backed off," Schippers said. "I still have in the back of my mind some thought that Filegate had something to do with it."

"Filegate" refers to the still-unresolved scandal of the FBI's illegal transfer to Clinton political operatives in the White House of the secret, personal background files of at least 900 Republican former officials. Those files, security experts say, are filled with raw, unverified information of the most personal and often lurid kind. Schippers says he believes the White House or its designees used leads from some of those files to blackmail lawmakers on Capitol Hill.

What would an individual's FBI file contain? According to *Insight,* individual security background files can be full of the most embarrassing and damaging information—and disinformation—imaginable, say those involved in the security-clearance process. Almost everyone has a skeleton in the closet. It's up to government lawyers and review panels to try to determine what aspects of one's present or past might preclude someone from holding a sensitive post.

"Background investigations turn up raw, raw data," says a senior U.S. intelligence officer. "Hearsay, vendettas—that's raw stuff. That stuff doesn't get filtered." For people holding senior posts, the investigations are even more intrusive. "Your spouse is investigated, too. Your personal life, your bank accounts, your investments, everything is in there . . ." Neighbors, friends, relatives—anything can get into the file. Many people have an inordinate respect for power, and they feel like they have to tell everything to investigators. It all goes in the file.

Schippers connected the dots and believed there was a connection to the Filegate scandal and the Republicans in the Senate going into the tank after the House impeached Clinton. If so, it appears that Clinton learned from one of the great mistakes of Richard Nixon. Years after being booted out of office, Richard Nixon remarked how his biggest mistake as president (aside from not destroying the "smoking gun" tape while it was legally in his possession) was forcing J. Edgar Hoover into retirement, an incredible achievement considering how many of his predecessors could only fantasize about doing such a thing. Nixon remarked that had Hoover still been around during Watergate, the Democrats would have never moved against him, knowing that Hoover had dirt on every one of them, which he would have gladly shared with Nixon.

With Hoover and his files on every member of Congress long a thing of the past. It appears possible that the Clinton White House had the next best thing; the pilfered FBI files, which could have explained how they had the goods on senate Republicans who declined to remove Clinton from office.

Even Clinton allies believed this was what was happening. George Stephanopoulos talked of a Clinton "Ellen Rometsch strategy." This refers to the Kennedy

Administration's use of FBI files to blackmail Republican leaders who wanted to investigate Kennedy's liaisons with Rometsch, an East German spy. Salon.com even reported that "diehard Clinton loyalists" were spreading the word that Clinton's survival strategy was the threat of exposing the sexual improprieties of Republican critics both in Congress and beyond.

A close Clinton ally was even spreading threats of a "Doomsday Machine," saying this: "Once the Doomsday Machine is set in motion, there will be no stopping it. The Republicans with skeletons in their closets must assume everything is known and will come out. So the question is: Do they really want to go there?"

Even before impeachment, Bob Mulholland, a Democratic national committeeman from California and chief spokesman for the state party, had already openly threatened the judiciary committee. Mulholland said that if the committee decided to initiate impeachment proceedings, he would release to the media his findings from divorce records and civil lawsuits involving the GOP congressmen. Friends nationwide would help him. "Many of the House Judiciary members were divorced, and their divorce papers contain a lot of interesting information, and we'll be sharing that with the American people."

Schippers takes aim at the scared Republicans in the Senate, beginning with Senate Majority Leader Trent Lott.

When we finished in the House—the managers, the staff, and myself—we honestly believed that once the actual evidence was presented in a trial atmosphere where the

American people could see and hear what happened *without* [italics mine] the use of the word "sex" they would see the witnesses, the victims, the documents, the films. We had four to five weeks' worth of evidence. We thought that once this was presented and the American people saw the truth the Democrats would be required to vote their conscience. We thought we would convict and remove him.

Schippers reports that when Hyde came to the Senate to give the senators all the material they had on Clinton proving the president was guilty, Lott replied, "Henry, you're not going to dump this garbage on us." When the House managers would remind Senator Lott that he had "sufficient votes to dictate the procedure and certainly to ensure presentation of evidence," Lott would balk and say he might not even have the votes to allow witnesses to be called.

Schippers also takes aim at Republican Senator Ted Stevens of Alaska: "Time was said to be too precious for the senators to waste on even a marginally protracted trial of the President of the United States," according to Stevens. The Alaska senator informed Henry Hyde, chairman of the House Judiciary Committee: "Henry, I don't care if you prove he raped a woman and then stood up and shot her dead—you are not going to get sixty-seven votes."

Schippers wrote, "not just the Democratic leadership. The Republican leaders—they're really the ones we couldn't believe. Our own guys, selling us down the river!"

House managers pleaded with senators to consider the evidence. "But it turned out that, as the sign-in sheets reveal, not one single senator took the time to review the evidence we were clamoring to present openly." Schippers explained to NBC's Brian Williams:

That was—that's when—I just shook my head. This was after the oath had been taken. We were in the—we were in the Senate—one of the Senate offices, and Henry Hyde was making a pitch to these six senators—these six Republican leaders that we needed (live) witnesses, "Please let us put our case on. At least let us—give us a trial," and, at one point, Senator Stevens said, "Henry, we're just trying to keep you from embarrassing yourself. You know that there's no way you're going to get sixty-seven votes." And Hyde said, "Well, you know, Senator, you haven't seen all the evidence."

Stevens also said "I'm reconsidering whether we need witnesses at all." According to Shippers, Senator Conrad Burns, Republican from Montana, was no better, saying, "We want to bring this thing to a close as fast as we can and as fair as we can." Same for Senator James Jeffords, Republican Senator from Vermont, saying, "After careful consideration, I have concluded that President Clinton has not committed an offense that indicates the President is not fit to serve. Therefore, I will not vote to convict President Clinton."

Senator Richard C. Shelby, Republican from Alabama, said he was inclined to vote against witnesses unless House prosecutors managed to make "a compelling case" that a particular witness would "change the dynamic." "Now, are witnesses going to change the whole tone of the trial and tenor, that's something else. I don't believe they're out there," Shelby said. Senator Gordon Smith, Republican from Oregon, said he had heard enough to "'raise a reasonable doubt' about whether the prosecution had proved its case." In short, all these Republican senators were in the tank even before they heard or saw any of the evidence against Clinton.

An important point lost in this story is that Schippers was looking at much more than Monica Lewinski. He believed the most egregious offenses by Clinton were related to the illegal Chinese campaign contributions to Clinton allegedly in exchange for military secrets. The Senate investigation into that more serious matter had been headed by Republican Senator Fred Thompson of Tennessee, who as of this writing has just entered the 2008 presidential race. According to Schippers, "We were reaching out for more information (from the Thompson Committee), and we were told, "Stop, it's over."

Schippers reflecting how Fred Thompson's committee on the Chinese money scandals going into the tank was eerily reminiscent to me of the committee investigating Whitewater, headed by Republican Senator Alphonse D'Amato, another investigation that tanked.

The Republicans in the Senate were not the only ones scared. It was the same situation in the House, according to Schippers, speaking to *Insight* magazine, who said that while Republican Congressmen Christopher Cox and Dick Armey were helpful, Gingrich was another story.

According to Schippers:

Gingrich, in particular, was a problem for us. We would have meetings with Gingrich and reach an agreement, "We're going to do it this way," but by the time we'd get back to our offices he would be with Minority Leader Richard Gephardt doing exactly the opposite.

Schippers then explained how Gingrich's leaking all the Monica material to the press caused the media to ignore all the other nonsexual misdeeds he was investigating. Schippers continued to blame Gingrich for not allowing the nonsexual scandals to be investigated:

Our original plan was not to make anything public, to keep it under the tightest security, until we made our reports. But it was Gephardt and Gingrich who decided they were going to let out all the crap. Unfortunately most of it was that sex stuff the media immediately fastened on to send up the battle cry that "It's only about sex....Had it not gone to the media, and had I been able to list fifteen felonies, you'd have seen almost no sex in it. It was the felonies on which we focused.

Schippers continued on, about the absence of leaks until Gingrich got involved:

Gingrich could not get in there until much later. We had an ultra-secure room with ultra-secure evidence, no leaks coming out. Then, in that two weeks after the House leadership authorized the release of the sex-scandal material, everybody was having a feeding frenzy on all that garbage.

When asked if Gingrich and Gephardt discredited the impeachment investigation, Schippers replied "Oh, yes. They were the ones who against our wishes put out President Clinton's grand-jury testimony."

Well, we already know why Gingrich was in the tank. But what about the other senators? As mentioned above, prior to the impeachment hearings, the Republican-controlled Senate held two major investigations. First, Republican Al D'Amato of New York led the Senate hearings on Whitewater, and second, Republican Senator Fred Thompson of Tennessee investigated the more serious Chinese money scandal that David Schippers wanted to add to his impeachment investigation.

First let's take a look at Mr. D'Amato. He dumped his first wife of twenty-three years, Penelope, with whom he'd had four children, shortly after he was elected to the Senate in 1980. Both of them being practicing Catholics, they didn't get a divorce right away, but instead separated. D'Amato continued to live in the couple's basement until their eventual divorce in 1995, right around the same time D'Amato's Whitewater hearings began. During this period, the "separated" D'Amato was allegedly quite the ladies' man in New York, while still technically married. (Remember, New York State is roughly 60 percent Roman Catholic and D'Amato had to run for re-election in 1998, when he ultimately lost to Chuck Schumer.)

Was this the reason the Whitewater investigation went into the tank? Or could it perhaps have been because Al D'Amato had so many ethical problems in his past ? For instance, while he was running for the U.S.Senate in 1980, D'Amato and the Nassau County Republican Party were investigated by a federal grand jury amid charges that county employees were required to kickback 1 percent of their salaries to the Republican organization. D'Amato testified to the panel that he had indeed donated some of his salary because he wanted to be a "team player," but he denied that he ever required any of his employees to donate money, and no charges were ever brought against him. *The Village Voice* also reported during the campaign that D'Amato had been involved in a long series of political irregularities, including accepting low-interest campaign loans from companies doing business with Nassau County. Again, no charges were brought.

In a strange twist, after finally getting his divorce, D'Amato was briefly engaged to Claudia Cohen, a Democrat and former wife of Ronald Perelman, the flunky of Vernon Jordan who had secured a job for Monica Lewinski for which she had no qualifications. Small world.

Now lets take a look at the newest entry into the 2008 presidential derby, former-Senator Fred Thompson of Tennessee, who headed the Senate hearings into "the "China Connection."

After being elected to the Senate, Thompson was immediately considered potential presidential timber by most political pundits. His real-life story as a successful prosecuting attorney putting away crooked politicians and his equally successful career as an actor gave him a special stature when he entered the U.S. Senate in 1995. Thompson's mettle was first tested when he was chosen to chair the hearings into "the China Connection" in 1997. This was without question the most serious of the Clinton scandals, involving supposed trading of military secrets to the Communist Chinese government in exchange for illegal campaign cash for Clinton's 1996 re-election.

Thompson flunked the test. From the beginning, he went straight into the tank. Instead of holding legitimate hearings, Thompson idiotically argued that the Independent Counsel statute allowing his hearing to take place *should not be allowed to exist*. Thompson took this inanity to an even more astonishing level when he claimed the investigation should be held by none other than–are you sitting down?—Janet Reno! The same Janet Reno who in the end made a plea agreement with the two "ringleaders," John Hang and Charlie Trie, giving both men zero jail time! Thompson was rebuked by members of his own committee, even Democrat Joe Lieberman.

Maybe this is pure coincidence, but Thompson was also one of the few Republican senators to vote that Clinton was "innocent" on the article of impeachment regarding Clinton's committing perjury. Maybe also coincidence was the fact that Thompson had dumped his first wife of twenty-six years, Sarah Elizabeth, with whom he had three children, to date, among others, county music star Lori Morgan before marrying Jeri Kehn, a thirty-five-year-old political media consultant, twenty-four years his junior.

On a personal note, the sight of Fred Thompson gladly letting himself be used as fodder for left-wing propaganda on the TV show *Law and Order* really makes me want to lose my lunch. On most episodes, Thompson plays the dim-witted, rightwing, southern-talking prosecutor as compared to his sophisticated liberal New Yorker assistant prosecutors who are usually prosecuting right-wing fanatics; killers of abortion doctors, killers of Jews, blacks, Arabs, etc. The show generally portrays conservatives as bigots and criminals, while the prosecutors rarely, if ever, prosecute left-wing criminals. Even before Thompson joined the cast, the show's left-wing agenda was flagrant and highly criticized for mixing reality with fiction when one of the main characters sarcastically derided President Bush, referring to him as "that dude who lied to us about WMDs."

Finally we came to the Senate "trial" after Clinton was impeached in the House.

Clinton survived not because he did not commit "high crimes or misdemeanors," but because the Republican Party was politically very weak at that time, possibly even politically weaker than Clinton during his darkest moments.

The Republican Party was weak because it was rotting from the inside, collapsing from the weight of its own flagrant hypocrisy during Clinton's impeachment. The GOP would be exposed so thoroughly as phonies that Clinton looked sympathetic to the public in comparison. (Once again reinforcing the fact that negatives drive American politics far more than positives.)

Were the Republican senators being blackmailed? Was there really, as George Stephanopoulos suggested, an "Ellen Rometsch strategy?" Did Clinton really have the goods on them? Well, I can't say for sure, and no one yet can. But as the old saying goes: "If it looks like a duck, and it walks like a duck, it's probably a duck."

Two key senators in particular stand out for being ready to remove Clinton one minute, then mere days later protecting him: one a key Republican and one a key Democrat

The key Republican was the fancy-dressing Orin Hatch from Utah. On August 17, 1998, after Clinton's first botched his "Mea Culpa for Monica" speech (when he apologized for ten seconds and attacked Ken Starr and the Republicans for ten minutes) Orin Hatch clearly believed Clinton had committed "high crimes and misdemeanors," telling Larry King, "There's not much doubt in my mind that there's been an abuse of power in this instance . . . It could mean some obstruction, it could mean some subornation. It could mean a number of things that you could call abuse of power . . . there are a lot of things that could be used to show a pattern of deceit, a pattern of dissembling, a pattern of not telling the truth and a pattern of misusing the law to—gain one's own ways." Hatch was also caught off the air saying of Clinton, "Boy, I'll tell you, what a jerk."

So you would think Hatch was clearly in the anti-Clinton pro-impeachment camp. Well, Hatch changed his tune only eight days later on August 25, 1998, again on *Larry King Live,* saying "Let's hope it (impeachment) doesn't reach that far" His warped reasoning was: "I doubt seriously that you can really go through this process in the remaining twenty-plus days that we have in the Congress"

Strangely enough, the same thing happened with Clinton's biggest Democratic critic in the Senate, Robert Byrd of West Virginia. As mentioned earlier, Byrd was crucial for the Republicans, since if he defected, other Democrats would have the political cover to follow suit. But shortly after threatening Clinton not to *"Taaampaahhh with this juuurreee!!,"* Byrd looked ashen-faced as he (like Hatch) pulled the old switcheroo. Byrd sounded equally ridiculous as Hatch:

I do not think that this is just a reflection of the American people's traditional bias for the underdog, but rather, of the much more basic American dislike of unfairness. Many people, perhaps even most people, do not believe that this process has been a fair process. We have known for weeks that the votes were not here to convict this President. And yet some wanted to press on, in a desperate attempt to bring witnesses onto the Senate Floor. What a dreadful national spectacle that would have been! That is one reason why I offered a motion to dismiss the proceedings.

Did Clinton get to Orin Hatch and Robert Byrd? You decide.

Hatch had plenty of ethical issues of his own, including his close ties to Teamsters Union Boss Jackie Presser, and his close ties to, and the shady settlement he reached with, the corrupt Bank of Credit and Commerce International (BCCI) for drug money laundering (the bank had ties to dictators and terrorists). Hatch sought to persuade BCCI to give a $10-million loan to his investment partner, and also intervened with federal S&L regulators on behalf of the same partner. Hatch's actions were later investigated by the FBI (though no charges were ever brought)—and we discussed earlier where those pilfered FBI files may have ended up.

Senators Stevens of Alaska, Shelby of Alabama, and Domenici of New Mexico also have a history of serious ethical issues. Stevens used his committee post to save a $450-million military housing contract for an Anchorage businessman, who happened to be Stevens' business partner in a series of real estate investments that turned the senator's $50,000 stake into at least $750,000 in six years. Also, an Alaska native company that Stevens helped create landed millions of dollars in defense contracts through preferences he wrote into law. The company subsequently paid $6 million a year to lease an office building owned by Stevens and his business partners. But there's more: An Alaskan communications company benefited from the senator's activities on the Commerce Committee, and his wife, Catherine, earned tens of thousands of dollars from an inside deal involving the company's stock.

Stevens was also accused of violating Senate ethics by accepting money from a defense contractor in return for advertising its products on television, raking in $60,800 from the defense contractors while head of the Defense Appropriations Subcommittee. Stevens has also been ridiculed over the years for his $315 million "bridge to nowhere," which serves a community of 8,900 people in Alaska. Keep in mind that Alaska *chose* to build its airport on an island, which is served by a ferry and has a year-round population of fifty people! Ironically, as of this writing, Stevens and his son are being investigated by the FBI in a major bribery scandal, although no charges have yet been filed against Stevens.

Senator Shelby of Alabama also has ethical issues regarding what appeared to be a conflict of interest. In his role as chairman of the Senate Banking, Housing, and Urban Affairs Committee, he opposed legislation that would have helped reform the title insurance industry and helped reduce the homeowners' costs, particularly when they refinance a mortgage. The conflict was that Shelby was earning between $100,000 and $1,000,000 per year from Tuscaloosa Title Co. Inc., a title insurer he founded in 1974.

Senator Domenici of New Mexico also had some ethical questions raised regarding campaign contributions from banking interests in what looked like a quid-pro-quo for Domenici's passing legislation weakening corporate crime and fraud laws, referred to by critics as the "Crooks and Swindlers' Protection Act."

Then there was Republican senator and big family man

Larry Craig of Idaho, who as if this writing is shamelessly trying to extricate himself out of a gay sex scandal. Considering rumors about Craig being gay have been floating around since the 1980s, it wouldn't be such a stretch to believe that info may have been gleaned from the pilfered FBI files.

And why did Trent Lott go into the tank with all the other Republican senators after impeachment? It may be coincidence, but Bill Clinton and Trent Lott at that time shared the same political advisor, the infamous Dick Morris. If there was anything on Lott, Morris would know, which means Clinton would probably know.

So if it's true that Bill Clinton was able to save himself by taking advantage of the sexual and ethical shortcomings of his political opponents, what does it all mean? As I've said before, and will continue to say, this is yet more proof that the negative (and not the positive) drives American politics. It also means something very important: Clinton being forced to go that route to save his bacon may not have necessarily been such a bad thing. While it's certainly a bad thing that Clinton's going that route may have thwarted stricter justice being imposed on him, lets take a look at the flip side: Is it so terrible that Clinton's political opponents were unable to hold Clinton accountable while they themselves tried to remain unaccountable for *their own* sexual and ethical transgressions?

So in the end, should Clinton have been removed from office? It's not such an easy call. After the passing of some time, and the cooling of some heads (including mine) it would appear that as I've said earlier, Clinton's punishment in the end fit the crime. His behavior definitely deserved impeachment, but probably didn't deserve removal from office. As I said earlier, on the one hand, the Republican were right that he had committed "high crimes and misdemeanors." But then again, the Democrats were just as right that Clinton's offenses (the provable ones, anyway) were "all about sex." Therefore, impeachment without removal was the logical compromise.

And despite my feelings back in the day, (when I was still a hard-core Republican true believer), that Clinton deserved removal and should have been hung by his balls, in retrospect I believe that Clinton's punishment was correct. His place in history is tarnished. Years from now, long forgotten will be his achievements in regards to moving the Democratic Party back to the political center, booming the economy, eliminating the national deficit, and bringing America welfare reform; all most people will remember about Clinton was that he was impeached and humiliated. The fact that Gore lost in 2000 was also a repudiation of his legacy (although that will of course change should Hillary get elected in 2008) so Clinton paid an incredible price for his actions and stupidity.

It's fascinating how history seems to just work itself out, in this case due to the flagrant arrogance of President Clinton, and the equally flagrant hypocrisy of his Republican detractors. But that's not the end of the story. There's another element to the Clinton years that, as far as I know, no-one has brought up until now—that is, how the scandal changed the nature of American politics forever in unprecedented ways:

• Who would have believed even ten years ago that the

President of the United States of America would be caught in a sex scandal, and that his main defender during the scandal would be one of America's most notorious pornographers? And that this sex-scandal-plagued president and the pornographer, Larry Flynt of *Hustler,* would come out as the *good guys,* and the *sympathetic* ones? And that the bad guys would be the opposing party, who were taken down by hypocrisy and dishonesty that the American public easily saw through?

- Who would have believed that this same president, who on his previous run for the presidency (which he won) had been caught on a "smoking gun" tape talking to his mistress (Gennifer Flowers) about their sexual affair, would easily survive the scandal by claiming his ex-mistress' tape and charges were bogus because the charges were made public by a pornographic magazine (*Penthouse*)?

- And who would have believed that the same American public that was in general sympathetic to Clinton during his sex scandal had, just sixteen years prior, disdained a presidential candidate who admitted having sexual *fantasies?* (This of course refers to Jimmy Carter blowing a fifteen-point lead in 1976 over Gerald Ford because, in an interview with *Playboy,* Carter admitted that while he's never cheated on his wife, he at times felt "lust in his heart?")

The most talented fiction writer couldn't come up with

this stuff. What's going on here?

Oppo Man could tell you what's going on here. In 1992, the number of married folks who cheated on their spouses was double what it was in 1976. By the time Clinton became president, adultery was much more commonplace in America than it had been when Jimmy Carter made his now-infamous remark. Many Americans were sympathetic towards Clinton because many, if not most, have been unfaithful at one time in their lives, either to a spouse or to a significant other.

During the Clinton scandal, many people thought "If not for the grace of God, it could have been me" as they witnessed the fate that befell Bill Clinton. I firmly believe that the vast majority of otherwise honest Americans would lie under oath in the same manner if it involved a sexual act, particularly involving infidelity.

I know this is true in my own life. If I were ever put under oath concerning my own infidelities, including some with married women, I probably would have lied as well. Not only has this been the reflexive response to lie when caught in these super-embarrassing situations, but even if in cases where there has been clear-cut evidence against me, I have continued to lie and deceive, compounding the original lie.

Also, women's attitudes in particular have changed dramatically during the past generation when it comes to sex. Here's the proof: During the 1960s, Nelson Rockefeller failed all three times he ran for president. He was rejected primarily by female voters. Why? Because he was divorced, with the widespread rumor that he had having an affair with his wife-at-that-time while still married to his first wife. Women found this an abomination in those days—the worst thing a man could do was to cheat on his wife.

By 1998 this had changed. During the Clinton scandal it wasn't the men being polled who were overwhelmingly supporting Clinton, it was the females (particularly under sixty) who were overwhelmingly supporting him, despite the fact that he had cheated on his wife.

America had changed indeed. And these changes will affect presidential politics forever. The attacks against Clinton so badly backfired that presidential candidates are now pretty much immunized by any attacks regarding sex.

For instance, in 2000, when rumors of George W. Bush's past drug use and womanizing were rampant, he simply told the press he wasn't going to talk about it, and that was that. The press never again questioned him on the subject, and neither did the Gore campaign. Clinton had immunized him.

It was the same for John McCain, whose history of infidelity with his first wife was well-documented and far worse than anything Clinton had ever done. And the same for John Kerry in 2004. He was known on Capitol Hill for having a history of being quite a ladies' man.

As for the 2008 presidential race, Giuliani will probably be immunized in the same way, all because of Clinton. (Giuliani had a disastrous and messy divorce from his second wife amid evidence of infidelity with both his former press secretary and his current wife).

Americans just don't want to know about their public leaders' sex lives. They may be interested in the sex lives of more important people—like Brittany Spears, for instance— but the sex lives of politicians are simply off limits. That is, unless you are a fraudulent "family values" right-winger. Then you're fair game, and deservedly so.

If America has entered a new era where presidents or presidential candidates guilty of infidelity are now thought of as sympathetic characters, are we just now reaching the level of the "sophisticated Europeans"? Or are we instead, as Robert Bork believes, "Slouching towards Gomorrah?" Who knows?

* * *

So with the unwillingness of the Republicans in the Senate to remove Clinton from office in 1998, the rot that would result in the demise of the Republican Revolution took hold for good. Although the party's demise would not take full effect until Election Day 2006. I was already beginning to re-think my core political views.

Once Clinton left office and I was more clearly able to analyze his presidency, the irony was not lost on me that Clinton was twelve years ahead of me in terms of my political thinking. As I've said earlier, my metamorphosis from New York liberal Democrat to right-wing Republican political hack would finally end where it is has remained to this day—right in the triangulated center, exactly where Bill Clinton envisioned America would end up years earlier.

The point is that I came into existence as Oppo Man in 1994 as a result of my blind hatred towards Bill Clinton. I decided to change careers and go into politics for the purpose of helping defeat Clinton and the Democrats.

Yet today, in 2007, I am at peace in the same exact political center as my former nemesis. Of course, I still strongly oppose much of what Clinton did as president, particularly in the area of foreign policy and in his being responsible for having lowered the bar for what Americans now expect from their leaders in the personal integrity department. Other events such as Chinagate, Waco, and Elian Gonzalez (both certainly more the fault of Janet Reno than of Bill Clinton) have made so much of the Clinton presidency leave a bad taste in my mouth.

But today I look at the big picture and realize my own hypocrisy in hating Clinton all those years out of blind political stupidity. I've done things in my own personal life far worse than what he did with Monica Lewinsky.

It wasn't until Bill Clinton left office in 2001 that I realized I agreed strongly with Clinton's concept of "triangulation" (being at that top central corner of a triangle politically represented by the hard-liberal-left and the hard-conservative-right at the other corners, able to defeat both the left and right corners of the triangle). These accomplishments were not inconsiderable. He fought the left by:

- Bucking the liberals in his own party to pass "welfare reform."

- Bucking the unions that had considerable control of the Democratic Party to pass the strongly pro-business NAFTA and GATT, which helped lead to the economic boom of the Clinton years. Also appointing the pro-Wall Street Robert Rubin—who turned out to be one of the best Treasury Secretaries of the twentieth century; and reappointing conservative Republican Alan Greenspan to head the Fed.

At the same time Clinton was fighting the wackos in the

left corner of the triangle, he was simultaneously fighting the wackos on the right—the right-wing Republicans in the House who had tried to pass legislation I mentioned earlier in the book such as the bills listed here (thankfully these bills were summarily tossed into the garbage can once they got to Bob Dole and the Senate):

- Bills that had been written word-for-word by businesses that had contributed big bucks to the GOP, which in turn allowed businesses to pollute at will. One such bill allowed sludge to be dumped into the pristine Chesapeake Bay in Maryland.

- Bills that would have cut off government funding to *legal* immigrants.

- Bills to cut the normal budget increases in popular programs such as Medicare, student loans, school lunches, etc.

I must also say that, since leaving office, Clinton appears to have come to terms with what happened to him and appears to be an emotionally stable man for the first time in his life. Good Luck, Bill—and thank you, for you were the one man in America who inadvertently led to my true calling, and to a more reasoned political thinking.

★ ★ ★

I had a great chance to witness flagrant Republican "family

values" hypocrisy up close in 2002 when the Bible-thumping minister and Republican senator from Arkansas, Tim Hutchinson, was running for re-election. Oppo Man was brought on board by a client wanting me to dig up dirt on both Senator Hutchinson and his Democratic opponent, then-Arkansas Attorney General Mark Pryor. Pryor was the son of the former Senator David Pryor, whom Hutchison replaced in 1996 when the elder Pryor retired.

Hutchinson's original victory in 1996 had made him the first Republican U.S. Senator elected in Arkansas since Reconstruction. Now here it was, six years later, and Hutchinson hit the campaign trail for re-election as Oppo Man hit the state of Arkansas to dig up the dirt. (This was also my first chance to visit the home state of former President Clinton, where so much Clinton folklore had originated, making the race even more interesting for me.)

My first stop was Little Rock, right smack dab in the middle of the state, to research Pryor. Most of the juicy "hits" against Pryor came from his tenure in the Arkansas state legislature, before he became attorney general. Looking at Pryor's voting record in the state legislature, I found the usual crap you find with just about *any* Democrat in *any* state legislature—including votes to raise taxes and votes showing him to be soft on crime.

This type of legislative voting record would normally spell instant doom to a statewide candidate in a southern state. But this race was hardly normal, thanks to the Republican incumbent Hutchinson. After researching Pryor, my next step was to research Hutchison, who resided in Bentonville, Arkansas, in the most northwest county in the state, bordering Oklahoma. That's when the real action began, and where I saw up-close evangelical right-wing religious hypocrisy at its worst.

I already knew going in that Hutchinson had divorced his first wife of twenty-nine years, Donna, to marry a young ex-staffer in his office, Randi Fredholm, who was fifteen years his junior. His second marriage came just a year after his divorce was final. This on the surface was no big, considering Arkansas has one of the nation's highest divorce rates. Divorcing your wife of twenty-nine years to marry a much younger woman only one year later, and just as you've achieved the power of a U.S. senator, didn't exactly pass the smell test (particularly considering Hutchinson had been one of then-President Clinton's strongest critics during the Monica fiasco, blathering "family values" left and right). Nonetheless, it at first appeared Hutchinson would survive this, as he had claimed he had never been unfaithful to his first wife.

But it *was* a major problem, as I soon would see from routine research. While Hutchinson had claimed he had been faithful to his wife before the divorce, everything I saw pointed in the opposite direction, although it was admittedly all circumstantial evidence.

First, I took a look at his travel records as senator. He listed several trips from DC to Arkansas, visiting different cities during each visit. All hotel receipts for the senator and all his staff were public record. During each visit, then-staffer Randi Fredholm was submitting invoices for hotels in the exact same cities on the exact same dates as was the senator. On the surface, this would not be unusual; staffers often travel with members of Congress when they visit their home state, and even stay at the same hotels. But it certainly raised questions in my mind

Next, I took a look at Hutchinson's divorce, registered at the Benton County Courthouse on July 29, 1999. The alimony payments were a joke—there was no child support, since the children were grown, and they split the proceeds of their modest $40,000. The newly elected U.S. Senator, who had been relatively poor his whole life and was finally now making good money as a U.S. senator, wouldn't even give his wife the full value of their dump of a house. So much for "family values"!

I then found that Ms. Fredholm had been promoted by Hutchinson from legislative director to state director during the tail end of her stint working for him from 1993–1998 (she later quit to go to law school and practice law for the firm Dickstein Shapiro LLP in Little Rock and in DC). The promotion—and accompanying salary hike—*may* have been legitimate. But considering the circumstances, it didn't exactly pass the smell test either, and at the very least raised the appearance of impropriety. It also raised the question of whether Ms. Fredholm got the promotion on merit, or if she was having an affair with Hutchinson as early as 1998? If Hutchinson was having an affair while attacking then-President Clinton during impeachment, then he was a family values hypocrite. I couldn't prove that Hutchinson *was* one, but the facts were interesting.

In any case, his actions were astounding. Hutchinson could have at least gone through the motions of *appearing* to be faithful and avoided even the *appearance* of impropriety, if he'd had the discipline to let a civilized amount of time lapse before marrying Ms. Fredholm; and at least wait until after his re-election campaign in 2002. Instead, he married her only a year after the divorce in a private ceremony in an undisclosed church. According to press reports, the hypocrisy in his personal life and the clumsy way he handled it during the campaign did him in. Hutchinson asked his children not to attend out of respect for their mother. To make matters worse, when he ran for re-election in 2002, Hutchinson's new wife was nowhere to be found.

When these events didn't pass the smell test, Hutchinson lost support with his right-wing evangelical base. On Election Day, many of them stayed home. But it wasn't his getting a divorce, nor even his marrying a younger woman, that did him in. It was his apparent hypocrisy that made the voters turn against Hutchinson.

Hutchinson was an ordained minister and had a reputation as a family man. He graduated from the infamous right-wing evangelical Bob Jones University, preached at several churches, and started a Christian radio station before entering politics. He eviscerated Bill Clinton for his marital troubles and ethical failings, and voted to impeach him. The Christian Coalition gave him a "Friend of the Family" award.

Hutchinson's hypocrisy was *so* blatant and *so* flagrant that his opponent Pryor took immediate advantage with an ad that featured Pryor reading the Bible to his children, while his wife and children appeared with him in many TV ads and public appearances. Hutchinson clumsily responded with an ad featuring his grandson, but it backfired. "How can any Arkansas voter watch that Hutchinson TV ad with the cute grandson without wondering where Grandma went?" commentator Gene Lyons wrote in the *Democrat-Gazette*. In addition, Hutchinson's new wife not only stayed out of the public during that 2002 re-election race, but she also never appeared in any of the television campaign ads for the former preacher man.

The hypocrisy was just too much for the voters of Arkansas. So much so that, on a great election night for Republicans nationwide and as George W. Bush parlayed his popularity in the wake of 9/11 into Republicans regaining control of the Senate, Hutchinson was the *only* incumbent Senate Republican in America to lose that night in 2002.

Final Result: Mark Pryor 53 percent, Hutchinson 47 percent.

Good riddance.

Chapter Seventeen

ONLY IN LOUISIANA: CYNICAL POLITICS AT ITS WORST

I n the wake of Hurricane Katrina, the mayor of New Orleans, Democrat Ray Nagin, became the most disgraced politician in America. However, despite all the controversy surrounding the poor handling of the disaster in his city, Nagin didn't resign—he stayed on the job as New Orleans tried to rebuild.

In 2006, Nagin was running for re-election. My thinking at the time went like this: "Well, he's a smart guy, and he's definitely learned from the mistakes made during Katrina. Plus he appears to still connect with the people of New Orleans, and would therefore be the best man for the job should something like Katrina happen again." I also liked Nagin for the same reason I liked him back in 2002 when he first got elected: He was the most conservative, pro-business candidate in the bunch.

Oppo Man decided to work for a client who wanted me to dig up dirt on Nagin's chief opponent, another Democrat,

Mitch Landrieu. Landrieu was Louisiana's lieutenant governor at the time and had previously spent sixteen years in the state legislature. He was also the brother of current U.S. Senator Mary Landrieu and the son of a former New Orleans mayor, the beloved Moon Landrieu. Most of Oppo Man's work involved researching Mitch Landrieu's votes in the legislature, and there were many votes useful to the cause—votes to let criminals and prisoners back onto the streets, votes to raise taxes, the usual liberal garbage. However, due to Landrieu's popularity and credentials and Nagin's mishandling of the hurricane aftermath, I didn't really expect that Nagin would be re-elected.

Then, in the April 22 runoff election, something unexpected happened. Nagin actually came in first, with 38 percent of the vote. *Landrieu* came in second with 29 percent. So, for the general election, I continued to research Landrieu's record, still working for the man whom I believed was—despite all the mistakes of Katrina—smart enough and tough enough to lead New Orleans back to its former greatness.

Then a bomb fell that proved that Oppo Man wasn't nearly as bright as he thought he was. I had previously thought nothing of Nagin's prior racially divisive statement that New Orleans needed to be "more chocolate" (referring to African Americans), thinking it was a just an innocent slip of the tongue or a joke. I was so wrong.

Shortly before the election, whilst speaking before a gathering of the NAACP in Houston, Nagin had these pearls of wisdom: "I have twenty-three candidates running for mayor and very few of them look like us." Instead of being contrite and showing some courage and taking some blame, the guy that botched Katrina instead reverted to a "divide and conquer" racial posture? Suddenly it hit me: *I was working for the wrong guy!*

Landrieu, while certainly liberal, was nonetheless a good guy with a long, respected record in state government. His family tradition was impressive. In retrospect, I should have seen him for what he really was at the time: the perfect candidate to unite blacks and whites, not divide them along racial lines, as Nagin so flagrantly and shamelessly was doing. Making matters worse, Nagin was doing it during such a time in the city's history, less than one year after Katrina.

I couldn't believe it. I had deluded myself that Mitch Landrieu was just a liberal low-life when in fact he had the experience, the know-how, the temperament, and most importantly, the *brains* to be the mayor New Orleans needed at that critical time.

Now all I could do was to sit and wait—and hope somehow that Landrieu would pull it off and undo my mistake. I hoped that somehow the voters in New Orleans would come to their senses and see that Nagin was a sham. Wishful thinking: Nagin 52 percent, Landrieu 48 percent. Nagin also achieved a dramatic shift in the racial breakdown of the vote. In this election, he received 80 percent of the black votes and 20 percent of the white votes—a complete reversal of his support base in the 2002 election.

In the end, exit polls showed voters voted strictly on the issue of race. Making it a complete farce was the fact that many blacks voting for Nagin weren't even voting from New Orleans, having fled after Katrina, with no guarantee they would ever return to New Orleans! Many were in other parts of Louisiana and Texas. Tens of thousands of voters in Houston and Austin, Texas—who may never set foot in New Orleans again—were deciding who would be New Orleans' next mayor.

I also couldn't believe how badly Nagin had conned Oppo Man. Nagin won the only way he knew how to win, which was possibly the *only* way he could win: by employing a racially divisive, 100 percent cynical political campaign. Nagin was ridiculous; Oppo Man letting himself get conned by this fraud was equally ridiculous.

* * *

Besides the Nagin debacle, I was also hired by a client working on behalf of another Democrat in Louisiana in 1999, Shane Guidry. Guidry was trying to unseat Jefferson Parish councilman Butch Ward, his Democratic opponent, and I was brought on board to dig up dirt on Ward. Once again, as was the case with Ray Nagin, Oppo Man found himself working for the wrong guy. In Louisiana, counties are called "parishes" (due to the state's French roots), and Jefferson Parish is a blue-collar residential series of white neighborhoods bordering New Orleans and Orleans Parish. Butch Ward had represented the parish for twenty years and was considered "Dean" of the entire Louisiana council.

Now you are probably wondering why I was working on such a rinky-dink local race in Louisiana. Well, in Louisiana, the position of Parish Councilman is a powerful one (far stronger than its name implies), and there's a lot of money in Jefferson Parish, just like in Orleans Parish. The person elected to the position becomes responsible for doling out millions of dollars in government contracts. And my clients pay basically the same regardless of the office, since Oppo Man's services are needed no matter who needs to be researched and no matter what office they're running for (in some cases, running from).

Shane Guidry was a parish reserve deputy with a lot of family money—he would go on to spend an unprecedented $3 million in the race. He had the backing of Sheriff Harry Lee. However, he also had serious problems.

In the end, all that money did him no good: He and his father, Robert Guidry, were ensnared in the federal bribery case against former Governor Edwin Edwards. Edwards had been found guilty of soliciting bribes from casino owners and Robert Guidry, owner of the Treasure Chest casino, pled guilty to paying Edwards $1.4 million in bribes to obtain a casino license. He received five years probation. Shane Guidry, on the other hand, received immunity when he testified before a federal grand jury investigating the case. And although the Guidry campaign kept repeating that his father's mistakes shouldn't reflect on the rest of the family, Guidry was sunk.

The research we had on Butch Ward was nothing compared to Guidry's involvement with the most discredited politician in modern Louisiana (and it's quite a feat to achieve *that* title in *that* state). In response to Guidry's attacks, Ward sent out a mailing displaying a photo of former Governor Edwin Edwards, the Treasure Chest Casino, Shane Guidry, and his father, Robert, and announcing "*Shane's Ship Arrives.*" This was excellent oppo work by the opposition. Final results: Ward 61 percent; Guidry 39 percent.

To make matters worse, when the election was over, many of the Guidry campaign consultants were stiffed out of their pay. Some joined together in a lawsuit; the case was settled out of court almost a year later. (Fortunately for me, I had been paid and wasn't affected by this.) Then, as a surreal ending to an already painful story, two years after the election, in 2001, Shane Guidry, his father, and his brother were all arrested at a Morton's Steak House after a shouting match with Popeye's Famous Fried Chicken founder Al Copeland degenerated into a brawl. Shane was charged with battery, but the charges were later dropped.

Once again, Oppo Man was wrong about who was good and who was bad. In reality, Oppo Man's "bad guy" was just a run-of-the-mill clubhouse politician. And Oppo Man's "good guy" was a clown.

Another Louisiana phenomenon was that, while I worked on that 1999 Guidry/Ward race, two incumbent statewide commissioners, who were both under indictment, were running for re-election. I had nothing to do with either race, but it's still important to mention to clearly depict the context of everything political that goes on in Louisiana. Besides that year's indictment of former Governor Edwin Edwards, 1999 also brought the indictments of Elections Commissioner Jerry Fowler and Insurance Commissioner Jim Brown. Fowler was indicted for filing false records and conspiracy to launder money, and Brown for conspiracy to improperly help a failed insurance company. Yet the two of them just kept campaigning for re-election, as if nothing happened. Brown won; Fowler lost. Where do they dig up guys like Ray Nagin, Shane Guidry, Jerry Fowler, and Jim Brown? Only in Louisiana.

✷ ✷ ✷

One final anecdote regarding research in Louisiana: In all my travels as Oppo Man, it's the only state in America where I was regularly followed. Not by professionals; if they were professionals, I would never have known I was being shadowed. But in New Orleans and in Gretna (which is in Jefferson Parish), amateur surveillance was the order of the day. Desk clerks at the hotels where I stayed would tell me after the fact that sometimes, after I entered the hotel and was in the elevator, one or two men would ask if they knew anything about "Mr. Marks' business in Louisiana."

They knew my name, but apparently not much more. My name was probably provided by some political hack at the Orleans Parish or Jefferson Parish courthouse, since I would have had to sign my name to request copies of any court documents and show my ID. They would trail me and try to find out what I was up to. Whether or not they ever did, I'll never know—but they certainly never stopped me.

Yes, only in Louisiana.

Chapter Eighteen

ONLY IN NEW JERSEY: TWO CONSECUTIVE SITTING GOVERNORS RESIGN IN DISGRACE

R ight after the historical 2000 presidential recount, my next stop was New Jersey, in 2001, to work on that state's race for governor. In many campaigns, opposition researchers are leaked weird rumors that have to be checked out, no matter how outlandish or unlikely. Sometimes they turn out to be true, but the vast majority are bogus. Nevertheless, you always have to check them out.

The 2001 New Jersey governor's race was the only campaign I've ever worked where every one of the "rumors" leaked about a particular candidate turned out to be true. By the time it was all over, I was unceremoniously tossed out of a New Jersey courthouse, while then-Acting Governor Republican Donald DiFrancesco was being unceremoniously tossed out of office, forced to drop out of his re-election bid for governor in mid-campaign.

It all began in 2000 when George W. Bush became president. He named popular Republican New Jersey Governor

Christy Todd Whitman as his new Environmental Protection Agency (EPA) director. There is no lieutenant governor in New Jersey—the governor is the only elected statewide official (New Jersey is the only state in the U.S. with such an absurd political situation). Therefore, the next-in-line to take over the job was then-State Senate President Donald DiFrancesco, the friendly, back-slapping politician known quasi-affectionately in New Jersey and in neighboring New York City as "Donnie D."

In 2001, Donnie D. was running for governor in his own right and was the heavy favorite to win. I was hired by a client wanting me to dig up dirt on DiFrancesco; the client was working on behalf of DiFrancesco's Republican opponent, Brett Schundler. Schundler had gained fame nationwide because he was able to get elected as mayor of Jersey City even though he was a right-wing Republican in a minority-dominated urban city with very few Republican voters. Schundler had since been a fine mayor, cleaning up Jersey City and making a national name for himself by making the city one of the first in the nation to institute a successful school voucher program.

Before all the wild rumors concerning Donnie D. began coming in, my work was relatively low-key. I was doing routine research in Donnie's hometown of Scotch Plains, New Jersey, a nice, quiet suburban town about an hour away from New York City. Right away there was action: a slew of delinquent property tax payments against Donnie D.

As was the case mentioned earlier regarding Haskell, Texas, I couldn't be anonymous in the Scotch Plains courthouse as I looked for dirt. In Donnie's hometown, property tax records were not in the county courthouse (which is the norm) but instead were in the tiny, close-knit municipal building of

Scotch Plains. Everyone working in that building is or was Donnie D.'s neighbor.

In most cases, when I have to research someone in their own backyard, almost any request for public information regarding the town's fair-haired boy (or girl) is met by the bureaucrats with, at best, nasty looks, and at worst, flat-out refusals to fork over the public records. In Scotch Pains, though, the weirdest thing happened. The clerks were delighted to give me whatever I was asking for, even handing over material damaging to Donnie D. that I hadn't asked for. He had obviously pissed off some of the folks that knew him best.

Then the real action began.

My next stop was the Monmouth County Courthouse. A rumor had emerged about Donnie D. having a number of lawsuits against him regarding his real estate dealings in the county. It was all true. Not only were there lawsuits resulting from multiple delinquencies on properties Donnie D. owned, there were even properties that had gone into default. One of the failed estate deals was funded through a personal loan from a family friend who ended up with a portion of a state contract. I had also confirmed multiple questionable real estate deals involving DiFrancesco's brother, Paul DiFrancesco, as well as confirming that the woman DiFrancesco's had chosen to be state treasurer had been fired from Citibank in New York after misusing travel expenses so she could pursue an extramarital affair.

I submitted my findings to my client, and the next thing I knew they were leaked to the *New York Times*, which ran a big story on the subject. The *New York Post* followed up on the story with their usual *National Enquirer*-like headline:

"Donnie D.-Faults." This was a lot of scrutiny, and pressure was mounting within GOP circles for Donny D. to drop out of the race.

The next thing I knew I was checking out another "rumor," which turned out to be one of the most off-the-wall experiences I ever encountered in my life as Oppo Man. The rumor to be "researched" was that DiFrancesco had been named in a divorce case in some obscure South New Jersey county, with documentation in the case file. After finding the divorce case number on the public terminal in the county courthouse, I simply went up to the counter to ask one of the clerks to please retrieve the file for my perusal. This is a commonplace request at every county courthouse. People ask to see files, and the clerks retrieve the files. The only potential problem I anticipated was the possibility that DiFrancesco had already gotten to the judge of the divorce case and that the judge had sealed the file (they were both Republicans likely to know each other personally, and Donnie D. was fighting for re-election—subject to question, this would have still been within the judge's legal discretion.

I requested the file . . . and all hell broke loose.

Instead of the desk clerk coming back with the file, a middle-aged, courtly, and polite woman approached me with the file in her hand. She stuck out her other hand and introduced herself as the county clerk (county clerks are elected officials and the highest-level persons in every county courthouse across America). It was peculiar, getting personal attention from an elected official at a county courthouse, but I just figured that everyone there knew why the file was so sensitive and that the county clerk (also a Republican) was just trying to politely find out who I was and what I was doing.

Since she was so polite and well mannered, I didn't think there would be a problem. Then, after a few pleasantries, she said to me, "Mr. Marks, this police officer will escort you to the chamber of the judge who handled the case. He'll take it from here."

What? The judge's chambers?!

In all of my years as an opposition researcher, this was a first. Since the county clerk and judge were both Republicans, and Donnie D. was the acting governor and most powerful Republican in the entire state, it should not have been a surprise. Ok, that's politics as usual. What was *not* in any way usual was their handling the situation by bringing me into a judge's chamber simply because I asked to view a public record.

I didn't know the half of it.

A young police officer led me up to the second floor and into the judge's chamber, his hand on my elbow gently but firmly, almost as if he was making sure I didn't bolt. The next thing I knew, this fat, jovial judge with a ruddy complexion and broad smile—sans robe—wobbled towards me to welcome me into his office, sticking out his hand and giving an impressively friendly handshake. In his left hand he held the file—which I wanted with increasing fervor as this bizarre situation played out.

Motioning for me to sit down in a nice leather chair in front of his desk, the judge began our palaver with some idle small talk. He remained friendly as he got to the point: "What is your business here, Mr. Marks?" I simply replied that I was a member of the public exercising my right as a citizen to view a public record in accordance with state and federal open records laws. "If the document is sealed," I continued, "then just show me the seal, Judge, and I'll be out of your hair. However, if it's not sealed, I would like to see the file."

At this point, the conversation went downhill fast and the fat judge's smile turned to a scowl. The rest of the conversation went something like this:

"But why do you want to see the file, Mr. Marks?"

"Why I want to see the file is irrelevant, Judge. I'm a member of the public exercising my right as a citizen to view a public record in accordance with state and federal open records laws. If the document is sealed than just show me the seal, and I won't look at the file. However, if it's not sealed, I would like to see the file."

"And who are you working for, Mr. Marks?"

"Who I'm working for is irrelevant, Judge. I'm a member of the public exercising my right as a citizen to view a public record in accordance with state and federal open records laws. If the document is sealed than just show me the seal and I won't look at the file. If it's not sealed, I would like to see the file."

Finally the judge simply looked up at the police officer who'd escorted me into the room (I hadn't realized he'd been standing there the whole time). The judge made a motion with his hand to the officer, and all of a sudden I was physically removed from my chair and unceremoniously booted from the judge's office. I lost my temper slightly as I was being dragged out the door. My parting words were, "But Judge, it's a fucking public record!"

He simply laughed and replied "Not for you, pal."

The next thing I knew I was out on the street, having

not only been denied public information, but also being removed from a public building when I had done nothing to warrant ejection.

I was half in a state of shock and half laughing when I called my handler for the Schundler campaign and told him what happened. He laughed and told me not to worry, that a female *New York Times* reporter was going to go to the same courthouse and request the same file. There was no way these clowns would deny a *New York Times* reporter public information, nor was there any way that they would manhandle a female, much less throw her out of the courthouse.

The whole matter became moot, however, when shortly thereafter, DiFrancesco dropped out of the race just two months before the Republican gubernatorial primary. It's my belief that the divorce file in question was just the tip of the iceberg, and that there were more "rumors" to come and even more damaging dirt on Donnie D. just waiting to be uncovered.

The incident was the first time my work was largely responsible for a sitting governor (well, "acting" governor, to be precise) dropping out of a re-election race even before the voters had a chance to decide his fate. It may have also been responsible for something even more important. Just a month prior to DiFrancesco's final demise, President George W. Bush had come to New Jersey to plug his "No Child Left Behind" education initiative, and it was assumed that he would use the visit to endorse DiFrancesco. During the 2000 presidential race, Donny D. had been Bush's New Jersey state chairman as Bush was battling John McCain, so there was some loyalty and camaraderie there. However, while Bush did a photo op with DiFrancesco at a public school to push his education agenda, there was no endorsement, possibly due to the dirt I had dug up on Donny D. and its subsequent publication in major New York papers. My work may have saved President Bush from making an embarrassing and potentially damaging endorsement.

Brett Schundler went on to win the Republican nomination, despite the establishment Republicans replacing DiFrancesco on the ballot with respected former Congressman Bob Franks—which was done with sleight of hand, since the switch was done well past the legal date for any new candidate being allowed onto the primary ballot. But what the hell, it's New Jersey, right?

Schundler subsequently lost the general election to the handsome, likeable Democratic nominee Jim McGreevey, who was at the time mayor of Woodbridge, New Jersey. McGreevey, however, didn't remain governor for long. On August 12, 2004, he was forced to announce his retirement in the middle of his term, exactly as had his predecessor Donnie D.

Where Donnie's story was pathetic, McGreevey's was painful—this handsome young man with the beautiful family confessed his homosexuality. During the general election campaign, when Schundler lost to McGreevey, we'd all heard the rumors about McGreevey being gay, but no one ever could confirm it.

However, while being outed might have been a forgivable offense to the public, McGreevey was possibly also corrupt. The story being circulated at the time of his resignation was that McGreevey was being extorted by a male lover who was on the state payroll in a no-show job—meaning he collected a salary courtesy of New Jersey taxpayers for doing no government work.

Two New Jersey governors with different reasons to resign in the middle of their respective terms within a few years of each other—no one can say this job didn't have its fascinating moments.

Only in New Jersey.

* * *

One other confrontational experience with so-called Republicans points to an odd and often overlooked aspect of politics: Politicians occasionally put themselves not only above the voters, but also above their own political parties.

It was the summer of 1996, and I was researching the opponent of New York Congressman Jack Quinn, a Democratic New York state legislator named Fran Pordums. I was in Albany checking out Mr. Pordums's voting record in the legislature when I walked into the offices of the Republican Assembly Campaign Committee (RACC). In most states, both parties keep records of their opponents' key votes in the state legislature, so I assumed the RACC would have records on how Pordums voted, particularly votes that would hurt him politically. I was surprised when a woman in RACC's office told me they kept no such records. While she was polite, I was certain that she was mistaken.

I asked to speak to the supervisor of the office. Before I knew it, I was in the middle of a shouting match with a high-level RACC official who also vehemently denied that RACC keeps records of how their opponents vote in the legislature.

In the New York State Legislature, Republicans have always (at least as long as I can remember) controlled the state

Senate and have been in the majority, while the Democrats have always controlled the state House, where the RACC was supposedly helping the Republican minority pick up house seats. When I finally left the office in frustration, I shouted some ungracious parting words: "I can see why you guys have been in the minority for the past fifty years," as I believed this was a significant oversight of the RACC in helping Republicans win these races for the state house.

As soon as I walked out I realized I had made a mistake. While what I said may have been true, it didn't matter—you don't alienate political allies, even when they're inept. So I decided to apologize—but not in person, since just walking back into the office was likely to cause a serious confrontation. I instead called the office and personally apologized to my RACC nemesis. Trying lamely to explain that I didn't mean what I'd said (which was bullshit), I apologized profusely for my rude and obnoxious behavior.

His response went like this: "Apology accepted. However, next time you enter this office you will be leaving on a stretcher."

At the time, I didn't think there was any logical reason why this RACC goon was acting this way toward me. However, I eventually remembered what so many political observers had been saying for years: Democrats and Republicans had a "gentleman's agreement" in the New York State Legislature—the Democrats wouldn't seriously challenge the Republicans in the state Senate, while the Republicans would extend the same courtesy towards the Democrats in the House. This could have explained my weird experience with RACC.

However, that one experience makes me wonder how commonplace that sort of thing is all over the country—a "gentleman's agreement" to preserve the status quo (even if it means threatening a few researchers). My own guess is that it is not as common as it once was, considering the collapse of many political machines across America during the past twenty or thirty years, particularly in larger cities like New York where machines were at their worst. If not, it's an abomination and just one more way that the two parties circumvent the political system and thwart democracy by "legally" rigging elections for mutual benefit.

During these two episodes—being thrown out of a county courthouse by a judge in New Jersey, then challenged in New York by my RACC nemesis—all I could think was "These are *our* guys?" Republicans, as was I? I can honestly say that, in the dozens of confrontations I've had over the years with Democratic political hacks and bureaucrats, even when I was illegally being denied public information, I was never, I mean *never*, treated with the disrespect and arrogance I met with during my time in New Jersey, and certainly never threatened with physical violence as I was in Albany, New York.

I feel compelled to add here that, years later, in 2000 and again in 2002, I did some work for RACC themselves researching some key New York legislative races. At that time I had completely forgotten the 1996 incident; I hadn't even made the connection they were the same group.

I don't know if they had new management, but in 2000 and 2002 they were a great bunch of folks, very professional, and it was a pleasure to work for them. I found it hard to believe it was the same outfit, but for some reason, they had changed for the better.

Chapter Nineteen

COCKFIGHTING AND IMPLODING CANDIDATES: ACTION IN KANSAS AND OKLAHOMA

After longtime Wichita, Kansas Mayor Bob Knight announced his retirement to run for governor in 2002, the two frontrunners to take his place were movie-house magnate Bill Warren (the heavy favorite) and Carlos Mayans, the Cuban-born former state legislator. Both men were Republicans. Warren was a local celebrity, owning just about every movie theatre in Wichita. (If you ask someone to go to the movies in Wichita, you ask "Wanna go to the Warren?") Mayans was a nice, likeable guy, but had very little campaign cash. I spoke to both campaigns and the decision to work for either Warren or Mayans came down to one issue: money. Warren had lots of it; Mayan didn't. So in the end I was hired by a client working on behalf of Warren, wanting me to dig up dirt on Mayans.

So Oppo Man went to work, digging up all Mayans' bad votes in the state legislature. There were so many bad votes that I figured it would be relatively easy to knock off Mayans.

Then, suddenly, things started to change. Only two days after announcing his candidacy, Warren got a judge to seal court records in which Warren's fiancée made allegations of abuse, threats, extortion, and slander. No criminal charges were ever filed. Warren and his fiancée, Susan Miller, claimed they had reconciled. Also, a civil suit against Warren involving Wichita State University women's basketball coach Darryl Smith was dismissed. Miller briefly dated Smith when she was estranged from Warren, and according to court documents that weren't sealed, Smith phoned in a report to Wichita police on March 19, 2002, accusing Warren of making harassing phone calls and threatening him with bodily harm. The next day, Miller filed for a court "protection from abuse" order against Warren. The order was granted on a temporary basis, pending hearings on whether to make it permanent. It was later dismissed.

Five days after the protection order was filed, Warren's company, American Cinemas Inc., filed a civil suit against Miller, claiming she was trying to damage the company and was demanding a $1 million settlement to desist. The suit said Miller was fired as manager of a theater after telling Warren in a recorded conversation that she was going to "ruin your white-trash, trailer-trash theater out here." Warren followed up the civil suit with a Wichita police report accusing Miller of blackmail and extortion. In October, Warren also sued Darryl Smith, claiming that the coach had filed a false police report against him.

The press was going wild with the story. After all, how often do you see this much Jerry Springer-type action in Wichita, Kansas? (That's not a slight of Wichita, which is a great mixture of blue collar and white collar, urban and rural—

right on the Oklahoma border, it's one of America's great half-Midwestern/half-Southern cities.) The brewing scandal and its constant coverage in the news proved too much for Warren to handle emotionally. Despite still being the front-runner, and despite his huge financial advantage over his opponents, he had a meltdown. While chatting with some reporters about his recent experiences, Warren lost it. Claiming he now hated Wichita, he said he was going to shut all his movie theatres in the city. After the blow-up became front-page news, Warren backed off, claiming he was simply being "sarcastic" when he made the remarks.

Warren then blamed the press for "exaggerating" his melt-down and accused them of favoring his opponent, Carlos Mayans. He went on to claim that Mayans had told him that, if elected, he (Mayans) would harm Warren's businesses, prompting Warren to call Mayans "unethical" and a "lowlife."

Final results: Mayans 53 percent to Warren 15 percent.

* * *

Same year, same state, same mayhem. Adam Taff of Lake Quivia, a beautiful suburb of Kansas City, had all the tools to be a great politician: he was a war hero, had looks right out of central casting *and* the cover of *GQ*, and was charismatic, like-able, and smart.

In 2002, Taff challenged Jeff Colyer in the Republican primary for the right to face veteran Democratic Congressman Dennis Moore in Kansas' Third District. Oppo Man was hired by a client working on behalf of Colyer, but there wasn't much dirt on Taff—only some slight "resume inflation," whereby he claimed to be an All-American football player at his college, when he in fact he'd received honorable mention only. A white lie, no big deal. However, it made me think: Why lie about that, when the truth—honorable mention as an All American—was still mighty impressive, as was the rest of Taff's resume?

Colyer, the favorite, had the backing of the Republican establishment in Washington (plus some of their money) despite the national party's generally remaining neutral in GOP primaries. Colyer was also a celebrity of sorts, having gained national prominence for providing free plastic surgery to burn victims during wars in foreign countries. Colyer was a great guy, but Adam Taff had that intangible "star quality," like a rock star. The final result on Primary Day: Taff 52 percent to Colyer 48 percent.

In the general election, it looked as if Taff could keep the momentum going and win. Another big factor in his favor was that 2002 was shaping up to be a big GOP year, as President Bush successfully turned the mid-term elections into a refer-endum on the "War on Terror" (at a time when Bush was polling strongly in the wake of 9/11). However, for whatever reason, the national GOP refused to help Taff in the election's closing days (although Vice President Dick Cheney did fly in for a last-minute Taff fundraiser). Taff lost the election to his Democratic opponent by 3 percentage points, 50 percent to 47 percent.

Taff tried again in 2004, but lost the Republican primary by fewer than one hundred votes to law professor Kris Kobach, another razor-thin decision. Since Taff was liberal on some social issues, most notably abortion, the right-wingers were able to get the vote out and just barely defeat him. So Taff had to endure two very close defeats back-to-back in 2002 and 2004. But he still appeared to me to have a great future. I also believed he had the tough military demeanor necessary to handle the adversity of losing those races.

I was wrong. He cracked. On August 18, 2005, Taff was indicted by the feds for fraud—he had used campaign contributions to obtain a loan for a $1.2-million home. He was sentenced to fifteen months in federal prison. (And in the meantime Jeff Coyler has since been elected to the Kansas state legislature.)

* * *

In 1994, Steve Largent had a plan that seemed perfect. The NFL Hall-of-Famer would retire from the Seattle Seahawks and return to his native Oklahoma to run for Congress. Largent entered the *Republican* primary for the Tulsa-based seat, won the nomination, and then easily won the general election. Once in Congress, Largent took a self-imposed term-limit pledge to serve no more than eight years in Congress, meaning he would retire in 2002.

The year of Largent's first congressional run was the first year that Republican Frank Keating was elected governor—so, when Keating had to step aside because of his own two-term limit in 2002, Largent would just be retiring from Congress. By that time, Largent would have solidified his support throughout the state, which would have become even more of a Republican stronghold than it was in 1994. Largent would be a shoo-in—he would just walk into the governor's mansion.

It was a perfect plan. And Steve Largent was the perfect man for the job, an evangelical who not only talked the talk, but walked the walk.

For instance:

- When he caught his teenage son smoking dope, Largent summarily brought the boy down to the police station and made a "citizen's arrest." Against his own son!

- One night when his teenage daughter was acting as a designated driver, she and her friends were stopped by police after some of the girls were spotted with open containers in the car. Upon entering the police station, Largent was told by the cops, "Don't worry, Steve, your daughter was the designated driver and wasn't drinking. We're not charging her with anything. You can take her home." To that, Largent replied: "She was driving all her drunk friends around town? Lock her up with the rest of them!"

- While still a football star with the Seattle Seahawks, Largent found himself attracted to one of the waitresses in a coffee shop he was patronizing with some teammates. Despite being the most famous celebrity in all of Washington State, he nonetheless introduced himself to the coffee shop's manager and asked for permission to ask the waitress out on a date. Incredible as it may seem, Largent, the equivalent of Michael Jordan or Shaq in his day, wanted *permission* from the manager to date the waitress. And that's how he met Terry, his wife of more than thirty years and the mother of his four children.

Yep, that's Steve Largent. In 2002 it looked as though his eight-year plan was going perfectly—he was easily elected in every race from 1994 to 2000, never failing to get less than 60 percent of the vote. That year, Oppo Man came to town to dig up dirt on Largent's likely Democratic opponent for the governorship, Vince Orza, chairman and CEO of a popular restaurant chain called Eateries. Then something unexpected happened.

During the battle for the Democratic nomination, underdog State Senator Brad Henry jumped all over Orza's proposal to eliminate taxes on individual and corporate incomes and make up the revenue—about $2.2 billion—with increased taxes on consumers. Also, right before the primary, the August issue of *Restaurant Business* magazine named Orza one of 2001's "10 Worst-Performing CEOs." Then Orza also got nailed when it was widely reported that, despite a money-losing year for his company, he had pocketed a $325,000 salary and $118,000 in additional compensation from Eateries, Inc. The result: In a huge surprise victory, Brad Henry defeated Orza 53 percent to 47 percent.

Now we had a new Democratic opponent. Consequently, Oppo Man was hired by a client working on behalf of Largent who wanted me to dig up dirt on Henry, an obscure state legislator. I was stuck pouring though all of Henry's votes in the Oklahoma legislature, which yielded all the usual liberal leanings: taxes, crime, abortion—votes that would not be popular in an overwhelmingly Republican state. But no one gave any thought to actually using any of it, since it was assumed Largent would always be so far ahead. Candidates generally do not go negative if they have a big lead; only if the race is close or if they're behind. Everything looked like it was under control, and Largent maintained a huge lead in the polls over Henry.

Suddenly, though, it was one crazy thing after another for Steve Largent.

A Republican lawyer named Gary Richardson, who had already entered the race as a third-party candidate, decided to drop $2.1 million into the campaign, which would siphon off Republican votes (mostly moderate) from Largent.

Largent happened to be on a hunting trip on 9/11 and didn't find out about it until two days later. He therefore missed a vote in Congress renouncing the terrorist act. Again, no big deal, since it was one of those unanimous votes to make a point over America's shared grief, not to pass any important legislation. Nevertheless, "Independent" candidate Richardson ran TV ads stating that Steve Largent was the only member of Congress to miss the vote renouncing the 9/11 terrorist act against America.

When an Oklahoma City TV reporter aggressively asked Largent about his whereabouts on 9/11—and about insinuations that he didn't care enough to cast the vote in Congress— the usually unflappable Largent, who had never lost his temper in public, much less used foul language, blurted out "That's bullshit! That's bullshit!"

This time it *was* a big deal, as Largent's tirade was caught on camera—and Americans tend to believe far too much of what they see on TV. The same footage was later used in a Gary Richardson TV ad, which showed the World Trade Center collapsing, accompanied by the Alan Jackson song "Where Were You (When the World Stopped Turning)."

Later, the same ad showed the footage of Largent using the expletive, doing terrible damage to the image of straight-laced, evangelical Largent.

On Election Day, despite losing ground in the polls due to his profanity-laced tirade, Largent was still expected to win easily. **2002 was shaping into a great year for Republicans nationwide, and Oklahoma was a hard-core Republican state. So it never occurred to us that things might end differently for Steve Largent.**

Final results: Brad Henry 43.27 percent, Steve Largent 42.61 percent, Gary Richardson, 14.12 percent.

The outcome was a shock, and not until the exit polls were analyzed did anyone remotely understand what the hell had happened. How could Steve Largent have possibly lost?

It turns out he lost because of an issue that wasn't even on the political radar screen, an issue only the most demented yahoos could give a damn about: *cock fighting!* Largent had made an off-hand remark that, since Oklahoma was one of only two states with legalized cock fighting, as governor he would change the law to make it illegal, joining the rest of civilized America, sans Louisiana. Unfortunately for Largent, there was a cock-fighting initiative on the ballot, which brought out every wacko in the state to vote against him, since to these voters there was no more important political issue than the continued legality of cock fighting.

There's no hard number indicating how many Oklahomans actually voted against Largent on this single issue. But Chad Alexander, chairman of the Oklahoma Republican Party, was quoted at the time as saying, "I do think cockfighting led to rural turnout, where those votes went to Henry."

Either way, it was enough—along with Richardson's siphoning off 14 percent of the vote—to sink the unsinkable Steve Largent, the most hard-core conservative candidate the state has probably ever seen, who one time took a liberal and humane position on one issue because he knew it was the right thing to do. As a result, the candidate who would have been best for the state gets voted out.

There are some things you would just never expect to make a difference in an election. Cockfighting is one.

Chapter Twenty

OPPO MEN VERSUS OPPO MEN: BLINDSIDED IN NEW HAMPSHIRE

I n early 2002, I received a call from the campaign of Gordon Humphrey, the former two-term U.S. senator from New Hampshire was now running for governor of the Granite State. His Republican primary opponent was Craig Benson, a gazillionaire businessman, and it sounded like a fun race since researching wealthy businessmen often turns up all kinds of dirt. Shortly after receiving the call, however, I was told that my services might not be needed. The two Republican opponents had entered into a gentleman's agreement with the mutual promise of no negative campaigning. If this were the case, Oppo Man's expertise would not be necessary.

There was also a third Republican candidate who later entered the race—Bruce Keough, an under-funded college professor who was considered a joke with no chance of winning. After all, his opponents were a former U.S. senator and an ultra-rich businessman. And Keough wouldn't have had a chance, except there was a major problem with the Humphrey/Benson "non-aggression" pact. One of Oppo Man's best friends, and a fellow Oppo Man (we'll call him Oppo Man #2) had already been hired by Benson to dig up dirt on Humphrey. So Oppo Man knew that Benson was lying. He had promised not to go negative against Humphrey for one obvious reason: he had already hired Oppo Man #2 to dig up the dirt on Humphrey, and he was going to blindside Humphrey.

Not unexpectedly, the non-aggression pact quickly fell apart when the Manchester *Union-Leader* reported that Benson had already hired Oppo Man #2, in effect breaking this so-called "non-aggression" pact. Now, it is indeed true that many campaigns hire Oppo Men to dig up dirt with no intention of ever using it, but simply as insurance in the event the opposition goes negative first. But Humphrey didn't trust Benson enough to believe this was the case. So when the story broke, I was immediately hired by Humphrey in retaliation.

Benson's Oppo Man #2 then hired yet another Oppo Man (hereby referred to as "Oppo Man #3") to travel to New Hampshire to dig up dirt on Humphrey. What made this funny was that Oppo Man #3 was also a good friend of mine—all three of us, Oppo Men 1 through 3, had worked together at different times through the years.

Then, after I discovered that much of the dirt against Benson involved shady stock transactions regarding his company, Cabletron, I was forced to hire yet another friend and Oppo Man (hereby referred to as Oppo Man #4) who had expertise in that area to help me. So here was the ridiculous situation: Four Oppo Men, all friends, were working on the same race, #1 and #4 for Gordon Humphrey, #2 and # 3 for Craig Benson.

It's not uncommon for opposing Oppo Men in certain campaigns to know each other—most campaigns, regardless of where they are, go to Washington to hire Oppo Men, and there aren't that many of us. On the Republican side, for instance, there are only about fifteen to twenty of us that I know of. So it's not all that rare to have friendly Oppo Men working for opposing sides of campaigns, But two Oppo Men versus another two Oppo Men was extremely unusual, to say the least—particularly in a campaign that started with a non-aggression pact.

Either way, the research yielded plenty for Oppo Man #4 and I to work with for Humphrey—there was so much dirt on Benson it was ridiculous. He had created the company Cabletron, a computer products/networks firm that became the largest employer in the state of New Hampshire. But things quickly went south for the firm, as massive competition had taken a heavy toll on Cabletron's profits and stock price. Wall Street analysts turned from cheerleaders to hecklers. Making matters even worse, Benson's management style was widely viewed as arrogant, erratic, and demoralizing. He resigned as CEO in 1997, then reappointed himself as CEO in 1998, then resigned again in 1999.

To attempt to salvage *some* shareholder value, Benson and his board of directors broke up Cabletron into four smaller companies, and Benson was reported to have pocketed a cool $100 million by cashing in his stock options. His partner, Robert Levine, was reported to have been involved in sales of stock of up to $180 million. Levine, an odd bizarre character who drove around town in a tank and showed up at corporate meetings in camouflage fatigues, was forced to retire, on

December 1, 1997, at the ripe old age of thirty-nine, after his abrasive, obnoxious personality proved "too hot to handle" for Benson and other Cabletron execs.

In an eerie parallel to Enron, stockholders had filed a class-action lawsuit against Benson and Cabletron in 1998, after allegedly being misled about Cabletron's financial health. The case was later settled. In 1994, Cabletron lost a high-profile sex discrimination lawsuit when a federal court ruled that Benson had fired a manager simply because she was a woman. A federal jury ordered a payment of $2.5 million, citing testimony that Benson had said, "Put a guy in there." However, despite this and other unsavory acts too numerous to mention, Benson was still the favorite to win, because he had unlimited funds.

As we attacked Benson non-stop throughout the spring and summer of 2002, Benson returned fire by attacking Humphrey's voting record in the U.S. Senate (in particular a bad vote regarding Social Security) using some good material gleamed by Oppo Men #2 and #3. The race became so nasty between Humphrey and Benson that the third-party candidate, Bruce Keough, began moving up in the polls. He didn't have to do anything to advance—he just sat back and watched the other two kill each other.

In the week or two leading up to the September 17, 2002, primary, we continued to attack Benson relentlessly, hoping to somehow overcome Benson's huge financial advantage in campaign funds. While Humphrey raised an impressive $3.75 million, Benson, using mostly his own personal funds, was able to spend $9.5 million on the race— by far the most ever spent for a gubernatorial race in the history of New Hampshire. As the election neared, polls showed the race to be neck-and-neck between Benson and Humphrey.

So the Humphrey campaign continued attacking until the very end, with Benson responding in kind. In the end, however, the voters were grew sick of watching the two candidates throw grenades at each other and the resulting explosions just translated into votes for the third candidate, the little-known Bruce Keough. Final results: Benson: 36.6 percent, Keough: 33.7 percent, Humphrey: 27.9 percent.

Our attacks worked against Benson, but unfortunately did not translate into Humphrey votes. Instead, the attacks benefited the third candidate Bruce Kehough, who appeared above the fray and far from all the mud being thrown back and forth.

Benson went on to easily win the general election against his Democratic opponent, State Senator Mark Fernald, who suicidally campaigned on a platform of imposing a state income tax in New Hampshire. Not surprisingly, Benson didn't last long as governor, being defeated after just one term of two years. Despite intelligently settling the class-action lawsuit with Cabletron shareholders shortly after being elected and starting his term as governor with a clean slate, Benson's crass behavior continued and he served his term under constant controversy.

For us political hacks, there were two morals to this story that we could learn from:

Moral #1: Negative campaigning, despite being highly effective, does not necessarily translate into votes for the candidate doing the attacking, as was illustrated here with the unexpected showing of the third-party candidate in the race, Bruce Kehough. Another memorable anecdotal example of this phenomenon occurred during the 1996 Republican primary in New Hampshire, when Bob Dole's and Steve Forbes' relentless attacks against each other resulted in many of the votes going to the eventual primary winner, Pat Buchanan.

Moral #2: If a person with a shady past is elected to public office, he or she is quite likely to continue doing unsavory things despite their new job, resulting in their inevitable political self-destruction.

Chapter Twenty-One

THE UNPREDICTABLE NATURE OF OPPOSITION RESEARCH AND NEGATIVE CAMPAIGNING

Opposition research is employed so often in American politics for one reason: for the most part, it works. But one of the most interesting elements of opposition research is how unpredictable it is. While opposition research and negative campaigning are overall wildly successful, there is never a complete guarantee that they will work as expected. There are many different scenarios that could result from them, good or bad for the campaign. And you never know where the opposition hit is going to come from—American politics is, at times, completely unpredictable.

1. Good Research Doesn't Always Translate into Defeating Your Opponent

You never know for certain how voters or campaigns will respond to research. For instance, in 2003, a local Mississippi prosecutor, Democrat Jim Hood, was running for state

Attorney General. I was working for a client who wanted me to dig up dirt on Hood, so I scoured seven different county courthouses where Hood's office had prosecuted cases and found literally dozens of plea bargains in which Hood gave serious sexual predators probation or zero jail time.

The charges in the indictments (or "informations," as they are also called) were very graphic in nature, with language, such as "Mr. Smith then proceeded to put his penis in the mouth of twelve-year-old Miss Jones." And it wasn't just one isolated case—there were so many of them it was ridiculous. In addition, there were many other bad plea bargains in which other serious criminals pled guilty and received little, if any, jail time—far too many to mention here.

Since Hood had such a terrible record as a prosecutor and was running as a Democrat in Mississippi, probably the most right-wing state in America, Oppo Man was certain Hood had zero chance of winning. But he did, easily defeating Republican Scott Newton 63 percent to 37 percent—once again proving that in American politics, anything is possible. Either the voters of Mississippi didn't care about these sexual criminals getting no jail time or the Newton campaign didn't use the issue strongly enough.

It was the same thing in the 2002 races for governor involving gubernatorial nominees Kathleen Sebelius in Kansas and Gennifer Granholm in Michigan. I was hired by a client to dig up dirt on both of them. Sebelius easily won her 2002 gubernatorial elections against Republican Tim Schallenberger, despite her ultraliberal voting record in the state legislature, which included voting against tough sentencing for sexual offenders and acts harmful to minors;

against capital punishment in a state where the voters over-whelmingly supported it; against mandatory minimum sentencing; against repealing the insanity defense; against prosecuting juveniles as adults; against tough sentencing for crimes involving drug dealers, including those near schools; in favor of looser parole laws; in favor of benefit funds for incarcerated criminals but against appropriations for a crime victim reparations board; and also against criminal restitution.

These votes alone, not to mention her votes on taxes and social issues, was one of the worst records Oppo Man had ever seen in any gubernatorial candidate. Her record as state insurance commissioner was also a joke, as premiums skyrocketed. I didn't believe she had any chance of winning, especially considering Kansas was a Republican state, and as mentioned earlier, 2002 was shaping up to be a big Republican year nationwide. But Oppo Man was wrong again, just as I had been with Hood. Sebelius won easily, 53 percent to 45 percent.

In Michigan, Granholm, had formerly been a federal prosecutor and had a "Willie Horton"-type problem. She had given soft plea bargains to dozens of serious criminals, including one William Day. In a plea agreement for an armed robbery charge, Day, who could have been sentenced up to twenty-five years in federal prison, was instead given a sentence of seventy-one months by Granholm. Instead of putting Mr. Day behind bars for a long time, Granholm let him walk early. Upon his release went on one of the biggest bank-robbery sprees in the history of Detroit, robbing seventeen during a four-month span.

Like Hood and Sebelius, Granholm also had an overall poor record as a prosecutor when it came to putting bad guys in jail, and also had very liberal policies towards crime. This smelled like certain disaster to Oppo Man. But once again, Oppo Man was wrong, as Granholm went on to easily defeat her Republican opponent, Dick Posthumus, despite the lieutenant governor being able to run on the coattails of the popular Republican Governor John Engler, and once again despite 2002 being a big Republican year nationwide.

Another common reason for such anomalies is that good opposition research is wasted larger nationwide issues are in play. For instance, in the 2006 elections, plenty of subpar Democratic candidates won simply because voter dissatisfaction with President Bush over Iraq trumped all. A great example was in New Jersey, where Democratic Senator Bob Menendez was re-elected despite the fact that he was up to his ass in serious corruption allegations. Menendez also had the problem of running against Republican Tom Kean, Jr., the son of the most popular governor in the state's history, and a Republican critic of President Bush's Iraq policy who had called for Don Rumsfeld's head to roll. But none of it mattered—voters were so angry at Bush that they took it out on all Republicans, whether or not they supported Bush on Iraq. The same thing happened with Clinton in 1994; many Democrats went down because of Clinton's low popularity ratings.

2. Unpredictable Research: Good Research on Paper Sometimes Backfires in Practice

Sometimes what appears to be good research on paper just doesn't register with the voters. Even when polls show a certain issue will hurt a candidate, it doesn't always happen that way. Here are some examples of what appeared to be good oppo resulting in the opposite of its intention.

On Election Night 2006, the Democrats had gained five Senate seats but needed six to take control of the U.S. Senate. There was one race too close to call as the night ended, but two days later, it was official: Democrat Jim Webb had defeated the popular incumbent Republican George Allen.

One year prior to Election Day, Allen had decided to run for president, taking his 2006 Senate re-election for granted. He had always easily won his prior elections in Virginia for Congress, governor, and then U.S. senator. In his prior race for the Senate, he had knocked off two-term Democratic Senator Chuck Robb. Allen and every other political observer believed (as did I) that Allen's 2006 race for re-election was just a tune-up for his presidential run in 2008.

Wrong.

Most of the media blamed Allen's loss on his ridiculous "macaca" racial slur, when he twice referred to a dark-skinned man filming him with a camcorder at one of his rallies as a "macaca," which literally means "monkey." But there was another reason for Allen's loss. His campaign opposition research produced an issue against Webb that backfired.

Webb had written some pulp fiction books with strong sexual overtones. The Allen campaign believed that Webb's fictional descriptions of incest and pedophilia would hurt him politically. But when Allen tried to make a campaign issue of it, it backfired. Prior to this ad, Allen had been holding a slight lead in the polls. His lead was blown after the ad aired. Allen remained dead even or behind for the remainder of the campaign, and ended up with the Senate's narrowest loss of 2006.

Why did the ad against Webb backfire? Well, voters knew Webb's books were fiction, and the fact that Webb had different talents outside politics (where he was a respected former Secretary of the Navy) was appealing. Being a "renaissance man" of sorts was a novelty and was considered a plus by many voters. Candidates with multiple talents are always attractive, such as Senators Bill Frist of Tennessee and Tom Coburn of Oklahoma (doctors), Sonny Bono (singer), Arnold Schwarzenegger and Ronald Reagan (actors), Congressmen Steve Largent and J. C. Watts of Oklahoma (football players), and Congressmen John Glenn of Ohio and Bill Nelson of Florida (astronauts). Being a pulp-fiction author carries a mysterious aura. So Allen blew it, both with the racial slur and his emphasis on the wrong issue.

3. Misleading Attacks Often Backfire

Sometimes campaigns don't do their homework and don't double-check their opposition research. In these situations, opposition research can backfire.

A good example mentioned earlier was Bob Dole's ad against Steve Forbes during the 1996 New Hampshire primary, which probably cost Dole that state (won by Pat Buchanan). Dole had put out an ad claiming that Steve Forbes' flat tax would result in higher taxes for Americans, which was bullshit. The voters saw through the falsity of the ad and it backfired badly against Dole, particularly since Dole was already vulnerable on the tax issue, having supported and voted for many tax increases while in the Senate. Unfortunately for Steve Forbes, however, the slander against his flat tax did not result in those anti-Dole votes going to Forbes; they went primarily to Buchanan (who finished first) and Lamar Alexander, (who finished in third place, slightly behind Dole).

Another misleading ad also mentioned earlier was probably responsible for Republican Jeb Bush losing to Democrat Lawton Chiles in 1994 during their contest for governor. Bush's ad featured a mother who blamed Chiles for the fact that her daughter's convicted murderer was not on death row. Unfortunately for Bush, the convict's case was still being appealed; a death warrant had not reached Chiles' desk. Using bad or misleading oppo research can be deadly.

One more example was in the 2006 race for Congress between Democrat Mike Arcuri and Republican Ray Meier of New York. An ad by the National Republican Congressional Committee (NRCC) on behalf of Meier backfired badly when it blamed Arcuri for using a hotel phone to call a sex-chat line while on a taxpayer-funded trip. In fact, records indicated that Arcuri hung up immediately and dialed the New York Department of Criminal Justice Services, whose number was one digit different from the sex-chat number.

Arcuri was able to prove that the call was an innocent mistake, and Republican Meier was forced to denounce the ad. The charges in the ad were so flagrantly wrong that several television stations in New York rightfully refused to run the commercial. Final result: Arcuri won 54 percent to 45 percent.

4. Implausible Attack Ads Can Backfire

George Bush the First was the target of attack ads that backfired in 1988 (courtesy of Michael Dukakis) and again in 1992 (courtesy of Republican challenger Pat Buchanan).

In 1988, in response to effective Willie Horton ads used against Dukakis, the Dukakis campaign responded with a similar attack ad of their own against Bush. The ad claimed that Bush was responsible for the murder of a pregnant mother, referring to an escapee from a federal halfway house who (like Willie Horton) went on to commit a heinous crime after escaping. However, the tie from the escapee to Bush was indirect and tenuous at best. Consequently, the public saw the ad for what it was: a desperate and disingenuous attempt to respond to the effective Willie Horton ad. The ad backfired because the public simply refused to believe Bush was soft on crime.

Fast forward to four years later and another attack ad against Bush I, this time courtesy of the Pat Buchanan campaign in the Georgia primary. The ad accused the Bush administration of using taxpayer money to fund pornographic art. Once again, the ad seemed desperate and the voters simply refused to believe it. Like the Dukakis ad four years prior, this ad backfired against Buchanan, and for the same reason; it was implausible.

5. Bad or Misleading Research Can Sometimes Still Work

As mentioned earlier during the 1992 presidential primary in Florida, Bill Clinton used bad research to make the wild claim that his opponent Paul Tsongas was anti-Israel. Even though the claim was fully discredited, and Clinton even took back the claim before the primary, it didn't matter. The ridiculous claim did the trick nonetheless. The claim petrified Jewish voters, and even though Clinton's claim was bogus, those Jewish voters just weren't taking any chances; they voted for Clinton anyway.

Probably the most famous misleading ad that worked was the infamous "daisy ad" of 1964, when Lyndon Johnson was trying to scare Americans into believing that Barry Goldwater was just itching to blow up the world. The ad didn't affect the result of the election, since Johnson was going to win anyway. But it is believed that this devastating ad—shown only once, on September 7, 1964—may have turned Johnson's victory into a rout.

In the ad, a young girl is picking daisies in a field. "Four, five, six, seven," she intones. An announcer's voice (actually the voice used to count down the space launches at Cape Canaveral) begins another, ominous count: "Ten, nine, eight…" At zero the camera has zoomed in on the child's eye. A nuclear bomb explodes. Lyndon Johnson's voice is heard: "These are the stakes. To make a world in which all God's children can live. Or to go into the darkness. We must either love each other. Or we must die." Until the tag line appears, that ad has no explicit partisan content. "Vote for President Johnson on November 3. The stakes are high for you to stay at home."

6. Attack Your Opponent's Religious Views at Your Own Peril

As was the case in 1960 with the JFK issue, attacking a candidate's religion is usually the easiest path to disaster. Senator Rudy Boschwitz learned this the hard way in 1990. Running against fellow Jew Paul Wellsonte, a Boschwitz ad went something like this: "Both candidates were born as Jews and historically this may be a first. But from there on the difference between them is profound. One, Paul Wellstone, has no connection whatsoever with the Jewish community or our communal life. His children were brought up as non-Jews . . . The other candidate is Rudy Boschwitz, whose sense of his people was deeply imbued into him by his parents. They brought Rudy to the U.S. at the age of five, just ahead of the Holocaust, in which many of his family perished. His grandfather was a Rabbi, as were six preceding generations of Boschwitzes. Because of his intense interest in all things Jewish, Rudy is known as the 'Rabbi of the Senate.'"

All of the claims in the ad are true, but voters have never tolerated questioning a candidate's faith or religious beliefs. Wellstone won, 51 percent to 49 percent. (It will be interesting to see in 2008 whether or not Mormon Republican presidential candidate Mitt Romney—the former governor of Massachusetts—will have any problems with Southern evangelical Christians.)

7. You Never Know Where Bad Press Will Turn Up: Good Camcorder Research Often Works

It's routine nowadays to have an anonymous person attend your opponent's campaign events and film his or her speech. This is because when candidates are "preaching to the choir," they often say dumb things in the heat of the moment. When giving a speech to a group the candidate knows is strongly supportive, in their effort to stir up the group, the candidate will sometimes say something that, although good fodder to that particular group, will be offensive to the swing voters that candidates need to court in order to win. If the candidate says something off the wall or something that would not be liked by swing voters, the footage can be deadly. Think Howard Dean and "The Scream Heard Around the World."

In 1998, two-term governor of Alabama and Democrat-turned-Republican Fob James had just defeated Winton Blount in a nasty Republican primary. Once James won the tough primary, he seemed like a shoo-in in the general election against Democrat Lieutenant Governor Don Siegelman.

But there was problem. James had been caught on a camcorder at a meeting of the Alabama Board of Education, strongly opposing public schools teaching the theory of evolution. To mock those who believe humans evolved from apes, the distinguished governor started walking around like an ape, making chimpanzee noises and gestures. In all my years as Oppo Man, I've never seen anything so ridiculous (and hilarious). Result: James went on to lose to Siegelman, 58 percent to 42 percent.

8. Humor Can Actually Soften an Attack Ad and Make It More Acceptable to the Public

There are many excellent examples of oppo being used effectively in humorous ads, but I'll stick to two favorites.

In the wake of his involvement in the Keating 5 scandal, Alan Cranston was vulnerable in his 1986 re-election race for the Senate against Edwin Zschau (pronounced "Shau"). You know those corny "Greatest Hits" albums you see advertised on TV in the middle of the night, either for some has-been who hasn't had a hit song in twenty years or some guy no one's ever heard of? You know how they scroll the song titles down the screen as they play snippets of the songs?

The Cranston campaign did a spin-off on this type of TV ad called "Ed Zschau's Greatest Hits," and it looked like a real commercial, with song titles scrolling down such as "I'm Gonna Raise Your Taxes Blues" and "Double Talk Zschau." The latter was a catchy country tune that opened up something like this: "I'm a' double-talking Zschau, talkin' out of both sides of my mouth."

It was hilarious. It accused Zschau of raising taxes and being a double-talker without being nasty—instead, it was funny and still clearly got the message across. Ingenious. The beatable Cranston went on to defeat Zschau 51 percent to 49 percent.

In 1982, Montana's Democrat senator John Melcher was attacked by his opponent for being "out of step" with Montana. His response, which was effective and very funny at the same time, featured speaking cows coming to Melcher's defense. In any other case, this would sound ridiculous, but in this case it worked since Melcher was also a veterinarian. One of the cows said "Did you hear about those city slickers out there bad-mouthing Doc Melcher?" and the other cow responds "One of them was stepping in what they had been trying to sell. He kept calling me a steer." The ad worked, as Melcher and his cows went on to victory; 55 percent to 42 percent.

9. Debate Research: Just Too Easy

Sometimes campaigns get lucky and good oppo is handed to them on a silver platter when their opponent says or does something stupid during a debate. The footage is right there; all you need to do is to put it in a television ad. The 2002 U.S. Senate race in Tennessee featured former Republican governor and former presidential candidate Lamar Alexander versus Democratic Congressman Bob Clement, son of the state's former governor. Now, it's a rule of thumb in political campaigns never to go negative if you have a lead in the polls of at least ten points over your opponent. However, sometimes a campaign leading comfortably will be given something too good *not* to use. That was the case in one of the Alexander-Clement debates.

During the debate, Alexander accused Clement of being formerly mixed up with the controversial Butcher Brothers, whose corrupt banking practices had led federal investigators down a paper trail of illegal loans, forged documents, and various other fraudulent actions. (Jake Butcher's United American Bank collapsed on February 14, 1983, the fourth-largest bank failure in U.S. history.) Clement angrily denied any involvement with the Butcher brothers, and the Alexander campaign couldn't believe Clement actually denied something just about everyone in Tennessee knew to be true. So, despite being up by over ten points in the polls, the Alexander campaign simply ran an ad that began with the debate footage showing an angry Clement denying involvement with the Butcher brothers. You could see the veins popping out of his neck. This footage was followed by a simple photo from the United American Bank's annual report, showing a smiling Clement on the bank's Board of Directors, with the smiling Butcher brothers at his side.

Either Clement was too dumb to realize his claim could be easily rebutted, or he was too dumb to remember that he was actually on the bank's Board of Directors. In fairness, I have to add here that Bob Clement is one of the nicest Southern gentlemen you will ever meet. Politically savvy, not so much; but very nice.

The same fate befell New Mexico Attorney General Patricia Madrid in 2006. Challenging Republican Congresswoman Heather Wilson, Madrid looked like a winner until the two women debated shortly before the election. During the debate, Wilson asked Madrid for a pledge not to raise taxes if elected.

Madrid's response? No response. Like a deer caught in the headlights, Madrid froze for twenty seconds, simply staring blindly into the camera. She finally responded by not answering the question, instead attacking President Bush.

Like Clement before her, Madrid was caught on camera looking totally clueless, and the footage was also effectively used in a TV ad at the end of the campaign. Final Result: Madrid lost by 875 votes. The gaffe was turned into a very effective last-second ad for Wilson, who went on to win by only 1,500 votes.

10. Doctored Photos and Misleading Visuals: Sometimes Bad Research Works and Sometimes It Doesn't

Probably the most notorious use of a doctored photo to win an election was way back in 1950, when Republican John Butler was challenging Democratic senator Millard Tydings of Maryland. Tydings had chaired a Senate committee hearing, where he had questioned Communist leader Earl Browder. The Butler campaign had a photo of Tydings looking tough as he questioned Browder, but that's not the photo they used. Instead, the photo was doctored to make it appear as if the two were having a friendly conversation.

Something like this would probably backfire badly today, but back in the days of the "Red Scare" it worked. The doctored photo was effective and scary; making Tydings look as if he was being friendly to a communist. Final Result: Butler 53 percent, Tydings 46 percent.

Fast forward to twelve years later:

In 1962, an independent Republican group supporting Richard Nixon for governor in California really went off the deep end. Taking the Tydings chicanery one step further, the group published a pamphlet that featured a photo of Nixon's opponent, then-governor Pat Brown, bowing down to then Soviet Leader Nikita Khrushchev.

Except the photo was fake. Maybe this sort of thing would have worked in 1950, but by 1962, times had changed. The Nixon campaign, which had nothing to do with the photo, and the state GOP, chaired at the time by Casper Weinberger, repudiated the pamphlet and the photo.

11. The Best Opposition Research Ads of All Time: Ads That Single-Handedly Sank the Opponent

There are so many good one to choose from here, but, for simplicity's sake, I'll stick with the most obvious ones and my all-time favorites. The first winner is an ad by the Democratic National Senatorial Committee on behalf of Montana Senator Max Baucus in 2002 that forced his opponent, Republican Mike Taylor, to drop out the day after the ad was aired. The ad featured disco music playing in the background and footage of an ad Taylor ran in the early 1980s for his hair salon. The campaign ad pointed out that Taylor had diverted federal student loans when he ran a cosmetology school. Even more effectively, the ad showed footage of Taylor massaging another man's face, wearing a tight suit with an open shirt, and his hand reaching down in a manner that made it look as though he was reaching for the other man's crotch. Obviously, it falsely implied that Taylor was gay; Taylor dropped out of the race the next day.

The second winner is one I've already mentioned: the infamous 1988 Bush campaign's Willie Horton/crime ad. This one is a winner because it enabled Bush to overcome an eighteen-point deficit and pull out to an eight-point lead, a lead he never relinquished. I cannot think of any single issue in any presidential campaign that affected the outcome so drastically—or any issue that so justifiably did so. The American people had the right to know that Dukakis' weekend furlough program for prisoners, the only one of its kind in the country, had led directly to a violent crime.

An Honorable Mention has to be given to Ed Koch in 1977. It always marvels Oppo Man how talented good political media people are. First they have to be able to take hundreds of pages of research material provided by Oppo Men and Oppo Women, then have the pollsters test the relevant issues to see which hits piss off the voters the most. Then comes the part where they really earn their money: Putting the most damaging research into thirty-second spots that the voters will clearly understand. I know from experience how difficult it can be to whittle down this information. Now try to imagine an ad man (or woman) creating an ad that lasts only ten seconds but could win an election for their candidate.

In 1977, Ed Koch was an unknown congressman from an upper east-side Manhattan district running for mayor of New York City. No one knew who he was in Brooklyn, Queens, the Bronx, or Staten Island. He was running in a field that included big names, all far more well known than Koch was: then-Lieutenant Governor Mario Cuomo; the radical congresswoman from Greenwich Village, Bella Abzug; the city's most popular Hispanic politician, Congressman Herman Badillo from the Bronx; the city's most popular black politician, then-Manhattan Borough President Percy E. Sutton; and the beleaguered incumbent, clubhouse politician Abe Beame, who had led the city to the brink of bankruptcy.

Koch's campaign theme was "competence," since the city had just suffered through twelve years of poor leadership; four years of Beame, and eight years prior of John Lindsay. Lindsay was the good-looking but incompetent mayor that brought all the crime, welfare, and high taxes to New York City and turned that once-great—and eventually to be great again—city into the dump it was back in the day.

So how did the unknown Koch get his message across in ten seconds? Media man *par excellence* David Garth did it thusly:

"After eight years of charisma [showing a picture of the handsome but failed Lindsay]; and after four years of the club-house [showing a picture of the failed Abe Beame], why not try some COMPETENCE [showing picture of Koch]."

Juxtaposing a positive message of Koch with the negative images of Lindsay and Beame (and by inference, the rest of the field) was sheer brilliance. **Positive and negative campaigning together in that one 10-second sentence . . . incredible**

✳ ✳ ✳

Early in this book I explained why the negative aspects of political campaigns are a necessary evil. That it's impossible to have an educated electorate if that electorate doesn't have all the information out there regarding the candidates they have to choose from. Once voters have all the information—the good, the bad, and the ugly—they can then pick and choose for themselves what matters and doesn't matter.

For instance, as I also mentioned earlier, most Americans didn't care that President Clinton was getting "lip service" from an intern. But Americans still *had the right to know.* Otherwise, where do you draw the line? Which elitists get to decide what's good for the voters to know and what's not good? There is no middle ground. The voters have the right to know as much as possible.

In his book *In Defense of Negativity*, Vanderbilt University Professor John G. Geer articulates this point with greater clarity than I ever could. Geer begins his book with these quotes by John Stuart Mill and one from Geer himself:

Mill: *Truth. . . has to be made by the rough process of a struggle between combatants fighting under hostile banners . . . Campaigns are not feel-good exercises; they are pitched battles for control of the government. The stakes are often high and the competition is usually fierce. The real issue should be whether or not candidates present the information in campaigns that is useful to voters. The tone of that information should be a secondary issue, at best.*

Geer: *There is a consensus among policy-makers and political elites that attack advertising in campaigns, like crack cocaine, is dangerous to the well-being of our society . . . The public shares this distaste for negative advertising. In poll after poll, data confirm Bartel's observation. In July 2000, nearly 60 percent of the public, according to a Gallup Poll, was dissatisfied with how candidates conduct their campaigns (Brooks 2000a).*

Then Geer answers all the naysayers:

Why are political commentators so troubled by negativity? Any deliberative process usually benefits from having criticism and debate . . . Politics is rough and tumble; why isn't attack advertising thought of in those terms? Why are we so worried about "civility" in campaigns? If some aspect of a candidate's record is alarming, is it not important to raise that concern in an attention-grabbing fashion? Shouldn't the public understand the seriousness of the problem?

Negativity plays an important and under-appreciated role in democracies. In fact, I will argue that the practice of democracy requires negativity by candidates. In other words, the give and take of democratic politics demands that we know both the good and bad points of candidates and their policy goals. The opposition is well-suited to discussing the weaknesses of the other side. Therefore, in order to learn about the risks and problems associated with potential office holders, we need the opposition, in effect, to "go negative." When going negative, candidates can actually advance the debate, not undermine it. This simple point seems forgotten in many of the discussions about the subject.

There is an asymmetry between negative and positive campaign appeals. For a negative appeal to be effective, the sponsor of that appeal must marshal more evidence, on average, than for positive appeals. The public, like our legal system, operates on the assumption of "innocent until proven guilty." A candidate cannot simply assert that their opposition favors a tax increase. They must provide some evidence for that claim or it does not work and may in fact backfire on the sponsor of the attack. By contrast, that same candidate can claim he or she favors a tax cut, with far less documentation.

Geer then explains why negativity promotes democracy:

But I want to say more than just that democracy can survive negativity. I'm making a bolder claim: negativity can advance and improve the prospects for democracy. Without negativity, no nation can credibly think of itself as democratic.

Geer then again quotes John Stuart Mill:

If the (dissenting) opinion is right, they are deprived of the opportunity of exchanging error for truth; if wrong, they lose, what is almost as great a benefit, the clearer perception and livelier impression of the truth, produced by its collision with error. ("On Liberty," 79)

Second, criticism can increase the quality of information available to voters as they make choices in elections. To make good decisions, they need to know the past record of candidates and what they propose to do in the future. A central part of that information involves understanding the shortcomings of candidates.

The bottom line is that criticism is important because those out of power must have the right and ability to raise doubts about those in power (and visa versa). Otherwise, the public does not have access to full information "about the relevant alternative policies and their likely consequences" (Dahl 1998, 37).

Geer then explains how negativity increases the quality of information given to the voters in order for them to make an educated vote:

Imagine for a second buying a car without knowing about its problems. That would be a significant risk. In American election, we usually have to choose between two candidates. Each candidate will happily provide voters with their good points, but they are unlikely to supply their bad points. That, as noted earlier, comes from the opposition often in the form of attack advertising.

Geer then finally makes the important point that negative advertising holds political candidates accountable for their actions:

If the public wants to have accountability, someone has to do the accounting and that accounting is not done through positive, feel-good appeals, but through harsh political attack where voters are made aware of the problems of the incumbent.

Any effort to curtail negativity is far worse than enduring harsh rhetoric, since it means that the ability of the opposition to hold the other side accountable for their actions would be weakened. If negativity ever happened to disappear from our electoral battles, we can safely assume that so would our freedoms and any chance we have to lay claim to being a democratic nation.

Chapter Twenty-Two

TOM DELAY, RONNIE EARLE, AND OPPO MAN

O ne of the most memorable events in my career involved the battle between Tom DeLay and Ronnie Earle. On September 28, 2005, Travis County (Austin, Texas) prosecutor Ronnie Earle indicted Texas Congressman Tom DeLay for "conspiracy to violate Texas state election laws." It all had to do with the "Texas Republican Majority PAC (TRMPAC)," a political action committee (PAC) DeLay had created. Allegedly, DeLay had been laundering money from that PAC, through the federal Republican National Committee, and back into state races in Texas. This helped Republicans gain control of the Texas legislature in 2002 for the first time since Reconstruction. Along with DeLay, eight corporations were indicted for making illegal campaign contributions to DeLay's PAC. The indicted companies were Sears, Roebuck, and Co., Bacardi USA, Cracker Barrel, Westar Energy, Diversified Collection Services, Williams Companies, the Alliance for

Quality Nursing Home Care, and Questerra Corp.

In January 2006, I was hired by a client to dig up the goods on DeLay's prosecutor and nemesis, Ronnie Earle. Ironically, Oppo Man had one prior experience down in Texas doing research that also involved Tom DeLay. Back in 2000, DeLay's re-election campaign was confused when they were suddenly and unexpectedly challenged in the Republican primary by a guy named Michael Fjetland. No one had any idea who he was. Was he a serious challenger? Was he some kind of wacko? No one knew. So Oppo Man was asked to inconspicuously attend a GOP meeting that Fjetland, DeLay, and other local Republicans were attending in the courthouse in Sugarland, Texas (DeLay's hometown), keep a low profile, and find out what this guys agenda was. Since the meeting was open to the public, I figured it would be easy to remain inconspicuous among the regular folks.

It turns out Fjetland was no big deal, just a new guy in town wanting to meet other Republican politicians and get his foot in the door. He figured running against DeLay would at least get him noticed, which it sure did. He seemed like a nice-enough guy just trying to use his candidacy to hob knob with the local Republican politicos. (In the end he didn't run a serious campaign, losing to DeLay 83 percent to 17 percent).

So after attending the meeting and figuring out what Fjetland was up to, I reported my findings to the DeLay campaign, figuring I had done a good job and was inconspic-uous at the GOP meeting. Until the next day, when Tom DeLay's daughter and campaign manger calls me and asks, "Marks, are you crazy? You think you were inconspicuous last night?"

Well, I did.

She continued, half annoyed and half laughing: "My dad says he knew right away who you were."

I couldn't imagine how, since we had never met.

"Everyone in that room knew who you were. No one in Sugarland wears a suit jacket and tie. Not even in a court-house." She was right.

While this may have been an amusing anecdotal story from 2000, my later trip in January 2006 was no laughing matter. DeLay was fighting for his political life (which he would eventually lose) whilst at the same time trying to keep himself out of jail (which as of this writing almost two years later still remains up in the air).

So now I was in Austin trying to figure out what DeLay's nemesis and Travis County Prosecutor was up to.

At that point, four of the eight indicted companies (Diversified Collections Services, Sears, Roebuck, and Co., Cracker Barrel, and Questerra) had reached settlements with Earle's office in which they agreed to donate money to one of Ronnie Earle's pet political projects.

As I saw from courthouse documents in Austin, in their settlement agreements with Ronnie Earle's office, the four companies agreed to contribute over $200,000 to "financially support a nonpartisan, balanced, and publicly informative program or series of programs relating to the role of corporations in American democracy." This program that Earle suggested was at Stanford University and was called the "*Center for Deliberative Democracy*," a group supposedly designed to "educate" voters before casting their votes. One of the companies objected to this and it was ultimately agreed that the money would go to the

University of Texas. But it is telling that Earle wanted the money to go to the Stanford program.

As I would soon find out in my research, the "Center for Deliberative Democracy" (CDD) was a liberal outfit run by professors James Fishkin and Robert Luskin, and hardly "non-partisan."

The CDD's stated goal was to "create more educated voters" by holding town meetings across the country in which voters would be polled on a number of political issues. This would be followed by several days of having the participants listen to "experts" on both sides of relevant political issues. At the end, the voters would again be polled, which would show they now were more "educated" voters. This was the group's ostensible aim. However, Oppo Man's cursory initial investigation found that their agenda had nothing to do with creating "educated" voters. Quite the opposite.

Far from creating more "educated" and "sophisticated" voters, its real purpose was voter intimidation into an Orwellian-style "groupthink," with all of their "deliberative polling" appearing to be designed to move voters in only one direction: *to the left*. A recording Oppo Man retrieved from the CDD itself recorded one panel of so-called "experts" whose political views were overwhelmingly against George W. Bush's policies. The agenda of the Fishkin/Luskin "Deliberate Democracy" is further exposed by their own published statistics, where on *every single political issue*, "deliberative polling" moved the voters to the left and to the Democratic Party side of the debate.

For instance, consider the following crime issues that were polled, and how those polled felt before and after being educated by the CDD's so-called "experts":

- Sending More Offenders to Prison is Effective Way to Fight Crime: Before 57 percent; After 38 percent
- Stiffer Sentences Generally as an Effective Way of Fighting Crime: Before 77 percent; After 64 percent
- Favoring Compulsory Training and Counseling [Instead Of Prison]: Before 49 percent; After 63 percent

Same type of poll questions regarding foreign affairs, economic issues, and other social issues. The voters are always "educated" to change their votes to the liberal position.

So now you have a clear picture of the agenda of the "nonpartisan" group Ronnie Earle originally wanted the settlement money to go to in the TRMPAC case.

But it gets worse.

I found that the wording of Earle's own settlements with the four corporations was contradictory. The settlements were worded exactly like this: "The defendant, after discussions with the district attorney, has decided to financially support a nonpartisan, balanced and publicly informative program or series of programs relating to the role of corporations in American democracy." The companies that settled also acknowledged that corporate contributions "constitute a genuine threat to democracy."

Now first of all, Ronnie Earle's original choice as beneficiary for the settlement money, the "Center for Deliberative Democracy" was far from "nonpartisan" and "balanced." Secondly, how can this statement possibly use the words "nonpartisan" and "balanced" when the settlements also required the companies acknowledge that corporate contributions are a "threat" to democracy? The word "threat" alone is not "nonpartisan, nor balanced," but indeed extremely *partisan, unbalanced, and clearly against* the role of corporate money in American democracy.

So how did Ronnie Earle, a county prosecutor, get all this political power to indict Tom DeLay in the first place? Under Texas law, the Attorney General does not have the power to prosecute infractions dealing with state campaigns or crimes against the state. Instead, that responsibility lies with the Travis County DA (Ronnie Earle), under the state's Public Integrity Unit Law. This Texas law gives statewide prosecutorial powers to prosecute "political crimes" to only *one* county prosecutor, the one serving Travis County (where Texas' state capitol Austin lies).

And Mr. Earle was doing it with relish. Against the most hated man in Texas Democratic circles: Tom "The Hammer" DeLay; hated for being largely responsible for the Republicans taking control of the Texas legislature for the first time since the Reconstruction. Even worse, when this new Republican-controlled legislature would convene in January 2005, they would draw new U.S. congressional lines throughout the Lone Star State, which would make certain that the Democrats would *lose* congressional seats, while the Republicans would *gain* congressional seats.

This process is referred to as "gerrymandering," where every ten years, after the census is taken, each of the fifty state legislatures redraws that state's U.S. Congressional district lines. Whatever party is in power takes advantage of that power and draws the lines in usually-convoluted ways that will maximize the number of congressmen from their party winning congressional seats. For instance, a hypothetical state of 6 million voters would have twelve congressional districts, with roughly 200,000 voters per district. If the party in power had roughly 2/3 of the voters on their side, the fair thing to do would be to carve out twelve districts where roughly eight would be dominated my the majority party's voters and four by the minority party's voters. That would be fair.

But what if the party in power drew up twelve congressional districts where *every single district* was 2/3 majority voters and 1/3 minority voters? In that case, the majority would win *all twelve* congressional seats! And win them all easily, roughly 67-33 in each district.

Now, to the best of Oppo Man's vast knowledge, no state legislature has ever had the stones to do something so brazen. However, it's totally normal for the party in control of state legislatures to take advantage of the gerrymandering process.

For 130 years, when the Democrats took advantage of the process and were able to "gerrymander" the congressional lines however they damn well pleased in Texas, no one complained. But look what happened as the Texas legislature was ready to convene in 2005 and the "gerrymandering" would now finally be done by the Republicans. Did the Democrats accept it? Granted, they had some reason to complain, since middle-of-the-decade gerrymandering is highly unusual. Yet, they couldn't handle it.

Eleven Texas Democratic senators (soon to be known as "The Texas Eleven") decided that, instead of convening the legislature as all adult legislators do every two years in all fifty states, they would instead flee the state to bordering Oklahoma, so the Texas Senate wouldn't have enough members to vote on *any* legislation (the minimum number of members needed to pass legislation is referred to as a "quorum"). They were able to get away with this nonsense because the governor of Oklahoma, Brad Henry, was a Democrat.

Eventually, the Texas legislators had to leave the state of Oklahoma. So did they go back to Texas like adults and finally convene the legislature? Nope. Instead these geniuses fled to a *different* neighboring state with a Democratic governor, New Mexico, and Governor Bill Richardson. While the Democrats hid in Oklahoma and later New Mexico, Texas Governor Rick Perry put out "Wanted" posters of the fleeing legislators on the Internet as part of the state's "Most Wanted."

Politically, the Texas Democrats looked like idiots to the public. Governor Perry made great political hay out of the fact that—because the legislature was unable to reconvene—much-needed legislation to help kids, health care, education, senior citizens, etc. was unable to become law because there was no legislative "quorum" due to the childish behavior of "The Texas Eleven."

Eventually, the political pressure on one of "The Texas Eleven" became too unbearable, as Texas Senator John Whitmire defected, returned to Austin, and gave Governor Perry and the senate the "quorum" they needed to go to work. The other ten degenerates eventually returned with their collective tails between their legs. So the Republicans now could pass any legislation they wanted, including the dreaded (to the Democrats) gerrymandering of the congressional districts to favor the GOP.

So it was against this backdrop that Ronnie Earle decided to indict Tom DeLay for conspiracy to violate Texas campaign finance laws. Can you imagine this?

Here we have Ronnie Earle, Fighter for Justice, taking on the evil Tom DeLay for alleged campaign finance abuses, while DeLay's only real crime appeared to be (to Oppo Man at least) that he had the political savvy to help the Republicans wrest control of the Texas legislature, and hence, the Republican gerrymandering of the congressional lines. Yes, money laundering is a very serious accusation. However, according to the *Wall Street Journal*, DeLay's scheme had been executed by the Texas *Democrats* in 1991, under Governor Ann Richards. The "Lone Star Fund–Texas," the leadership PAC of then-Congressman Martin Frost (D-TX), also contributed money to the national Democratic Senatorial Campaign Committee ($5,000 during the period of October 17 through November 25). During the period of October 29 through November 5, 2002, the very same DSCC made contributions to nine candidates for the Texas House of Representatives, totaling $40,000—almost exactly the type of transaction for which Earle was indicting DeLay for in the TRMPAC case.

So this is where Oppo Man comes in, trying to determine if this was a legitimate prosecution or merely a political prosecution. It appeared to be, on the face of it, pure bullshit. However, whether or not DeLay is actually guilty of the charges leveled against him remains to be seen. As of this writing, Tom DeLay has yet to be prosecuted, nor have the other four other companies under indictment reached any settlements with Ronnie Earle's office.

✶ ✶ ✶

So who was the real villain in this situation? Let's take a close look:

1. What About Ronnie Earle's Own Campaign Finances?

Ronnie Earle's crusade against Tom DeLay is supposedly against "the evil influence of money in American politics," which he has said is "*as serious as the dangers of terrorism.*" But what about Ronnie Earle's *own* campaign finances?

In 1996, Ronnie Earle accepted controversial campaign cash from a discredited lottery commission lobbyist and his wife, causing a state investigation. Although it was illegal for a state official to take money from the lottery commission's lobbyist, GTECH, Earle nonetheless took the cash while claiming he wasn't a state official. In 1997, the lottery commission investigated whether or not Earle's accepting the money violated the law, with Earle splitting hairs over whether or not he was considered a "statewide official," which in this capacity he was. The matter was dropped as moot when GTECH was forced to get rid of the offending lobbyist, former Lt. Governor Ben Barnes, but not before Barnes and his partner Ricky Knox pocketed a cool $23 million in a buyout agreement with GTECH.

Earle's friend Ben Barnes and partner Ricky Knox both received 4 percent of Texas lottery revenue while on the job. The grey area of whether or not Ronnie Earle was a state official seems unimportant. At the very least, Earle flagrantly violated the spirit of the law, if not the letter of the law, when he accepted campaign cash his friend the lobbyist who was run out of town after making so much money.

In addition, Barnes and his wife contributed $4,000 to Ronnie Earle's 1996 campaign for Travis County DA. Not only that, Barnes continued to help Earle financially years later, being one of his fund-raisers in 2000, and contributing another $1,000 to Earle.

Even more remarkably, Barnes' chicanery continued unabated, as he was a key player in the discredited 2004 "60 Minutes II" hit job on President Bush's Air National Guard service. Barnes was Dan Rather's discredited "corroborative witness" against Bush, while also being a fundraiser at the time for John Kerry. And Barnes continues to be a big shot in Texas Democratic politics as of this writing, as if nothing ever happened.

2. Ronnie Earle's Biggest Contributors in Hotly Contested 1996 Race Were Lobbyists.

Watchdog group "Public Citizen" had this to say about Earle's campaign: "This is a really unusual pattern for a district attorney, one would always question the wisdom of taking large contributions from a group whose ethics you're supposed to police. Lobbyists are by and large his biggest contributors."

Earle's lame response to collecting all this lobbyist money? "Austin lobbyists live here, and they're as concerned about crime and the safety of their families as any other Austenite." This quote by Earle is truly insulting to anyone with an IQ over 17.

3. Ronnie Earle's Non-Prosecution of Attorney General Dan Morales

In July 2003, Texas Attorney General Dan Morales pled guilty to federal charges of mail fraud and income tax evasion.

Houston trial lawyer Joe Jamail claimed Morales asked for $1 million in campaign contributions from him in 1995 in exchange for his representation of the state in the tobacco lawsuit. Jamail said he thought it was a solicitation of a bribe and reported it to Ronnie Earle. Earle did nothing.

The wrongdoing by Morales was only prosecuted, after Earle left office in 1999, by then-Attorney General (now U.S. Senator) John Cornyn, who turned his evidence over to federal authorities. In March 2003, a federal grand jury indicted Morales for allegedly trying to secure hundreds of millions of dollars in bogus legal fees for one of his crony's attorney Marc Murr, in the state's anti-tobacco lawsuit. The panel also charged Dan Morales with "illegally using political funds to help purchase a $770,000," according to the *Houston Chronicle*. On October 30, 2003, Morales was sentenced to four years in prison.

This may be coincidental, but Earle received an endorsement from Morales in his tough 1996 re-election campaign mentioned previously.

So what to make of all of this Ronnie Earle/Tom DeLay debacle?

Well, as of this writing, Tom DeLay has yet to go to trial two years after his indictment. The conspiracy charge against him has been thrown out by the courts, but DeLay still faces the money-laundering charge. Also, the four corporate defendants who did not reach settlements with Earle's office have still not reached settlements, meaning they will fight Earle in court, or Earle will drop the cases against them. And the LBJ School has yet to spend the settlement money, as they've kept promising to do for two years now. According to an LBJ spokesman, the money will be spent on a yet-to-be-determined project regarding "ethics in government."

Finally, while Earle hasn't had the time or inclination to prosecute DeLay, he has somehow found time to star in a documentary film "The Big Buy," produced by film producer Mark Birnbaum, who has a long history of producing left-wing films, including one supporting the Communists in Nicaragua during the Cold War. In "The Big Buy" Ronnie Earle pontificates about how the threat of corporate money in American politics constitutes as big a threat to American democracy as terrorism.

It's bad enough how many reckless prosecutors in America try their cases in the media. This is the first one I've ever heard of being tried in a movie years before the accused even goes to trial.

Bottom Line: Whether or not Tom DeLay violated any laws remains to be seen. However, what has already been seen, and seen clearly, is an out-of-control politically motivated prosecutor by the name of Ronnie Earle.

Chapter Twenty-Three

ONLY IN OHIO: GOOD STATE GONE BAD?

O ver the years, I've spent a good deal of time in Ohio, which was one of my favorite states, researching everything from local legislative races to statewide races. Ohio always looked to be what oppo men refer to as a "good government" state. Ohio's governor and both U.S. Senators were all dull but apparently honest and competent guys: Governor Robert Taft, Senator (and former Governor) George Voinovich, and Senator Mike DeWine. All of the corruption of the past in Cleveland, Columbus, Cincinnati, and even Youngstown (after Congressman James Traficant was put away in 2002) seemed to have been cleaned up. In all the races where I'd done research, the winning candidate was never crooked (as far as I could tell).

That all changed in 2006, with scandals involving Governor Taft, House Speaker Larry Householder, and State Treasurer Joe Deters—all Republicans. I had researched Deters back in 2002 when he was the Hamilton County (Cincinnati) prosecutor running for state treasurer. During my research, I didn't uncover anything terrible in his past except for the usual bad plea bargains you'll find with just about any prosecutor.

Then came the case of Frank Gruttadauria, a broker for Cowen Corp., S.G. Cowen Inc., and Lehman Brothers in Chicago and Cleveland. He was sent to jail for fleecing clients out of $125 million by transferring money to various accounts over fifteen years. While he was negotiating his plea deal (which ultimately resulted in a seven-year sentence), he fingered three employees from Deters' office, claiming he raised $110,000 for Deters' campaign and in return was given plum government contracts, having been put on the #3 spot on a state list of preferred brokers, despite his lack of expertise in the type of trades in which the state was active. In fact, according to the court records, the broker bungled his first few trades with the state and needed help completing the transactions.

Three of Deters' associates were indicted. His chief of staff was fined a mere $1,000; one of his chief fundraisers (who helped the illegal "campaign dollars for government contracts" deal go through) was fined $5,000; and a third Deters flunky, a lobbyist, received probation. Can you believe these weak penalties for the serious crimes of giving favored government contracts to a major campaign contributor through an already-agreed-upon quid pro quo?! People generally go for long stays in jail for these types of crimes.

But it gets worse. Deters wasn't even indicted. He instead resigned his position as state treasurer and ran for his old job in Cincinnati as Hamilton County prosecutor. And despite the three guilty pleas of his flunkies, Deters denied it all and continued to stand by his associates and labeled the prosecution "bullshit" and a "vindictive" political witch-hunt. He even continued to employ one of them for more than $45,000 throughout the Cuyahoga County grand jury investigation and during his campaign to re-take the position of Hamilton County prosecutor.

As if this weren't bad enough for Ohio Republicans, in 2005 the squeaky-clean-appearing Republican Governor, Bob Taft, who was easily elected and re-elected in 1998 and 2002, pled no contest to four counts of receiving illegal gifts, and became the state's first governor to be convicted of a crime while in office. As a result, Taft had a 15 percent approval rating, the lowest in state history.

Then there was Republican Speaker of the House Larry Householder. I had previously been hired by a client working on behalf of Householder who wanted me to dig up dirt on key Democratic legislative candidates during different election cycles. Householder became embroiled in a scandal involving use of county employees to renovate a restaurant of which he is part owner, resulting in his resignation as speaker.

As a result of all these Republican scandals, every major Republican running in Ohio in 2006 got his clock cleaned. Not only did Ohio Republicans have to deal with George W. Bush's poor approval ratings, which were bringing down Republican candidates all over America, they were also plagued by all the corruption in their backyard.

I had also worked earlier in 2006 for a client who wanted me to dig up dirt on Democratic Congressman Sherrod Brown, who would go on to defeat the incumbent Republican Senator Mike DeWine. The research on Brown revealed some pretty damaging material for a campaign in a red state, such as his support for illegal aliens, higher taxes, and controversial lobbyists, but none of it mattered. Brown was a Democrat and DeWine was a Republican in an awful Republican year.

Maybe I was wrong all along about Ohio being a "good government" state, and corrupt things had been going on behind the scenes that I never knew about, particularly within the Republican Party. Either way, I have never seen any single state's politics go south so quickly.

Chapter Twenty-Four

THE BUSH BROTHERS (W. AND JEB) VERSUS KATHERINE HARRIS IN FLORIDA

I n the fall and winter of 2005, I had an unusual job working for a client who wanted me to dig up dirt on Democratic Senator Bill Nelson of Florida, who was running for re-election in 2006. His likely Republican opponent would be none other than (as far as the state's Democrats were concerned) the most despised and hated woman in Florida's history: Katherine Harris.

What I was shocked to learn from day one on the job was that Harris was not only despised by Florida Democrats, but she was *also* the most despised and hated woman by arguably the three most powerful *Republicans* in America at that time: President George W. Bush, then-Florida Governor Jeb Bush (who was finishing his last term, due to term limits), and GOP political guru extraordinaire Karl Rove.

In the end, my research on Nelson turned out to useless and didn't have much impact on the race. That's because there was a much bigger, weirder story taking place—Katherine

Harris's "Battle Royale" against the Bush brothers. The Bush/Harris brawl was the only game in town. The election wound up having zero to do with Bill Nelson's rich record (his time in the U.S. Senate and as Florida's State Treasurer and Insurance Commissioner) and became a referendum on Katherine Harris

No normal race has a Republican U.S. Senate nominee being vehemently opposed by the same state's Republican governor and the country's Republican president. At first it just seemed so bizarre to me. Harris had saved W. during the 2000 recount. She had also saved brother Jeb from the major embarrassment he would have experienced had Gore won the presidency because Jeb was unable to deliver his red home state to his brother.

Remember, it was Jeb who told his brother George "not to worry" about Florida as the polls were tightening during the final week of the campaign. In fact, Jeb had "guaranteed" George's victory. So unconcerned was Jeb with the Florida vote on Election Day, he didn't even bother to hang around Florida that night, instead spending the evening in DC with his brother and parents. Katherine Harris saved Jeb's bacon, as well as his brother's.

Finally, Harris saved Karl Rove from political oblivion, where he would have certainly been headed had Gore won the election. Instead, with W.'s victory, Rove became the most powerful political operative in the United States. So none of this made any sense. Why would these three guys be trying so vehemently and viciously to oppose the woman who saved all their asses in 2000 during the presidential recount in Florida?

I felt uncomfortable from the beginning. On the one

hand, I admired Harris and how she handled herself in 2000. I though it was incredible the way she stood firm under heavy vicious personal and political attack to make sure the votes would be recounted cleanly (of course, many liberals would say "to make sure Bush won"). So I wanted to do anything I could to help her to win that Senate seat. On the other hand, I felt intense loyalty towards both George W. and Jeb Bush. As mentioned earlier, I had worked personally to help both of them get elected. I had personally produced and aired 527 and "independent expenditure" negative TV ads against both Al Gore in 2000 and John Kerry in 2004. I had also worked briefly for Jeb Bush, doing press during his ill-fated effort to defeat Lawton Chiles for governor of Florida in 1994.

Was the Bush-Harris feud something personal I didn't know about? She still saved both brothers in 2000. Wasn't that the big picture? Nope, as I soon learned what happened.

After helping W. get elected, Harris was rewarded when the 2000 census came out and new congressional lines were re-drawn nationwide. In Florida, a new Republican district was carved out just for Harris, which she easily won in 2002. It was a safe Republican seat, and Harris could have been a congress-woman for life. Instead, she displayed incredible moxie by immediately showing the willingness to give up her safe congressional seat and expressing interest in running for the open U.S. Senate seat being vacated by Senator Bob Graham in 2004.

Behind the scenes, the Bush brothers and Rove made it known they wanted a different candidate in the Senate race: Mel Martinez, then Florida's Secretary of Housing and Urban Development. The reason they opposed Harris was out of fear that her presence on the ballot in Florida in 2004 (when W. was running for re-election for president) would drive Democratic voter turnout through the roof, which could have hurt the president's chances of capturing Florida a second time, as Florida would again likely be a key battleground state. The thought of déjà vu—with Florida coming back to haunt them again in 2004—was too much for the Bush brothers to bear. Harris had to be stopped.

So a backroom deal with Harris was cut: Harris would stay out of the 2004 race and the party would support her in 2006 if she ran for the other U.S. Senate seat against Democrat Bill Nelson. Republican Mel Martinez went on to easily win the U.S. Senate seat in 2004, and Harris was ready for action in 2005-2006. And action she got, though not the type she had in mind.

When she announced in March 2005 she would be running for the U.S. Senate seat held by Bill Nelson, two polls taken at the time showed her trailing Nelson by anywhere from twelve to seventeen points. Behind the scenes, the White House (with the blessing of Jeb Bush) refused to back Harris as promised and started looking for other potential candidates. When Jeb Bush was asked about Harris, he displayed a notable lack of enthusiasm, often talking as if she might not really be running.

Despite the lack of expected (and pledged) support by the White House and Jeb Bush, Harris pressed on, eventually winning the Republican nomination. Whatever momentum Harris may have received from winning the nomination was short-lived, though, as things went south for her quickly. First, Harris was put on the defensive regarding campaign cash she received from convicted felon Jack Abramoff. Just as that story was dying down, Harris got hit with a scandal that was much worse.

A prominent defense contractor, MZM Corporation, had been responsible for bribing California Congressman Duke Cunningham in order to get secure lucrative government contracts. As a result, Congressman Cunningham is now residing in the federal pen. Soon thereafter, the feds were again investigating MZM for bribery and campaign finance lawbreaking, except this time the target of their investigation was none other than Congresswoman Katherine Harris.

The Cunningham bribes were taken from Mitchell Wade, the former president of MZM, who, it just so happened, had twice dined with Katherine Harris. One meal at Citronelle in Georgetown cost $2,800, and Harris accepted $32,000 in contributions from the firm. Like Cunningham, Harris tried to help Wade, attempting to get an appropriation for $10 million to build a defense facility in her district.

Making matters worse, when Harris was hit with a Justice Department subpoena, she neglected to tell her chief political strategist, Ed Rollins (GOP political guru, and former Reagan Campaign Manager in 1984 when Reagan won forty-nine states). Rollins quit on the spot. Nevertheless, Rollins launched a private investigation hoping to clear Harris's name, but stated publicly his investigation was not able to exonerate her. Rollins later confirmed that Justice Department lawyers and FBI agents have recently questioned him and the Harris campaign about the $32,000 in MZM Corporation donations.

I've never met Ed Rollins personally, but we've spoken on the phone a few times. He's known by politicos on both sides of the aisle as one of the nicest, most decent men in the beltway, and his behavior here seems to reinforce that belief. He must have been sorry he got himself mixed up in this mess, sullying his good name in the process. And no sooner had I found out about Ed Rollins' unfortunate plight in the Harris affair than I learned yet another of Harris' campaign managers had quit. This one was a shocker to me. While the feds were investigating the Harris campaign, her campaign manager Jim Dornan resigned and announced he was cooperating with the FBI and Justice Department.

Jim Dornan? I couldn't believe it. I knew Dornan from back in the day when I first began my career as Oppo Man in 1994. We met that year in Oklahoma when I was researching the Democratic opponent of former Republican Congressman J. C. Watts. Dornan was Watts' campaign manager and a great guy. Jim was one of the most fun guys to be around in DC. He took his politics seriously, but never took *himself* too seriously, unlike most political hacks. Every Friday up on The Hill was "Dress Casual Day," and some Fridays right around lunchtime, I'd hear some commotion outside and would look out my window at the National Republican Congressional Committee, where I was working at that time, just a block from the Capitol. There I would see Dornan pushing a beer keg through the Cannon Building's revolving doors.

So now I find that the feds are questioning Dornan regarding possible bribes Harris may have received. It seemed as though anyone affiliated with the Harris campaign was having their name tarnished—in this case, two guys I firmly believed were honest. I *couldn't* possibly believe Dornan would have done anything so stupid, not to mention illegal, by involving himself with any skullduggery that haunted Harris.

And as far as Katherine Harris is concerned, I have no idea what to think. But here's what we know are facts:

- She accepted major campaign cash from the outfit that put Duke Cunningham in jail
- She had a lunch with these clowns that cost $2,800
- She used her position in Congress to help the shady defense contractor

In the spring and summer of 2006, Harris' third campaign manager quit and polls showed Bill Nelson ahead of Harris by thirty-three points. Though she had easily won the Republican primary, Harris was not invited to the Republican "Unity Tour" a statewide victory lap that featured virtually every prominent GOP candidate in Florida. Finally, on September 22, 2006, the Bush brothers campaigned for Harris at a fundraising event in Florida. Jeb Bush and President Bush, for the first time since Harris won the GOP Senate nomination, publicly complimented her and asked people to vote for her. Too little too late, wouldn't you say?

This had been a harrowing experience for Oppo Man— torn between loyalty to the Bush brothers on the one hand, but also feeling Katherine Harris was not given her due respect by them either. Trying to be totally objective, I would agree with the Bush brothers that keeping her out of a U.S. Senate race in 2004 was probably the right thing to do. It was a presidential election year, Bush was in for the fight of his life against John Kerry, and the last thing they needed was another headache in Florida, a la 2000. Loyalty or no loyalty, I believe they were right to make the deal they did in that instance, not only for President Bush's re-election prospects, but also because they were being forward-thinking—and engaging in smart politics—by stumping for an Hispanic Republican to become a Florida senator. Once that deal was done, the Bush brothers got everything they wanted. W. won the presidency for a second term, Martinez won the Florida senate seat, and Katherine Harris kept her mouth shut and upheld her end of the bargain.

Then came 2005 and 2006 and the Bush brothers broke their end of the deal. Were they justified? Instead of supporting her 2006 Senate bid against Bill Nelson, they openly and flagrantly thwarted her every move. I understand the political reasons for double-crossing her; the same high Democratic turnout that may have hurt President Bush in 2004 could have also potentially thwarted the expected victory of Jeb Bush's likely successor, Republican Attorney General Charlie Crist, in 2006. But this never happened as Crist won easily.

I'm not so crazy about the Bush brothers' double-dealing in the Harris matter in 2006, but I can see where that it may have been something they had to do. Still, I sympathized with Harris . . . until I considered the following:

- Even if she didn't take a bribe, her behavior in the MZM scandal did not pass the smell test.

- Good men like Ed Rollins and Jim Dornan have been tarnished by Harris' campaign's issues.

- Harris had record-high staff turnover—in her congressional office, four chiefs of staff and four press secretaries since 2003. On her campaign staff, seven campaign staffers quit, including four campaign managers. Something is fishy there.

- Harris accused Bill Nelson of taking contributions from Riscorp, an insurance company tied to a 1990s campaign-finance scandal in Florida. The problem was, Nelson, as insurance commissioner, had cleaned up that scandal, and Harris was the one who had taken money from Riscorp.

- Harris also accused Nelson of taking bribes, despite not being unable to offer any specifics regarding the alleged bribes.

- Harris gave a speech about a terrorist plot to blow up a power plant in Indiana, which turned out to be a figment of her imagination.

- In 2006, when Republicans tried to recruit former Florida congressman Joe Scarborough into the race against Harris, Scarborough was warned by Harris that if he ran, the mysterious death of a Scarborough intern in his congressional office in 1998 would become front-page news. This despite no evidence of any wrongdoing regarding said intern's death. Harris reportedly also tried the dead intern threat on Jim Dornan.

The moral of the story? Yes, politics makes strange bedfellows, but it also makes even stranger enemies.

Chapter Twenty-Five

MARK FOLEY, PEDOPHILIA, AND SEX CRIMES

I n May 2006, I received a call to do some research on Tim Mahoney, the Democratic congressional opponent of Congressman Mark Foley of Palm Beach, Florida, one of the wealthiest cities in America. It was a surprising phone call, since Foley had always been safe in his district. The district is slightly more Republican than Democratic, but not by much. However, Foley had been an extremely popular congressman in that district since 1994, and had never faced any serious opposition (winning every election with at least 58 percent of the vote).

The Republicans in the district are referred to in political jargon as "Rockefeller Republicans." Nelson Rockefeller was governor of New York from 1959 until 1973, before becoming vice president in 1974 under Gerald Ford after Watergate. Rockefeller was a Republican who was generally conservative on economic issues and generally liberal on some social issues—hence the term "Rockefeller Republican," used to this day to describe Republicans considered "moderates" as opposed to conservative or right-wing.

Palm Beach's Republicans always have been quintessential "Rockefeller Republicans," so most folks there never were bothered by the fact that Mark Foley was gay. Although he never came out publicly regarding his sexuality, almost everyone in his district, as well as on Capitol Hill, knew, but no one cared. He was a good guy and a fine congressman.

When Congressman Foley ran for the U.S. Senate in 2003, he was forced out of the Republican primary when the gay "rumors" surfaced, but it never hurt him in his congressional district. This isn't surprising, considering how much debauchery takes place in Palm Beach. Although on the surface it's a "proper" WASP city of rich folks (most of them fine people) and old money, behind closed doors it's Jerry Springer-land. So when I received the call to research Foley's opponent in 2006, I was surprised.

But shortly after being asked to look at Democrat Tim Mahoney, I was suddenly told to stop—that the research wasn't needed. So I forgot about the matter . . . until October 2006, when the Foley sex scandal suddenly broke. The allegations that Foley was sending sexually explicit emails to a congressional page genuinely shocked me. It was difficult to believe anyone could be so stupid and so flagrantly arrogant.

What makes it even worse is that he pursued a *congressional page*—at least in the private sector, he would have had a good chance of not being caught. But doing it as he did made many of his actions public record, not to mention potential federal crimes (as of this writing it is still under investigation whether or not Foley broke any laws, or if the page was under or over the age of consent at the time Foley was emailing him).

I was even more shocked by the Florida Republicans' choice to replace Foley on the ballot. State Representative Joe Negron was selected quickly after Foley's resignation from Congress, with the election less than a month away. By sheer happenstance, Oppo Man had researched Negron earlier in 2006, when he ran unsuccessfully for Florida Attorney General. Negron (in Oppo Man's never-humble opinion) was one of the worst Republican candidates around. The worst "hit" on Negron was that, as a criminal defense attorney, he'd had represented Henry Langltz, who was convicted of sexually molesting and killing a seventy-seven-year-old woman. In addition, a simple check of the Martin County Courthouse records (where Negron usually plied his trade) indicated that he had represented over one hundred low-life criminals, almost all of them convicted of the crimes with which they'd been charged with.

Can you believe this? Mark Foley resigns from Congress for allegedly being a pedophile, and the Republicans in Florida replace him with a trial lawyer who represented the sexual molester and killer of a seventy-seven-year-old woman. To this day, I have no idea if the geniuses who chose Negron knew about his defense of Mr. Langlitz. Nor do I know the reason I was asked initially to research the Democrat in the race, Tim Mahoney—then suddenly asked *not* to research him.

But that's not the point, nor even the craziest aspect of the Foley case.

For me the Foley case brought into much sharper focus my complete lack of conscience since becoming "Oppo Man." As an opposition researcher, it is your job is to research the opposing candidate(s) and/or the candidate for whom you are working. And your client always expects that you will find some dirt on the opponent, even when there *is* no dirt. Therefore, you *always* feel compelled to find something. And if nothing turns up, you either feel you've somehow failed, or you worry that your client will believe you're incompetent because you haven't found anything juicy.

Of course, there's always the fear you will look stupid if you miss something that later becomes public. For instance, none of the Republican opponents of George W. Bush during the 2000 GOP primaries found his DUI in Maine, but it was obviously found by the Democrats, since it was leaked to the media just five days before the presidential election of 2000, and it nearly cost Bush the election. (Bush's four- to seven-point lead in the polls before the DUI became public became zero points on Election Day.)

Because of this, *all* opposition researchers, Oppo Man included, are elated when they find something juicy on any political opponent. It makes you look good to the client. And the worse the dirt, the happier the researcher.

For this Oppo Man, there was nothing more ecstatic than finding a candidate who was or is in any way involved in a sexual crime, particularly one involving pedophilia. This will mean almost certain doom for the opposing candidate.

After the Foley scandal broke, I felt severe anger towards Foley—and great sympathy for his alleged victim. Then it finally hit me: How could I feel such anger towards Foley, and sympathy for his victims, while at the same time feeling pure ecstasy when as Oppo Man I discovered other innocent people have been victimized, such as a murdered and molested seventy-seven-year-old woman, who just happened to be represented by one of Oppo Man's targets?

Unfortunately, as mentioned previously, opposition research is a necessary evil. But it's certainly not necessary to feel ecstatic! Why *had* I felt so good about horrible sex crimes?

I guess for the same reason many Democrats, as of this writing, are elated that the war in Iraq is going poorly. I guess for the same reason a young woman ran into my office in the National Republican Congressional Committee, shortly before the 1994 election, and blurted out: "Did you hear the great news? Clinton sent the military into Haiti today and an American soldier was killed!!" I guess for the same reasons the Democrats get ecstatic when the economy is bad and good people are put out of work during Republican administrations (George Bush I in 1992, Reagan in 1981–1982), and vice-versa, such as when Republicans were ecstatic when we had 7.7 percent unemployment and 12 percent inflation under Jimmy Carter in 1980.

When it comes to political hacks like Oppo Man, and political ideologues of all stripes, politics always trumps reason. Real people and real tragedies seem great—if they help whichever political side you're on.

Chapter Twenty-Six

DON GOLDWATER FOR
GOVERNOR IN ARIZONA

One of my last missions as Oppo Man was also one of the most bizarre, a situation in Arizona involving Don Goldwater. To understand the context of Don Goldwater's 2006 gubernatorial campaign in Arizona, we really need to go back to 1964 and the shellacking his uncle Barry took from LBJ.

In the presidential election that year, Lyndon Johnson crushed then-Arizona Senator Goldwater 61 percent to 39 percent, with Goldwater winning only six states. Although he lost badly, Goldwater became, and has remained, a powerful and important political figure in America for one major reason: His political views, considered "ultraconservative" at that time—even borderline wacko—have since became mainstream political thought. Beginning in the 1970s during the Nixon years, Goldwater's ideas were cemented into the American mainstream by Ronald Reagan in the 1980s.

For instance, in the 1960s, to say we should build more prisons and lock up more criminals for longer periods was considered highly "unsophisticated" and "insensitive." To have said back then that we should try to make welfare mothers less dependent on government handouts also would have been considered cruel and uncaring. The ultraliberal thought that was mainstream back then has since been discredited not only by Republican presidents such as Reagan, but by moderate Democrats such as Bill Clinton, who did indeed finally institute reform and end welfare as we know it. Back in the 1960s, politicians were *proud* to call themselves "liberal," a word they now shun, preferring "progressive."

So, when Barry Goldwater ran for president in 1964, even his supporters were embarrassed in polite company to admit they agreed with his views, hence his very defensive campaign slogan: "In your heart you know he's right." (LBJ's campaign responded brilliantly with a slogan of their own: "But in your guts, you know he's nuts.")

Despite Goldwater's political defeat in 1964, history has recorded that campaign as strongly significant—for the very first time, conservative political ideas were at least being put on the table and into American political thought, despite the rejection of those ideas at the polls. Therefore, Barry Goldwater to this day is considered an icon among most Republicans and conservatives. And in Arizona, which he represented as a senator for a total of thirty years (1953–1965, 1969–1987), the Goldwater name is as revered as any other name in the state's history.

Which brings us to 2006 and the announcement that Barry's nephew, Don Goldwater, was going to run for governor of Arizona. At first blush, he looked like a shoo-in to win the

GOP primary against Len Munsil, an attorney and president of the Center of Arizona Policy, a right-wing think tank. Munsil seemed to be no match for a man carrying the great Goldwater name. The winner of the GOP primary would face Democrat incumbent Governor Janet Napolitano, elected four years prior in a very tight race. Therefore, it looked like Don Goldwater, if he waged a well-run campaign, would win.

Ironically, my first contact with Don Goldwater had nothing to do with opposition research, although that's where it ultimately—and sickeningly—led to. Oppo Man doubles as a radio talk-show host, one night a week. In May 2006, I interviewed Goldwater for KFNX in Phoenix. The interview was, to say the least, weird. Don Goldwater was even weirder, and any listener that night tuned in to *The Stephen Marks Show* could hear very clearly that this man was in way over his head.

When I politely asked Goldwater how he would respond to the charge that he was simply running on the coattails of his famous uncle's name, he responded defensively, almost angrily: "I earned this name!" The question was not meant to be confrontational. It was simply an obvious question you would ask of *any* candidate with a famous family name, such as Kennedy or Bush. The answer was so unexpected that I responded in a knee-jerk manner: "You earned the name? Oh really? I thought you were born with it."

I didn't know then, but realize now, that (possibly) part of the reason he reacted so defensively is that he was fifty years old and had never really accomplished much politically in his life. The many political titles he had held appear to have been either honorary or nonelected.

The interview didn't end there. Don Goldwater's major campaign issue, the one he genuinely felt passionate about, was illegal immigration. Of course, that's a major problem in states like Arizona that border Mexico. Goldwater's held the hardcore position that all illegal aliens should be immediately deported. But he went even further, dangerously further—he believed that all illegal aliens should be arrested, held in prison camps, and used as labor to build a wall on the Arizona-Mexico border! Goldwater had already attacked fellow-Republican President George W. Bush for taking a middle-of-the-road approach on immigration, parodying President Reagan's "Mr. Gorbachev, tear down this [Berlin] Wall!" with his own pearl of wisdom: "President Bush, build up this wall!"

At that point, just when I thought Goldwater's ideas on immigration couldn't possibly get any crazier, he began ranting about how all illegal aliens were criminals. The conversation quickly deteriorated:

Stephen Marks: "What percentage of illegal aliens do you believe are criminals?"
Don Goldwater: "One hundred percent of them. They all broke the law to come here illegally."
SM: "Not including the criminal acts of breaking federal laws to come to America illegally and to stay here illegally, what percentage of them are criminals?"
DG: "One hundred percent of them."

Would anyone in his right mind, much less a serious gubernatorial candidate, actually believe this? I figured he must have misunderstood my question. So I pushed him down even further, leaving no doubt as to what I was asking:

SM: "Mr. Goldwater, I'm referring to criminal acts that have nothing to do with breaking immigration laws. You know, like robbing a 7-11, for instance. What percentage of illegal aliens do you believe are those types of criminals?"
DG: "One hundred percent of them."

I realized two things at that point: This man was a bigot, and if he was lucky enough to win the Republican primary, his views on immigration would make him unelectable in a general election in Arizona, a state with many Hispanic voters.

My own opinion on the subject was never brought up during the interview, because that would have been inappropriate. But for whatever it's worth, it's quite simple: Unless your ancestors are American Indians, if you do not want to give today's illegal immigrants the same opportunities your ancestors had, you are a hypocrite. And if your ancestors had to deal with today's strict and draconian immigration laws, chances are you would not be living in America today.

But enough of my opinion. It's not important. Here's what is: in a bizarre twist the Goldwater campaign hired Oppo Man's firm to do some research, with Mr. Goldwater having no idea that the DC political operative he had just hired was the same person he had sparred with on a local Phoenix radio station. It just happened that way. And here's what made it *really* funny: Don Goldwater wanted research not on his primary opponent Len Munsil, nor on the Democratic nominee, Governor Janet Napolitano. Goldwater wanted research on *himself,* to find out what was out there that his opposition might find out about him. And when the job was done, he didn't know whether to laugh or to cry.

The first thing I found was that—right at that time, right in the middle of this tough political campaign—Mr. Goldwater was two full years delinquent paying taxes on one piece of property he owned, and one full year delinquent on a second property. Between the two delinquencies, Goldwater owed the government of Arizona almost $7,000 in back taxes, at the same time he was running to be governor of the state. This issue *alone* could have sunk his candidacy had it became public. (Out of morbid curiosity, two months after turning in the report to Mr. Goldwater alerting him of his delinquent taxes, I again checked the property tax records to see if they had been paid. They had not. As of this writing, they *still* have not been paid.)

Further research uncovered that Don Goldwater's father, Robert Goldwater, still alive at the ripe old age of ninety-five, had been busted by the feds repeatedly for being guilty of hiring illegal aliens! Not only that, but he had reportedly hired them by the hundreds, providing them with bogus Social Security numbers and forcing them to work in unlivable conditions that had led to worker strikes. The head of the U.S. Border Patrol in Phoenix at that time said Robert Goldwater "was, without a doubt, the source of our biggest headache." The press reported that these illegal aliens lived under plastic tarps, without toilet facilities, in the citrus groves in which they worked, cooked over campfires, and worked from dawn to dusk for as little as $5 per day. Finally, in late 1977, some two hundred workers went on strike at Goldwater's farm, seeking higher pay and claiming unsafe working conditions. The workers produced paycheck stubs showing that the farm had assigned them Social Security-type numbers when they were hired and deducted money from their pay, ostensibly for Social Security.

When questioned about his father's actions by the press, Don Goldwater pled ignorance and claimed he didn't know anything about it. If he's telling the truth (he would have been in his late teens to early twenties at the time), he's oblivious to what's going on in his family business. If not, he's a liar.

Either way, the issue meant that when his father passed away, Don Goldwater—the would-be governor who believes 100 percent of illegal aliens are criminals and should be forced into labor camps—would inherit Lord-knows-how-much dough largely from the wealth his father accumulated off the backs of illegal aliens. Like the deadbeat property tax issue, this issue—all by itself—could have single-handedly destroyed his candidacy had it became public during the campaign.

Oppo Man also found the usual political dirt against Goldwater, such as his apparent cynical and disingenuous flip-flopping on abortion. He also maintained that he had no opinion on the historic 1964 Civil Rights Legislation. (Not too bright, having no opinion on one of the most significant events in American history.)

After all my "research" on Mr. Goldwater was done, all I could think of was his belligerent quote during our radio interview: "I earned this name!" I was getting nauseated. In my opinion, Don Goldwater was a *disgrace* to that name. But I submitted my report to the Goldwater campaign like I was being paid to do, forgot about it, and moved on to other campaigns in other states. Meanwhile, the Goldwater campaign for the GOP gubernatorial primary continued.

Then came the scare. Suddenly it was only one week until the primary on September 12 against GOP opponent Len Munsil and I hadn't yet been paid by the Goldwater campaign for my work. I realized that if I wasn't paid before the primary, and Goldwater lost the primary, I would almost certainly get stiffed. This is a somewhat common problem with campaigns; after they end, any campaign can simply spend whatever money is left in the campaign's bank account however they please, and if any vendor or employee of the campaign is stiffed, there's no recourse. That's because no one in particular owes you money; it's the "campaign committee" that owes you the money. And if the campaign committee has spent all their money, you can only sue the committee, which is a waste of time because they are usually broke after the campaign is over. The Federal Elections Committee believes there is nothing wrong with this practice, so it is perfectly legal and not at all unusual for a "campaign committee" to stiff employees or vendors (see my chapter on Patrick Buchanan).

So I had my assistant, Mendy Caldwell, call the Goldwater campaign and politely ask to be paid for the work that had been invoiced more than a month prior. Suddenly it was the Thursday before the Tuesday primary, and there was still no check. When Mendy called them back to ask about the check, they completely blew her off, making it apparent they had no intention of paying the bill.

When Mendy told me they were blowing her off, I was flabbergasted—to stiff an opposition researcher who has all the dirt on *your own candidate* is pure suicide. That info, if given or sold to the opposition and/or to the press, would destroy that candidate on the spot, particularly in this case, since Goldwater's primary opponent had not gone negative against him. Therefore, all the damaging "research" I had on him was not yet known by the voters.

Oppo Man swung into action. I knew it would take just one simple phone call. I had Mendy make another call to them on that same Thursday, five days before the primary. When Mendy called, they didn't answer the phone, probably having checked caller ID. The voice mail message came on, followed by a beep, followed by Mendy's voice:

Hi. This is Mendy Caldwell calling again. You probably don't know what our invoice was for. It was for work we did when we were specifically hired by Don Goldwater to dig up dirt on himself. A report was submitted two months ago and you have ignored our invoices. If a check is not sent today via Fed Ex, a copy of this report, which includes Mr. Goldwater currently being two years of delinquent taxes and that Mr. Goldwater will profit financially from his father hiring illegal aliens, will be sent to Mr. Goldwater's primary opponents, as well as to the press, just in time for the Sunday papers two days before the primary. Goodbye.

I was on the phone, too, listening to Mendy leave the message. I knew her words would put the fear of God into them. Sure enough, Mendy got a call back within minutes. Not only would we receive the money but they were taking no chances with FedEx. They were *wiring* the money to us! In all my years as Oppo Man, this was the first time anyone ever wired me money. (For that matter, it was the first time I ever had to make this sort of threat to get paid.)

Finally, the GOP primary came on September 12. Final results: Munsil 48 percent, Goldwater 40 percent.

There is only one thing I can add in closing regarding Don Goldwater: Failure and adversity have brought down many men, but have made other men stronger and better. I hope that for Mr. Goldwater it's the latter.

Chapter Twenty-Seven

SYMMETRY AND IRONY

"Meet the new boss, same as the old boss."

("Won't Get Fooled Again," The Who)

There have been many ironies regarding my career as Oppo Man, but none as fascinating as this one. As I've mentioned, my career as Oppo Man began in 1994, when the Democrats controlled the White House, Senate, and the House of Representatives. During that election year, that Democratic Congress was taken over by the GOP for the first time since Herbert Hoover, because of the colossal unpopularity of then-President Bill Clinton.

Ironically, Oppo Man's career will end with the mirror image of its birth in 1994. The 2006 elections saw the exact same phenomenon we saw in 1994, but with the shoes on the other feet. This time the *Republicans* controlled all three branches of government, but lost control of both houses of Congress just as the Democrats had twelve years previously. This time it was because of the massive, colossal unpopularity of President George W. Bush. So once again we have a divided government because when either party has total control of the government, they just *can't help themselves*; they *have to* mess it up.

In my lifetime alone, the Democrats have held control of all three branches of government on three separate occasions, and all three times they screwed up so badly that they were voted out of power.

During the Kennedy/Johnson years from 1961 to 1968, the Democrats had total control. Yet the albatross of Vietnam around Lyndon Johnson's neck led to the election of Republican Richard Nixon in 1968, with the Democrats being voted out of the presidency. The shift already started two years prior, in 1966. During that mid-term election, the Democrats lost forty-seven seats in the House and three in the Senate, also because of voter dissatisfaction with Vietnam.

The second time the Democrats controlled all three branches of government during my lifetime was as a result of Watergate, with the election of Democrat Jimmy Carter as president to go along with Democratic control of both houses of Congress in 1976. As was the case in 1968, the prior off-year election (1974) also portended things to come, as the Democrats gained forty-nine seats in the House and four in the Senate. Even Gerald Ford's congressional district, which had been Republican controlled since the 1940s, went Democrat after Ford ascended to the presidency. But once again, as was the case with Lyndon Johnson, Carter screwed up so badly that the result was the election of Ronald Reagan as president in 1980 coupled with the GOP takeover of the U.S. Senate.

The third time the Democrats held total control of the federal government in my lifetime was during the first two years of the Clinton administration, 1993–1994. But once again, they just couldn't control themselves, with most of the blame this time going to Hilary Clinton's ill-fated healthcare debacle, coupled with Clinton's tax hike, the gays in the military controversy, and so on. As a result, the Democrats lost full control of both the House of Representatives and the U.S. Senate in 1994.

So here we are, after the 2006 election, with the exact same situation we had after the 1994 elections: once again, the party previously in total control of all three branches of the federal government (this time George W. Bush and the GOP) having *completely screwed up* and lost power. It apparently doesn't matter which side takes total power; once they gain those trapping of power it always seems to go to their heads. Good intentions quickly degenerate into sheer arrogance.

As they say, power corrupts . . . and absolute power corrupts absolutely. In the end, the Republicans were just as imperious as the Democrats were. But I was so blinded by my loyalty to the Republican Party that I never saw it coming. Not until the 2006 juggernaut.

In 2004, when Republicans gained complete control of government for the first time in my lifetime—with the re-election of George W. Bush, coupled with winning control of the Senate, and keeping control of the House—I really believed things would be different. That the Republicans would be different. By 2004, I was far past being the true believer I had been in 1994, and after ten years of being Oppo Man, I clearly realized that the Republicans were, on balance, probably as corrupt as the Democrats. But, still, I was certain that they could get this right.

This immediately reminds me of an old "Twilight Zone" episode featuring Peter Falk as a Castro-like character who leads a popular uprising against a corrupt dictatorship, only to become the same corrupt dictator his predecessor was. The "Twilight Zone" always ends with a moral, just like the "Aesop's Fables" of my childhood. In this particular episode, the moral was that a right-wing dictatorship being replaced by a left-wing dictatorship is really no replacement at all. They're equally as bad, regardless of their political leanings.

The Who's classic song, "Won't Get Fooled Again," also has an interesting lyric regarding public anger at the government leading to the overthrow of that government. At the end of the song, after a long, intense instrumental passage (representing the turmoil, fighting, and the "old guard" finally being defeated and replaced by the "new guard"), the song ends with this telling line: "Meet the new boss; same as the old boss."

Those nine words perfectly capture what happened in America during my career as Oppo Man from 1994 to 2006. The "new boss" and the "old boss" were not the same in political ideology, but they certainly *were* the same in attitude: *Arrogance.* Pure, unadulterated arrogance. Maybe the folks in the Who's fictional song were indeed "fooled again" after they said they wouldn't be, but the American public was clearly *not* fooled in 2006. The war in Iraq, which I believe was and still is a noble cause, has been a complete debacle of mismanagement, from the moment the president climbed aboard the *USS Lincoln* in his leather bomber jacket and proclaimed "Mission accomplished."

It's amazing how most politicians and the political elite have such contempt for citizens, yet history continues to prove, over and over again, that the public can see through hypocrisy and arrogance on the left just as easily as they see through the same garbage on the right. Just as the public threw out the Democrats in 1966 and 1968 over Vietnam, they threw out the Republicans in Congress in 2006 over Iraq. And they did so not so much doubting the Bush Administration's vision to wipe out terrorism (which I and many Americans deeply share), but disdaining its massive incompetence in the handling of it, and despising its arrogance in rejecting constructive criticism, even from their own generals in the front lines of battle. Arrogance, belligerence, stubbornness.

In 2006, just as in 1994, the American public "would not get fooled again." One of the major themes of the 1994 "Republican Revolution" and Newt Gingrich's "Contract with America" was the issue of term limits. This is the issue that, to my thinking, is the true test of Republican integrity and is also the perfect microcosm of all that went wrong with the 1994 revolution. While federal term limits legislation failed to get the two-thirds majority needed to become the law of the land after the 1996 Republican takeover of Congress, many Republican members nonetheless gave themselves "self-imposed term limits," meaning they promised their constituents that they believed so strongly in term limits they would step down voluntarily after a certain number of terms, even though they didn't have to.

Most of them didn't live up to their word—the trappings of power were just too much to give up. Republicans Nethercutt, Cubin, and Gutnecht were particularly egregious in breaking their pledges. Nethercutt became the poster boy of the term-limits movement in 1994. Campaigning largely on this issue, in a true David versus Goliath story, the underdog Nethercutt defeated then-Speaker of the House Tom Foley. Nethercutt vowed to serve three terms and step down in 2000. But he did not.

Cubin (same old story, with a slightly different wrinkle), also elected in 1994, stated she would abide by her state's legislative term limits laws and serve only three terms. But those laws were declared unconstitutional, so when 2000 rolled around, she weaseled her way out of her earlier promise and made a new, "revised" promise: That she would serve no more that six terms, which would have her retiring in 2006. Once again she did not, breaking her promise twice. And Gutknecht had this to say (get a load of this pearl of wisdom from the ex-congressman from Minnesota): "Does it make any sense to keep a stupid promise?"

In almost all of these cases, the constituents couldn't care less and kept repeatedly re-electing them to office. Why do voters put up with this flagrant hypocrisy and lust to retain power? The answer is simple. All polls show that voters have an overwhelmingly low opinion of Congress in general, but think their own congressman is great. And as far as breaking the term-limits pledge, the reason the voters put up with it is purely selfish: They know that a member with seniority will bring home more bacon for their state than someone new. Same old story—all the voters are against government waste, unless it's in their district. Then it's no longer "waste," but quality of life and jobs. Consequently, every election cycle, roughly 80 percent of Congress members face no serious challenges.

Especially sickening is hearing Congress members who have broken their promise on term limits bragging about how great they are and why they need to stay in Congress. Read the words of Republican Kurt Weldon of Florida:

One of the greatest privileges I have is being able to help thousands of my constituents each year who are having problems with federal agencies, including helping seniors with Social Security or Medicare benefits, helping homeowners with federal regulations, helping constituents with visa issues, and assisting veterans in getting their benefits or long-overdue medals.

Visa issues, Mr. Weldon? Does that mean helping illegal aliens?

Well, here's the bottom line: If their constituents are as cynical as their congress members are, and don't mind them breaking their term limits pledges, I guess that's democracy.

But since so much of this book is devoted to the negative side of politics, I believe it's important to give credit here to those who went against the grain and cared more about their country and their personal integrity than their personal power. Kudos to the following promise keepers:

- Former Republican Senate Majority Leader Bill Frist of Tennessee promised when he ran in 1994 that he would only serve two terms and then retire. Which he did. How many guys are there out there who would give up not only a U.S. Senate seat, but a high leadership position, as Frist did? He was a true citizen-legislator in the finest sense of the term. Job well done, Bill.
- Republican Mark Sanford of South Carolina, who later became governor.

- Republican Jim DeMint of South Carolina, who later became a U.S. senator.
- Republican John Thune of South Dakota, who later became a U.S. senator.
- Republican Bob Riley of Alabama, who later became governor.
- Republican Tom Coburn of Oklahoma, who later became a U.S. senator.
- Republican Richard Burr of North Carolina, who later became a U.S. senator.
- Republican Greg Ganske of Iowa, who later lost a Senate bid.
- Republican Nick Smith of Michigan, who stepped down.
- Democrat John Balducci of Maine, who later lost the race for governor.

* * *

The uncanny symmetry bookending Oppo Man's career between the 1994 mid-term elections and the 2006 mid-term elections hasn't been the only remarkable alignment of my life and politics. Consider first the strange pattern of the years served by the presidents in my lifetime juxtaposed with my life, even before becoming Oppo Man:

- President John Kennedy is killed and LBJ becomes president: First year of elementary school for Stephen Marks
- Bobby Kennedy is killed and Richard Nixon becomes president: First year of junior high school for Stephen Marks

- Nixon resigns and Gerald Ford becomes president: First year of college for Stephen Marks
- Ford is defeated and Jimmy Carter becomes president: Stephen Marks begins working in Manhattan, New York, and moves from hometown Brooklyn to Woodside, Queens
- Carter is defeated and Ronald Reagan becomes president: Stephen Marks moves from Woodside, Queens to Forest Hills and Manhattan, New York
- Reagan retires and George Bush I becomes president: Stephen Marks moves from New York City to Nashville, Tennessee
- Bush I is defeated and Bill Clinton becomes president: Stephen Marks becomes Oppo Man and moves to Washington, DC
- George W. Bush becomes president: Oppo Man vows to quit the business (believing that after helping elect Bush, he can move on with his life) but winds up continuing as Oppo Man. As Bush's presidency nears its end and the 2008 presidential primaries approach, Stephen Marks finally does retire to write this book.

I know this all sounds like a stretch, and that the presidential terms often correspond with the natural changes in *any* person's life, so all of the above may be pure coincidence. Yet consider the following symmetry between New York City mayors during my lifetime:

- Robert Wagner: Stephen Marks is born during the Wagner administration and spends the Wagner years going through elementary school.

- John Lindsay: Elected mayor as Stephen Marks enters junior high school
- Abe Beame: Elected mayor as Stephen Marks enters college
- Ed Koch: Elected mayor as Stephen Marks begins working in New York City
- David Dinkins: Elected mayor as Stephen Marks moves from New York City to Nashville, Tennessee
- Rudolph ("Rudy") Giuliani: Elected mayor as Stephen Marks leaves Nashville and goes to the nation's capitol to begin his career as Oppo Man

* * *

Not only was there symmetry between my career as Oppo Man and all the above-mentioned political events taking shape during my lifetime, there was also the symmetry and transition I mentioned earlier in my personal political leanings—the transition from liberal New York City Democrat to Beltway hardcore Republican political hack to what I am now: a middle-of-the-road, mainstream moderate who still leans Republican but who is a political Independent.

Why do I not consider myself a Republican despite agreeing with the party's positions most of the time, and despite my absolute contempt for liberals?

First, allow me to explain that my contempt for liberals has nothing to do with their political views, many of which I agree with, such as on the issues of abortion, stem cell research, gay rights, tort reform, union rights, and minimum wage. It's the fact that most right-wingers, with whose political opinions I do not agree, are completely honest about their political agendas, don't hide behind euphemisms, and are proud to call themselves "conservatives," whereas the vast majority of liberals rarely if ever admit their true agenda and almost never use the word "liberal" to describe themselves (instead preferring to hide behind high-sounding euphemisms such as "progressive"). I feel that, in general, liberals are dishonest in a way I cannot abide.

For instance, on the emotionally charged issue of abortion, pro-lifers (of whom I am *not* one) are *always* intellectually honest enough to use the word "abortion" as part of the debate. On the other hand, the pro-choice folks, despite having the majority of American voters in agreement with them on this issue, almost *never* use the word "abortion" during the political debate. They use instead such words and phrases as "choice," "right to choose," or my favorite, "I'm personally opposed to abortion, but I don't have the right to make that choice for another person."

Do you know of any other political issue where either side spouts such drivel as "I'm personally opposed to armed robbery, but it should be every American's right to make that choice" or "I'm personally opposed to bestiality, but it should be every American's right to make that choice"?

Their phoniness is what I hate about so many liberals. No different than the phoniness of so many conservatives. (Of course, there *are* some honest liberals who are not ashamed to admit they are liberals, such as Bernie Sanders, Russ Feingold, and the late Paul Wellstone.)

This is not to imply for one moment, however, that liberals and Democrats hold a monopoly on phoniness and hypocrisy. I've already explained in morbid detail the massive hypocrisy of many conservatives and Republicans when it comes to issues of family values, sex, and fidelity. The Republican and conservative hypocrisy on this issue easily eclipses *any* liberal hypocrisy.

Thus, I no longer consider myself a Republican, despite my political leanings being usually in that direction and despite my long record as Oppo Man having helped so many Republicans get elected and re-elected to public office. To some degree, you could say I even hate the Republican Party and would feel ashamed to be affiliated with them. The reason for this can be described in just two words: tort reform. And it's personal.

"Tort reform" is the political movement (headed and supported mostly by Republicans and right-wingers) to limit damages awarded in court to those who file lawsuits. The main objective of "tort reform" is to limit the amount of money given to plaintiffs who sue doctors for medical malpractice. Thus far, the Republican-led House of Representatives (before it was taken over by the Democrats after the 2006 elections) has passed a bill that would cap "pain and suffering," or what's referred to as "punitive damages," at $250,000. President Bush, a strong supporter, vowed to sign the legislation but he never had that chance. It never made it through the U.S. Senate, despite its being (like the House at that time) under Republican control.

Imagine that some doctor screws up a routine medical procedure on a three-year-old girl, which results in her being crippled and confined to a wheelchair for life. Should she only be entitled to $250,000 *for the rest of her life* for "pain and suffering" caused by that doctor's malfeasance? That would mean the three-year-old victim, if she lived seventy more years, would get a grand total of $3,570 per year for the rest of her life to compensate for being unable to walk because of human error. Oh, and that's minus the one-third her lawyer would get, leaving her with a whopping $2,380 per year for life.

Tort reform laws like this one, that never made it through Congress, nonetheless have crept through several state legislatures. In Texas for instance, tort reform law caps noneconomic damages at $250,000. According to press reports, this had the added effect of making it more difficult to find a law firm that will take your case—their payment (dependent on the settlement) may not be worth their time. Since the Texas bill was signed into law by then-Governor George W. Bush in 1995, personal injury suits filed in the Lone Star State have plummeted 40 percent, despite a dramatic rise in the state's population. As a result, victims of crooked businesses and quack doctors in Texas now can't find lawyers to take their cases, even though a 2002 federal study found, for example, that 40 percent of Texas nursing homes committed violations that caused harm or put residents at risk of death or injury, and 90 percent didn't meet federal staffing standards. Medical malpractice lawsuits have dropped 80 percent in Texas since "tort reform" was made law. This is crazy.

The entire system has been politically corrupted by both sides, with trial lawyers giving gazillions of dollars in campaign cash to Democrats, whilst the entire medical industry gives gazillions to Republicans. Both sides may be corrupt, but passing tort reform to cap damages at $250,000 will make doctors and other healthcare professionals even more unaccountable for their actions; in this case, resulting in little, if any accountability for harm that comes to their patients through malpractice.

This finally brings me to the story of why I can no longer in good conscience refer to myself as a Republican. None of the things I hate about liberals have affected me personally, with the exception of having to pay higher taxes during my lifetime. On the other hand, what has been done to me by *one doctor* (I'll refer to him here as "Dr. O") in particular, along with several other doctors on a smaller scale, has been enough for me to want to vomit every time I hear the Republicans spewing their support of tort reform. I cannot go into great detail because I will be in litigation with this particular doctor as this book goes to print. When someone severely affects your health in a negative and irreversible way and is not adequately held accountable for it, that is possibly the most unacceptable injustice.

Now, having spewed the diatribe above against doctors and their political flunkies who favor tort reform, you're never going to believe this one. Guess who some of Oppo Man's best clients were? Tort reform groups!

That's right—Oppo Man dug up dirt against legislators who were fighting for my side on this issue; who, like me, were opposed to and hated tort reform. Taking money from those whose agenda is to elect legislators that will pass legislation that, to me, is the most wretched legislation ever created by humankind—how could I do such a thing? I would explain it thusly.

The New York Yankees defeated the Los Angeles Dodgers in the World Series in 1977 and again in 1978. The two teams faced off yet again in the World Series in 1981, and when the Yankees won the first two games, it appeared as if history would repeat itself.

But then something strange happened. Yankee owner George Steinbrenner had a vicious hatred towards the team's great star, Reggie Jackson, and wanted to prove to the world that he, George Steinbrenner, not Reggie was the reason the Yankees were great. Steinbrenner ordered Yankee manger Bob Lemon to bench his star player so Steinbrenner could show the world that the Yankees could win the World Series *without* Reggie.

Bob Lemon objected, stating the obvious: Jackson was practically single-handedly responsible for the Yankees having won their prior two World Series, not to mention the fact that Jackson was one of the all-time greatest players in World Series history—hence his nickname "Mr. October." Steinbrenner responded with an ultimatum to manager Lemon: "If you play Reggie, I will fire you after the World Series, win or lose, and you'll never again get another dime from me. However, if you bench him as I say, win or lose, I'll take care of you financially for the rest of your life."

It was an offer Lemon couldn't refuse, so he benched the great Reggie Jackson. Result: The Yankees lost the next four straight games and lost the World Series. After the series, when reporters asked the decent and well-respected manager Bob Lemon how he could do such a thing, his response was succinct, honest, and to the point: "Every hooker has his price."

So if you ask me how I, "Oppo Man," in good conscience, could work for tort reform groups whose agenda was the exact opposite of mine, and whose goal was to protect the corrupt and incompetent doctors I hate so much, my answer is much the same as Bob Lemon's: Every Oppo Man has his price.

✳ ✳ ✳

The earlier chapter discussing sexual hypocrisy as the driving factor causing the demise of the Republican Party in this generation takes on a special meaning in relation to my time as Oppo Man. Oppo Man can understand and relate to that level of hypocrisy; he has lived it in his own personal life. My own disingenuousness is in perfect juxtaposition to what I witnessed conducting research as Oppo Man since 1994, and yet another reason why I had to get out of the game.

My major vice in life—women—was coincidentally (or maybe not-so-coincidentally) the same as that of many politicians, as we have seen. Just like the politicians I researched, I usually had to hide my actions, or at least try as best I could to keep them secret. This is not because I was married (I wasn't). But lies and deceptions were a necessary part of my lifestyle; and I was usually dating several different women at the same time. It was often difficult to keep up with all the fabrications.

I made a twelve-year sojourn across America that was as self-serving as the behavior of the politicians I was researching. My womanizing took on a life of its own. It was out of control. The worst part of it all was the complete lack of conscience on my part.

Traveling from state to state, and from city to city, made it fairly easy to be anonymous in my personal life apart from Oppo Man. I thought that being anonymous made me unaccountable—but of course I was not. There were consequences to my actions. Unfortunately, it took me many years to figure this out, and by the time I finally did figure it out, it was too late to fix all the damage I had caused. And after hurting so many people, the last victim, of course, was me.

I dated hundreds of women. I had sex with many of them, and even fell in love a few times. But even when I was in love, it didn't matter. I couldn't stop myself. Whether it was arrogance, immaturity, sheer stupidity, or a combination of the three, it didn't matter. I couldn't remain faithful. There have been three or four women I've met with whom I would have been happy had I settled down with them. In different ways, they were all perfect for me. But I couldn't do the right thing.

As I mentioned earlier in the book, I took advantage of situations where women, some of them single parents, were stuck living in a certain place (usually rural or a small town) where it was impossible for them to meet any men that would interest them. These women live lonely existences, and when they met Oppo Man, he gave them false hope. Sometimes even married women are in this situation. I remember one in particular who pleaded with me to take me with her and was willing to leave both her husband and her child. I once met a beautiful married woman who wanted to be with me, but I turned her down. Had my conscience finally get the better of me? Of course not. It just so happened that when I met that particular woman, I had recently seen a film on TV where a married man tracked down his unfaithful wife's paramour and had him killed in the most gruesome way imaginable. I still had that movie in my head when I met this particular woman, thinking that maybe there was a reason for me having seen that movie, that it was a kind of warning. After I got over that fear, I regretted, for several years, not being with that woman.

369

There's no need to go further into the sordid details of my sex life. What's important and relevant is what this says about Oppo Man. He can justify his actions or rationalize them any way he chooses, but he still knows they were wrong. Using women is wrong. Dating married women is wrong. Even if the married women he saw were in bad marriages that were going to collapse anyway, that didn't mean Oppo Man had to compound the problem. There was no guilt or shame until it was too late.

In retrospect, my behavior as Oppo Man put me in a mindset that affected my real-life behavior. Being successful as Oppo Man required me to be disingenuous; thus, disingenuousness became justified in my mind and crept into my personal life as well, a cancer spreading from one side of my life into the other.

It has to end.

A major theme of this book is that opposition research and negative campaigning are necessary, even *required*, evils in politics. Unfortunately for me, the mindset required to be a good opposition researcher was one that simultaneously threw the rest of my life into complete chaos. I'm sure there are many good Oppo Men and Oppo Women out there that can do their jobs without it adversely affecting their private lives. In fact, I know this to be true regarding most opposition researchers with whom I have worked. May they carry on their good work!

It was once good for me; but no more. I finally want a normal life, and that requires me to put Oppo Man to rest.

R.I.P OPPO MAN . . .
AND THOUGHTS ON THE
2008 ELECTION

So how can we sum up the life of Oppo Man as he's finally put to rest?

In thirteen years he conducted research in thirty-eight states, having visited thirty-two of them, while researching hundreds of "targets." This book only scratches the surface of all the different jobs Oppo Man has done, but hopefully will give you good insight into the arena of American politics known as "opposition research."

His life began with the Republican Party takeover of Congress and ended with the Democratic takeover of Congress.

His life began with the downfall of the Democratic Party in the previous generation and ended with the downfall of the Republican Party in this generation.

His life was a metamorphosis; triangulating from New York liberal to Republican political hack to mainstream political centrist disillusioned with both the Democratic and Republican parties.

Oppo Man's life has also ended in a strange place histori-cally; with a Republican president's 30 percent approval rating coupled with a Democratic Congress' 20 percent approval rating. These numbers are by far the worst in my lifetime for both the president and the Congress. Just as my personal life has also reached an all-time low.

But as I am hopeful and optimistic regarding my personal life, I'm also hopeful that Americans will eventually become more optimistic about their leaders in Washington. These things tend to by cyclical, and the hopelessness Americans feel towards their government at different times in our history always seems to turn around. Although it does seem worse today.

The political left and the political right in America appear to be more isolated from the mainstream; and more ideologically extreme than ever. For instance:

On the issue of abortion, those on the right still see abor-tion as "murder" whilst those on the left still see no rights for the unborn child.

On the issue of guns, those on the right still want zero restrictions on any gun ownership, whilst those on the far left still want to ban most guns by defining them as "assault weapons."

On gay issues, those on the right still see gays as sub-human while those on the left continue to indoctrinate chil-dren on the virtues of homosexuality in public schools, television, and movies.

On the War in Iraq, those on the left actually root for American casualties, and for America's defeat, while those on the far right blindly continue to support failed policies.

These are all just anecdotal examples, but taken together illustrate that the schism in American politics between left and right today is at its worst.

What makes matters even more severe is that in the debates on all these issues, most Americans are somewhere in the middle, not aligned with either political extreme. However, there is, unfortunately, rarely any voice for the political center, as the extremists continue to define the debate. That is because those on the extreme left and right are usually the most passionate; passionate enough to get involved in the political process, with both extremes equally convinced of their right-ness and moral superiority.

And as we enter 2008, thus far neither party seems to have a vision of any sort. Despite President George W. Bush's massive unpopularity and inability to get anything done legislatively, the Democrats' answer thus far has been devoid of ideas, and has had nothing positive to offer. So we are left waiting to see if this will change once both parties choose their 2008 presidential nominees.

But whether or not the presidential nominees will have anything positive to offer the American people, one thing *is* for certain; there's going to be lots of "oppo" done on all the major presidential candidates, with plenty of negative campaigning. This is and will always be a given. For instance:

Hillary Clinton

Expect Hillary Clinton to be attacked for her support of taxpayer money being spent for a Christian-bashing display at the Brooklyn museum; for her non-attendance at police funerals after 9/11; for her accepting campaign cash from Arab interests; and for her legislative proposal in the wake of the 2000 election to do away with the Electoral College, which would in effect minimize the importance of the voters in thirty out of fifty states (the smaller states). Also expect some rehashing of old issues Hillary has yet to be held accountable for, such as her legal work on behalf of an infamous cop killer, and the still-unaccounted-for financial bonanza she made from her commodities trading.

Barack Obama

Also expect Barack Obama to be attacked for his support of the corrupt Chicago political machine; for his serving as an organizer for a group indicted by the feds for vote fraud as he calls for more ethical reforms in government; for his shady real estate transactions with a well-known crook; and for his legislative push for more federal spending to combat the avian flu at the same time he purchased stock in a speculative company developing a drug to combat that flu. Then there are racial issues, such as his Trinity United Church of Christ in Chicago, headed by a race-baiting radical; and Obama's remark in his book regarding his not marrying a white woman he was in love with for fear that he would gravitate towards "her world."

John Edwards

Expect John Edwards to be attacked for the shady sale of his old Georgetown mansion to folks under government inquiry for accounting practices who also faced legal complaints from the same labor unions that are now supporting Edwards; for another shady real estate deal with a lobbyist for Saudi Arabia, who Edwards claimed he didn't know was a Saudi lobbyist; for his using "junk science" to win large malpractice awards in controversial cerebral palsy cases; and for his owning the most expensive home in North Carolina, while working for high-dollar law firms and representing high-dollar plaintiffs while at the same time claiming he's all for the "little guy."

Rudy Giuliani

Expect Rudy Giuliani to be attacked by his fellow Republicans for his liberal position on abortion, gay rights, affirmative action, and gun control; for his endorsement of Democratic Governor Mario Cuomo in 1994; and for his flip-flopping on abortion and school choice. In desperation you can also expect his opponents, at some point, to bring up his high-profile philandering and divorce.

Mitt Romney

Expect Mitt Romney to be attacked for purchasing failing businesses, only to fire employees and hire them back at lower wages while gutting their health care plans; for his launching chain super-stores which resulted in putting mom-and-pop stores out of business; and for his questionable political contri-butions from a company indicted for fraud after supplying low-quality materials to the Big Dig Tunnel project in Boston. On social issues expect Romney to be attacked from both the right and the left; on the right for his former support of gun control, gay rights, transgender proms, gay adoptions, abor-tion, his Department of Educations' controversial publications relating to gays and AIDS, and his support for adding a box to driver's license renewal forms to indicate whether the appli-cant's sex has changed. Should he win the GOP nomination, expect Romney to be attacked from the left on these same social issues since he has flip-flopped on so many of them.

Fred Thompson

Expect Thompson to be attacked for his lobbying work for a pro-choice abortion group. This makes him appear disingenuous today as he claims to be taking up the conservative mantle within the GOP, particularly among southerners and evangelicals, whilst also claiming to be rabidly pro-life. This issue goes to the heart of his integrity, as does the issue of his maintaining a Political Action Committee since leaving the U.S. Senate, with this fund-raising group paying more money to his son than it has paid to help elect Republicans to Congress, its ostensible aim. Finally, Thompson will be attacked (particularly by Democrats should he be the presidential or vice-presidential nominee) for his role during Watergate. His actions as counsel for the senate committee investigating Watergate in 1974 appear to have been not so much concerned with getting to the truth (as has been widely assumed since 1974), but instead trying to protect then-president Nixon get through the crisis.

John McCain

Expect John McCain to be attacked (if he's still even a factor in the race) for his strong support of immigration reform, which is considered poison to most voters, particularly Republican voters; and for his "friendship" with mobster Joe "Bananas" Bonano. Also expect some rehashing of McCain's role in the "Keating 5" scandal, in particular regarding his ownership of a piece of property in Arizona paid for by the infamous crook. Finally, expect some sort of attack regarding McCain's lack of temperament, such as these remarks: "Why is Chelsea Clinton so ugly? Because Janet Reno is her father." and "Leonardo DiCaprio is an androgynous wimp."

Final Thoughts

So as we enter 2008, we can expect another typical negative and vitriolic presidential campaign. And as I've said repeatedly throughout this book, this negative campaigning is a necessary evil which will be needed if the electorate is to cast educated and intelligent votes (the voters are usually smart enough to figure out which negative attacks are meaningful and which are not). Hopefully the results will give us leadership in Washington that will inspire more confidence than we have today.

For me personally, I have two hopes:

I hope President Bush can somehow turn around his failures in Iraq and somehow leave office successfully with his original vision of a stable Democratic Iraq, leading to more stability and democracy in the Arab and Muslim world, and with victory in the War on Terror. How Iraq turns out in the end, and whether or not we ever capture Osama bin Laden will secure Bush's place in history as either another Lyndon Johnson or another Winston Churchill. I sure hope it's the latter.

I know what you're thinking: I'm a dreamer, just like George W. Bush. You're right. If you don't have dreams, you have nightmares.

My second hope is to see Bush succeeded in the White House by Rudy Giuliani. Like Reagan and Clinton before him, Giuliani's life story thus far seems destined to end with the presidency.

And in the end, the bottom line is this: As I've stated earlier, despite all the imperfections in our governmental system (and there are many), and despite all the negativity, disillusionment, and hopelessness many Americans feel, our government and political system today is still *by far* the most open, honest, and democratic in the history of the world. As I also stated earlier, as long as humans are imperfect, so will our government be imperfect.

And despite all my rantings in this book about the corruption and hypocrisy of both the Democrat and Republican parties, our strong two-party system is still superior to the multi-party parliamentary governments throughout the world. In Italy and in Israel, for instance, the parliamentary systems have led to weakened major parties, resulting in non-stop turmoil with governments constantly collapsing. The result in those countries have been governments far less stable and inspiring than what we have here in the U.S.

Finally, while most Americans may indeed be disillusioned with our government, they are not apathetic. In the last presidential election in 2004, American voter turnout was the highest in American history. So in the end, the American people, despite their disillusionment, are nonetheless always optimistic and hopeful. Which is part of what makes this country so great.

OPPO MAN AWARDS

This book would not be complete without an awards section to explain the strangeness of American political campaigns and the work of opposition research.

1. Most Ridiculous Candidate Researched by Oppo Man: Tie Between Fred Head of Athens Texas, and Jim Pancake of Athens Ohio

To qualify for the most "ridiculous" candidate, the candidate has to be ridiculous in name *as well as* being equally ridiculous in actions. In 2006, Oppo Man was hired by a client to dig up dirt on the Democratic nominee for Texas State Comptroller, a gentleman from Athens, Texas, by the name of Fred Head. A former state representative, Head was running against incumbent Republican Susan Combs.

Not only did Mr. Head have a questionable record as a state legislator (being defeated in 1980 after serving several terms in the 1970s), but also had a questionable record as an attorney, with the Texas State Bar reprimanding him four times for improper behavior towards his clients, including once putting him on probation. Head also had a questionable record with the IRS during a bizarre bankruptcy where many of his debts were left unpaid, including local taxes. To make this all even more bizarre, Head was once found guilty of "Obstructing a public highway" by "allowing his cows and cattle to roam and cross over said Highway 31 East."

Now in 2006, after not having held public office in twenty years, Head was coming back from the dead. Despite having zero chance of winning, Texas Democrats appeared to be desperate for a candidate and had no one better to run. My guess is that the Democrats knew they had no chance of winning and were just in this for a good laugh. Final result: Susan Combs 69 percent; Fred Head 27 percent.

Maybe it's the water in places called "Athens," but the co-winner for "Most Ridiculous Candidate" was also from an Athens, this one in Ohio. In 2002 Oppo Man was also hired by a client to dig up dirt on Democratic Township trustee running for the state legislature by the name of Jim Pancake. His record on the issues was decent and seemed well-suited for this blue-collar district, until I discovered that Pancake had been repeatedly delinquent in child support payments to his ex-wife, who was living in a trailer. Multiple judgments against him in this matter were there for the plundering in the Athens County Courthouse. Final election results: Jimmy Stewart (yes that's his real name, you can look it up) 58 percent; Jim Pancake 42 percent.

Honorable Mention must be given here to Mr. Bill Boner—although Oppo Man never worked in any race featuring Mr. Boner, this category would be incomplete without him. Boner was the former Democratic congressman from Tennessee who was elected mayor of Nashville in 1987. Only a few months into his term, Boner left his third wife to start fooling around with lounge singer Tracy Peel. (Peel proved Boner was well-named when she told *The Tennessean* he was "capable of seven hours of passion.") Once the affair became public, Boner announced he would not seek re-election. Nashville spent the rest of Boner's term in effect without a mayor, as Boner basically stopped doing his job, choosing instead to hang out with Ms. Peel, whipping out a harmonica as she sang at various clubs in the dregs of Nashville. The two were soon invited onto the Phil Donohue show, where Boner whipped out his harmonica as Ms. Peel broke into "Rocky Top," the super-corny theme song played at University of Tennessee football games.

So here they are, Fred Head, Fred Pancake, and Bill Boner. Even the most talented fiction writers could never come up with such characters.

2. Dumbest Candidate Ever Researched by Oppo Man: Phil Busey of Davie, Florida

Davie is a nice, small residential city just south of Fort Lauderdale. Busey was a professor of horticulture running for city council. His claim to fame was patenting a "super grass" that would supposedly do away with concrete. (Sounds like a Ralph Kramden idea, and it was just about as successful.) After being hired by a client to dig up dirt on Busey, I also found that Busey was involved in a nude beach. The beach's website led me to another Busey website that contained hardcore pornography. He didn't have the brains to shut down his porn site even for a few months while he was campaigning. Busey responded lamely to press inquiries that it shouldn't be a campaign issue. Thank God it was—Busey went on to lose by only sixty votes.

3. Most Corrupt State Researched by Oppo Man: Tie Between Louisiana and New Jersey

During Oppo Man's lifetime, much of America's political corruption has been rooted out. For instance, cities in the sixties and seventies that were famous for dirty politics—New York City, Chicago, Boston, Philadelphia, Atlanta, and Cleveland, just to name a few—are now cleaned up. However, two states still stuck in a time warp are just as corrupt as they have always been: Louisiana and New Jersey.

4. Cleanest State Researched by Oppo Man: Maine

Maine politicians are "citizen legislators" in the truest sense. Plus, there's just not enough money for corruption to exist. Legislators there are paid only $10,500 per session.

5. State with Most Political "Characters": New York Edges Out Texas

Most Americans like their politicians dull and boring. Not so in New York. Just in my lifetime, New York has had a governor who gave the finger to a hostile crowd and dropped dead in the middle of sex with a woman almost forty years his junior (Nelson Rockefeller); a governor who was known to enjoy his drinks and who would sometimes show up for work with multicolored hair (Hugh Carey); a mayor who couldn't understand why welfare mothers were so fat (Ed Koch); and a mayor who announced to the press that he was divorcing his wife without letting her know beforehand (Giuliani). Just to name a few more, Brooklyn Congressman Fred Richmond was convicted of tax evasion and forced to resign from Congress, while Brooklyn District Attorney Eugene Gold was a child molester. Gold, an old geezer, sexually molested a little girl—at a District Attorneys' convention, no less.

Then we have the Queens Borough President, Donald Manes, who chose suicide rather than face prosecution by then U.S. Attorney Rudy Giuliani for skimming money from city parking meters. His suicide attempt ended in failure, but then the hospital was subsequently crazy enough to send him home, where he finished off the job on his second try. And, of course, we can't forget the George Raft sound-alike Charlie Rangel, or former Police Commissioner Lee ("Out-of-Town") Brown, who, as his nickname suggests, rarely showed up for work. (This didn't stop the good folks of Houston, Texas, from later electing him as mayor after he was shamed into leaving New York.)

Nor can we forget the "Reverend" Al Sharpton, who enjoys respectability nationwide despite urging college students in New Jersey to kill cops ("Off the pigs," as he so eloquently put it); called America's founding fathers the "Scum of Europe"; defended high-profile murderers and rapists; was up to his eyeballs in the Tawana Brawley hoax; and claims that it was black folks who taught whites table manners back in the days of slavery, saying "Back in those days, when white folks wanted steak, they went out and bit the cows in the ass." Ahhhh—only in New York.

6. State with Pettiest Politics Dealt With by Oppo Man: Kansas Republicans

In normal states, after the primaries end, the different factions of each party come together and support the nominees. Not so in Kansas, or at least with the Kansas Republicans. The split among the moderate and conservative wings of the GOP in Kansas is by far the worst in America. After the primaries are settled, the losing side of the Kansas GOP always actively fights to elect the Democrat. Not only that, even within the moderate wing of the party, there's yet another ridiculous split. The liberal wing of the moderates is more left-wing than the Democrats in Kansas! The question is, who are the "real moderates"? Just ridiculous.

7. Dumbest Move Ever Made by Oppo Man

As mentioned in my chapter on Texas, getting mixed up with "crazy Samantha"—the femme fatal who somehow got a hold of my telephone records and called everyone on the list—had to be one of the major blunders in the life of Oppo Man. Screaming at every woman on the list in a jealous rage, and telling the others that I was an ax murderer, child rapist, or anything else that entered her fertile imagination, Samantha was truly bizarre.

However, there was one notable bonehead move even worse, if that's believable. In New Hampshire in 2002, I had to drop off an envelope in a FedEx mailbox, which happened to be located close to the state capital in Concord. As I was about to exit the car (which was parked illegally right in front of the mailbox) to deposit the items, a strong rain and wind came out of the blue. At this point, I was going through the worst year of my asthma, and the air at that moment became completely unbreathable. But since it would only take roughly five to ten seconds to get out of the car, drop off the envelope, and get back in the car, I figured it was no big deal to put my ski mask on for those few seconds, since it covered my nose and mouth.

I wore the mask only in extreme conditions, where the air is especially bad and cold at the same time. I also goes out of my way not to wear the mask in any sensitive area that would arouse suspicion. So I put the mask on and dropped off at FedEx as quickly as I could, then got back into the car to drive back to New York.

Roughly two hours later, somewhere near the Massachusetts/Connecticut border, my cell phone rang. It was a police detective back in Concord and he seemed very relieved to get me on the phone. He was in a completely frazzled state and was obviously trying to talk to me as calmly as he could. It turns out that several good Samaritans saw a very suspicious man get of his car with a ski mask on and quickly deposit a package in the FedEx mailbox in front of the state capital— roughly six months after 9/11. At least two of them got my license plate number. Since it was a rental car, the entire street was cordoned off by the local and state police, as every single item in the FedEx mailbox was checked for anthrax.

From my license plate number, the cops were able to call Hertz car rental and find out who I was. Was I a terrorist? They needed to find out. They eventually found the FedEx envelope I had put in the box, which had my phone number on it, and called me. After explaining to the detective why I had the ski mask on and that I was not conducting any shady or terrorist-related enterprises, he pleaded with me to come back to Concord so he could close the file on the case.

Since my job for *any* client as Oppo Man requires complete discretion and secrecy, this looked like it could turn into a complete debacle if it became known that the mysterious man who dropped off the FedEx envelope into the mailbox was in town to dig up dirt on the candidate favored to become New Hampshire's next governor (which, in fact, he did). Had I been exposed, it would have made me look like a total idiot to my client in New Hampshire—who would have been extremely embarrassed by the whole thing. As for my reputation as Oppo Man, I would have become a laughingstock.

The cops had my name but had not yet released it to the press, so I figured the best thing to do was go back and help them close their case without exposing my identity and my business. The detective gave me the option of going to a local police station near to where I was, but we both agreed it would be better if I drove back to Concord and straightened out the entire mess. His captain, obviously getting pressure from higher-ups, not to mention the media, was not going to let him go home until he closed this case. After driving two hours back the way I had come, I parked outside the police station and called the detective. He told me to go into a door where I wouldn't be spotted. Once inside, he was very professional and handled the case perfectly. He was able to pacify his police captain and convince him I was no threat, and let the press know it was just a false alarm.

So I dodged the bullet, but through no skill or intelligence on my part—just dumb luck. It was lucky that the police were able to contact me that night while the case was still hot, and also lucky that the cops were professional enough to close the case without any embarrassment for Oppo Man.

8. Smartest Move Ever Made by Oppo Man
Retiring from politics to write this book.

ABOUT THE AUTHOR

Stephen Marks has been a political opposition specialist for more than twelve years. He has appeared on numerous television programs, including *The O'Reilly Factor*, *Hannity & Colmes*, and *FOX News Now*. He also hosts *The Stephen Marks Show* on KFNX talk radio in Phoenix, Arizona.